50 CIRCUIT HIKES

A STRIDE-BY-STRIDE GUIDE TO NORTHEASTERN MINNESOTA

Howard Fenton

Pfeifer-Hamilton Publishers
Duluth, Minnesota

Pfeifer-Hamilton Publishers
210 West Michigan
Duluth MN 55802
218-727-0500
www.phpublisher.com

50 Circuit Hikes: A Stride-by-Stride Guide to Northeastern Minnesota

Printed in the United States of America

10 9 8 7 6 5 4 3 2 1

Editorial Director: Heather Isernhagen

Art Director: Joy Morgan Dey

Cover photographs by Tim Kaffine.

Cover background photograph by Dudley Edmundson.

Library of Congress Cataloging in Publication Data

99-62011

ISBN 1-57025-197-5

To Ruth

ACKNOWLEDGMENTS

I began this book in the summer of 1996 when I scouted all but a handful of the hikes described in these pages. From the beginning there have been people helping this project along, and I wish to acknowledge their contributions. First and foremost is my wife, Ruth, whose strong editorial skills and encouragement strengthened my drafts and sustained me through the long course. Tim Dawson was there when I needed a hiking partner, particularly one with a canoe, to scout the hike on the Kabetogama Peninsula in Voyageurs National Park. Sparky Stensaas provided valuable ideas for my book proposal. John Green graciously answered questions about the geology around Bean and Bear Lakes. I would like to thank the North Superior Ski and Run Club for permission to use their map of Pincushion Mountain, and the Minnesota Department of Natural Resources for allowing me use of their state park and forest maps. The reference librarians at the University of Minnesota–Duluth, the College of St. Scholastica, St. Louis County Historical Society, and the City of Duluth Public Library provided valuable research assistance. Finally, I would like to thank the hikers I met who encouraged and cheered me on in my efforts. It is always good to meet fellow travelers.

INTRODUCTION

"There are paths that can be followed, and there is a path that cannot—it is not a path, it is the wilderness."

–Gary Snyder

This guidebook is for hikers of all abilities—the novice as well as the experienced. But, above all, it is for lovers of the outdoors, particularly those who love northeastern Minnesota and want to learn more about this unique region.

Northeastern Minnesota boasts thousands of miles of trails. This guide offers you a selection of circuit hikes from a variety of landscapes and with various degrees of difficulty. Each hike ends right where it starts, incorporating a circuit as a major element of the route. Besides eliminating the need to run car shuttles, circuit hikes minimize the need to rehike trails, enabling you to spend more miles exploring new territory. And there is a lot to see.

I've chosen hikes with panoramic views of Lake Superior from ridges and mountain tops along the North Shore, hikes along rivers where the roar of cascading water drowns out all other sound, and hikes along lake shores where the call of a distant Blue Jay carries easily across the still waters. Some hikes will lead you along wide, gently rolling, grassy paths, while others will take you over rugged, rock strewn trails, or across the tops of beaver dams. Wildlife abounds for the quiet and watchful hiker, and there is much to learn about northland ecosystems, geology, and the history of its people.

The hikes are not all panoramas with excitement around each bend. There is plodding through mud, wading through streams, and contending with the ever-present mosquitoes of summer. However, if you want to experience and enjoy the one, you'll have to accept some measure of the other.

While I provide some hiking advice, this book is not meant to be comprehensive in that regard. There are plenty of good how-to books written about hiking, first aid, and map reading. I recommend that you read one or two of them before taking any of the hikes in this book.

Howard Fenton
1999

CONTENTS

The Hikes

HOW TO USE THIS BOOK

Each hike clearly identifies information you can use to select hikes suited to your abilities and mood. In addition to hike location, directions to the trailhead, map suggestions, and permit requirements for each hike, you will also find information on trail length, estimated hiking time, hiking difficulty, route-finding difficulty, and GPS coordinates.

Some hikes are easy and follow well-marked trails, while others, where the going is strenuous, or the route is a bit vague, are more difficult, and many fall in between these two extremes. If you have little or no experience, the easier routes give you an opportunity to develop good hiking skills. As your skill level and confidence improve, you can move on to the more difficult hikes.

Difficulty ratings are defined as:

- **Easy**—Short hikes of three miles or less with mostly gentle grades.
- **Moderate**—Hikes of three to six miles with gradual changes in elevation, although there may be one or two short steep ascents.
- **Difficult**—Six to eight mile hikes with some lengthy or steep elevation changes.
- **Strenuous**—Hikes of more than eight miles or with substantial elevation changes.

Route-finding difficulty is defined as:

- **Easy**—the trails are obvious, with trail-side maps at many intersections showing your location.
- **Moderate**—more intersections with few or no trail-side maps; trails are not well blazed.
- **Difficult**—trails are not always discernible requiring excellent route-finding skills.

I cannot emphasize enough the importance of a good map. Do not rely on the simple sketches in this book. They are intended as a general guide, not as a replacement for the quality maps that would be very handy if you should happen to get lost.

Also, be aware that conditions along these hikes may change due to logging, washed-out bridges, and overgrown trails in late summer. Before setting out, you may want to call the office with management responsibilities for the area you'll be hiking in. They can give you information on logging operations, missing bridges, or plans for clearing trails. See pages 209–210 for addresses and telephone numbers.

A quick-reference chart of the fifty hikes can be found starting on page xviii. This chart offers important trail information at a glance, including hike lengths, estimated hiking times, difficulty level, route-finding difficulty, as well as information about camping, cross-country skiing, and snowshoeing. It's the most helpful tool for deciding which hike is right for you.

WORDS OF WISDOM

The Boy Scout's motto "Be Prepared," is familiar to everyone. As with much of life, there are risks involved in hiking. To make your experience as pleasurable as possible, and to minimize the risks, there are three fundamental principles you should follow:

1. Know as much about the hike, and yourself, as possible.

2. Carry the twelve essential items (listed on pages xi–xiii) and wear appropriate footwear and clothing.

3. Understand emergency prevention and preparedness.

Knowledge is Power

Before selecting a hike, learn as much as you can about it and decide whether it's within your capabilities. How far is the hike? How much time will it take to complete, and how much time do you have? What is the terrain like? Is it flat with grassy trails, or steep and rocky? What are the current weather conditions, and how are they likely to change? Answers to these questions in light of past experiences on other hikes should help you gauge the suitability of a given hike on a given day.

Distance is relative when you go for a hike. You aren't going to walk at the same pace every time you go hiking. The terrain, the weather, your familiarity with the route, your mood and physical condition, as well as your agenda for a given hike will determine how long it is likely to take.

The Things You Carry

It is important to wear clothing and footwear appropriate for the weather and the trail. On some hikes, where the terrain is fairly smooth and not too rocky, or the trail not too long, you may feel comfortable wearing running shoes. Light, soft-soled shoes can be a pleasure to hike in, but they can also be an invitation to trouble. After awhile, feet can get tender and bruised. For longer distances over rougher terrain, sturdy shoes with stiff soles are important. And, if you want to increase your protection against twisted ankles, ankle-length boots are in order.

Given the propensity for quick-changing weather in northeastern Minnesota, it is important to be prepared for more than just the weather conditions that exist at the start of a hike. Use a layering system when dressing so that clothing may be removed or added as necessary.

Besides the clothes and shoes you wear, there are twelve essential items no well-prepared hiker should be without. These items are not listed in order of importance so don't think you need only carry those items at the top of the list and disregard those near the bottom.

1. **Candle or firestarter.** A candle or firestarter, when placed under a pile of small kindling and lit, will continue to burn until the kindling ignites and begins to burn on its own. A firestarter option is cotton swabs smeared with petroleum jelly. They can be stored very compactly in a water proof container such as a plastic film canister. Besides helping to start fires they can also be used to provide relief to chapped lips.

2. **Matches.** Be sure they are kept in a waterproof container.

3. **Compass.** In order to keep yourself from becoming lost, it is very important to have a compass and a map, and know how to use them. These route-finding tools are virtually useless in the hands of someone who does not know how to use them, and indispensable to someone who does.

4. **Map.** In addition to keeping you from getting lost, or helping to find out where you are if you do happen to get lost, a map is good to have handy as it helps you identify surrounding landmarks. Being able to identify the land features makes the hike more interesting and enables you to develop geographic connections between what you see around you and places on the map that lay beyond the horizon.

5. **Extra clothing.** The idea here is to plan for cooler or wet weather. If the weather gets hotter you can always take off layers, or stop and rest. But if it gets cooler, you will need to add layers of clothing. In the event of rain, it becomes especially important to wear something that will keep you dry. Getting wet dramatically increases the likelihood of developing hypothermia which, besides being debilitating in its own right, can compound other problems.

6. **Food and extra food.** Food provides your body with the fuel needed to stay warm and keep a clear head. Nuts, fruits, and grains offer both nutrients and a delicious snack.

7. **First aid kit.** As with the map and compass, it is very important to carry a first aid kit and know how to use it. Taking a basic first aid course would be a great idea. Be prepared for cuts and scrapes, blisters, frostbite, infections, dehydration, sunburn, and hypothermia, in addition to sprained ankles and broken bones. Going out on a day hike doesn't require extensive first aid training, but it does require being prepared for the most common types of medical problems.

   Your first aid kit should include the following items, which can be purchased individually and assembled into a kit, or purchased as a preassembled kit:

   - sewing needle
   - antibacterial ointment
   - butterfly bandages
   - gauze pads
   - triangular bandages
   - lightweight first aid instructional booklet
   - aspirin
   - antiseptic swabs
   - adhesive tape
   - adhesive strips (bandages)
   - moleskin
   - roll of three-inch gauze

8. **Flashlight.** Be sure to include extra batteries and a spare lightbulb.

9. **Pocketknife.** A pocketknife with various tools like those found on Swiss Army knives is useful.

10. **Sunglasses and sunscreen.** Sunglasses, even on cloudy days, protect the eyes from undue strain, and are especially important when there is snow on the ground. Sunscreen offers the short-term benefit of an enjoyable hike free of sunburn, and the long-term benefit of reduced risk of skin cancer.

11. **Water bottle.** Water, and plenty of it, is essential to finishing a hike in good condition. Dehydration can worsen fatigue, result in poor decision-making, and, in hot weather, be deadly. Drink often. Don't wait until your body sends you a thirsty signal. To make it more convenient for you to drink, carry a water bottle in your fanny pack. This makes it more accessible and you don't have to go through the tedious routine of taking off your daypack to get the bottle.

12. **Water purification** (chemical or filter). You can usually carry enough water with you to last a full day of hiking. However, if you are planning to spend the night on the trail (or if you end up needing to), you're going to need some way to purify stream or lake water. Iodine tablets are the lightest means of purification you can carry,

but you may not like the taste it gives the water. Purification systems that require pumping water through a filter that screens out bacteria are available on the market, are compact, and add only a little weight to your pack. They are more expensive then the iodine tablets so there is a trade off. Also, if you rely on tablets, be sure to buy a new supply every year as they can loss their effectiveness.

Avoiding Trouble

To make your hike as enjoyable as possible, it is important to avoid trouble. Know where trouble might be lurking and take precautions to avoid it. Such precautions create only a slight, if any, inconvenience to your hike, and can prevent a great inconvenience if not taken. However, it is important to realize that no matter how cautious you are, problems may still occur.

Pesky insects. Perhaps the number one annoyance in northeastern Minnesota in the summer are those pesky mosquitoes, blackflies, and ticks. They can be a bother to the point of madness, but there are things you can do to minimize their effect on your enjoyment of the outdoors. Insect repellent is one possibility. However, if you don't like the thought of chemicals on your skin, you may wear long-sleeved shirts and a mosquito-proof headnet.

In tick season, usually June and July, tuck your pant legs into your socks and keep your shirt tucked in. Make a close check of yourself as soon as possible after the hike. If you find a tick that has already embedded itself in your skin, don't try to pick it off as you will most likely succeed in pulling away the body of the tick while leaving the head embedded in your skin. It is best to use the hot end of a just extinguished match to get the tick to withdraw its head. Then you can safely pluck it off your skin.

If you are allergic to insect bites, be sure to carry the appropriate medicine with you in your first aid kit. Other people in your hiking group should be made aware of your allergy to bites and how to administer the medicine in case you are unable to do so.

Giardia lambia. This unpleasant little creature is an intestinal parasite found in animal feces, particularly beaver. As animals, including humans, may defecate in or near water, water is the usual source of infection by this parasite. An infection of giardia, known medically as giardiasis, causes severe gastrointestinal symptoms including painful cramps, gas, severe diarrhea, dehydration, dizziness, disorientation, and extreme listlessness, and fatigue. Medical treatment is required to get rid of the parasite and its attending disease. Drink only treated water to avoid giardia. It's not likely any symptoms will appear while you are on the trail, but you don't want to experience this disease in the comfort of your home either.

Black bears. Black bears are generally not a bother. You might go years hiking in northern Minnesota and never even see one. That doesn't mean they aren't there, just that they are very secretive and that they are just as afraid of you as you are of them. However, if you should encounter a bear there are some things you should know.

Black bears, as a rule, have a reputation far worse than they deserve. But don't push the envelope and provoke them either. Don't approach unattended cubs, chances are the mother is nearby. If you meet a grown bear on the trail, don't turn and run away. This could trigger a predator response and it could give chase. It is better to stand still or slowly walk backwards. Let the bear go about its business. If it becomes clear the bear intends to stay in a spot, such as a well-stocked blueberry patch that makes it impossible for you to continue on the trail, you may have to turn around and go back the way you came, or prepare yourself for a long wait.

Don't try to escape bears by climbing trees. Remember, black bears can climb trees too. If you should be attacked by a black bear, fight back by punching it in the face and kicking it, or throwing things at it. You may deter the bear from its attack.

Hypothermia. Hypothermia results from the cooling of the body's inner core and is the number one killer of outdoor recreationalists. The symptoms progress rapidly, starting with a weakening of reasoning powers, judgment skills, and hand control—eventually leading to mental and physical collapse. Symptoms include uncontrollable shivering, vague or slurred speech, lapses in memory, a lurching gait or frequent stumbling, exhaustion, and drowsiness. A person suffering from hypothermia is likely to show little concern for their condition, or for any need to get treatment.

Hypothermia is caused by a combination of exertion, dampness, and wind. Temperatures do not have to be freezing for hypothermia to occur. Most cases develop with temperatures between 30–50 degrees Fahrenheit. Anytime a person is tired from exertion and is exposed to windy, wet weather, there is a risk of hypothermia. If these conditions exist, watch for the first signs of any symptoms. Trust your own judgement of the symptoms you see rather than relying on what the victim tells you. If someone looks like they are suffering from hypothermia, treat them for it right away. Get the victim out of wet clothing and into dry clothes as soon as possible. If necessary build a fire to dry clothes and heat the victim if dry clothes are not readily available. In cold weather conditions it is a good idea to carry a space blanket as part of your first aid kit. Wrap the victim in the blanket until dry clothes are available. In extreme situations it may be necessary for another person to lay down with the victim in order to transfer body heat. Administer warm fluids to the victim if you have a way of heating them.

To defend against hypothermia it is important to stay dry. Wet clothes lose about 90 percent of their insulating properties. This is especially true of cotton. Wool is better than cotton if you should happen to get wet, and synthetic fabrics made especially for outdoor clothing are even better.

Heat stress disorders. Heat disorders run along a continuum from heat cramps, to heat exhaustion, to heat stroke. It is important to treat each of these conditions as they arise or else you run the risk of them getting worse.

Heat cramps are caused by the loss of salt through sweating. Treat the cramped area by stretching the affected muscles and administering athletic drinks or very lightly salted water. There are drink mixes containing electrolytes that can be combined with water for this purpose. During the summer months, you may consider adding a dehydration solution mix to your first aid kit.

Heat exhaustion, brought on by extreme heat and water loss through sweating, should be treated by seeking shade for the victim and again giving them slightly salted water to drink. Symptoms of heat exhaustion include a general weakness, unstable walk, fatigue, wet and clammy skin, headache, nausea, and physical collapse.

Heat stroke is a life threatening condition. Its symptoms include a high body temperature, a lack of sweating, convulsions, and delirium. It is a medical emergency. Permanent brain damage or even death may result if not treated properly. Immerse the victim in cold water, then lead them to a shady spot and fan them vigorously. Give them water treated lightly with salt or a dehydration solution to drink. Repeat the soaking and fanning as needed.

Lightning. Thunderstorms are common in summer, and may occur in spring and fall as well. For this reason it is important to pay close attention to changing weather conditions, listening for thunder and watching for lightning. If a thunderstorm is approaching it is a good idea to begin making your way back to the trailhead the quickest way possible. However, if you get caught in a storm and are still on the trail, try to avoid cliff faces, shallow caves, ridge tops, or tall trees and the roots that radiate out from them. It is better to crouch down, setting on your heels, than to lay down flat on the ground. Remove metallic objects from your body as they may cause severe burns if you should happen to get struck. If someone is struck by lightning, be prepared to administer CPR, mouth-to-mouth resuscitation, and treatment for shock.

Sunburn. Prolonged exposure to the sun can weaken the body's defenses against cancerous cells in the skin, increasing the risk of skin cancer. Wear sunscreen, even on cloudy days, as the tanning rays are able to penetrate clouds.

Getting lost. If you find yourself lost there are some things you should do. First of all try to stay calm. Relax. Sit down and study the situation. If you know how to read a map and you have one with you, study it and your surroundings. Look for familiar land features. In some instances you may be able to pick a nearby stream and follow it until you come to a house or cross a road. This is especially helpful along the North Shore where streams flow towards Lake Superior and eventually intersect U.S. Highway 61. But beware, in other cases a particular stream may take you further away from safety.

If you can't figure out what to do, the best thing could be to just stay put. If you are carrying the twelve essential items in your daypack, you should be prepared for an unfortunate, although tolerable, night in the woods. Don't attempt to walk out of the woods after dark. Try to put a positive light on the situation and settle in for the unique experience of a night out. Hopefully you told someone where you would be hiking and when you would be back. When you don't show up at the appointed time, help should be on the way soon.

Trail conditions. While it is important to always pay attention to your surroundings while hiking, there are times when trail conditions may warrant extra caution. Watch out for wet rocks or roots. Be careful making your way around fallen trees, and take extra caution whenever crossing logs. If your are unsure of your ability to balance on a log, get yourself a long staff that you can use as a third leg for better balance. None of the hikes in this book require you to wade any deep streams or rivers, but if you are ever met with the need to do so, cross them at the shallowest place you can find or where the water is the calmest. Rushing water that reaches your knees may be strong enough to sweep you off your feet.

Hunting season. Hunting is a fact of life in northeastern Minnesota. Be aware of the places to avoid during hunting season. Know when to stay out of the woods, or go hiking where hunting isn't allowed. Even then, it's a good idea to wear something that is blaze orange.

DATE COMPLETED	HIKE	DISTANCE (miles)	DIFFICULTY
	1 Quarry Loop Trail	1.8-3.6	Easy-Moderate
	2 National Christmas Tree Trail	2.6	Easy
	3 Remote Lake Solitude Area	5.6	Moderate
	4 Continental Divide—Savanna Portage	4.9	Moderate
	5 Rolling Hills	1.4-2.3	Easy
	6 Rogers Lake	6.0	Difficult
	7 Silver Creek—Bear Chase Trails	3.3-6.6	Moderate-Difficult
	8 Organtz Trail	2.0	Easy
	9 Mission Creek Trail	3.9-5.0	Moderate
	10 Magney-Snively	3.2-7.8	Moderate-Difficult
	11 Park Point Nature Trail	4.1	Moderate
	12 Summit Ledges	1.4	Easy
	13 Otto Lake	4.2	Moderate
	14 Laurentian Divide	4.5	Moderate
	15 Big Hole & Ridge Trails	3.9	Moderate
	16 Sturgeon River Trail—South Loop	8.1	Strenuous
	17 North Dark River	1.8	Easy
	18 Easy Bay—Norberg Lake	3.0	Easy
	19 Becky & Blueberry Lakes	4.2	Moderate-Difficult
	20 Bass Lake Trail	5.9	Moderate
	21 Ole Lake—North Star Run	8.0	Difficult
	22 Angleworm Trail	13.6	Strenuous
	23 Astrid Lake Trail	6.4-7.3	Difficult
	24 Echo River & Herriman Lake	6.0-9.7	Difficult-Strenuous
	25 Dovre Lake Trail	7.1	Difficult

ROUTE-FINDING DIFFICULTY	TIME	USAGE	PERMIT	CAMPGROUND	TRAIL CAMPSITES	CROSS-COUNTRY SKIING	SNOWSHOEING
Easy	2:00	Heavy	x	x		x	
Moderate	1:30	Light		x		x	
Moderate	3:15	Light			x	x	
Easy-Moderate	2:45	Moderate	x	x		x	
Easy	1:15	Moderate	x	x		x	
Difficult	3:30	Light				x	
Easy	3:45	Heavy	x	x	x	x	
Easy	1:00	Heavy	x	x		x	
Moderate	3:00	Light				x	
Moderate	4:15	Light				x	x
Easy	2:30	Heavy				x	
Moderate	1:00	Moderate					
Moderate-Difficult	2:30	Light			x	x	x
Moderate	2:45	Light				x	x
Easy-Moderate	2:15	Moderate	x	x		x	x
Difficult	4:30	Light				x	x
Easy	1:00	Light					x
Easy	1:30	Moderate	x	x		x	
Easy-Moderate	2:30	Light	x	x	x	x	x
Moderate	3:30	Heavy			x		x
Moderate	4:45	Light	x			x	x
Moderate	8:15	Moderate	x		x		x
Moderate	4:30	Light		x	x	x	x
Moderate-Difficult	6:15	Light	x		x		x
Moderate	4:15	Light	x		x		x

DATE COMPLETED	HIKE	DISTANCE (miles)	DIFFICULTY
	26 Ash River Falls—Loop B	4.1	Moderate
	27 Agnes, Ek, & Cruiser Lakes	9.9	Strenuous
	28 Gooseberry River	5.2	Moderate
	29 Split Rock River	4.6	Moderate-Difficult
	30 Corundum Mine Trail	3.1	Moderate
	31 Split Rock Creek	6.2	Moderate-Difficult
	32 Bean & Bear Lakes	6.4	Difficult-Strenuous
	33 Mic Mac & Nipisiquit Lakes	6.8	Difficult-Strenuous
	34 Mic Mac Lake—Mount Baldy	5.4	Difficult
	35 Matt Willis & Yellow Birch Trails	6.1	Difficult-Strenuous
	36 Manitou River	4.1	Difficult-Strenuous
	37 McDougal Lake Trail	0.9	Easy
	38 Flat Horn Lake Trail	2.0	Easy
	39 Eighteen Lake	2.7	Easy
	40 Divide Lake	2.1	Easy
	41 Hogback Lake	3.2	Easy-Moderate
	42 Ninemile Hiking Trail	4.3	Moderate
	43 Ennis, Blackstone, & Secret Lakes	3.7	Moderate
	44 Cross River Wayside	6.3	Moderate-Difficult
	45 Leveaux Peak	3.2	Easy-Moderate
	46 Oberg Mountain	2.3	Easy-Moderate
	47 Lookout Mountain	3.0	Moderate
	48 Cascade River	7.9	Strenuous
	49 Pincushion Mountain	4.4	Moderate
	50 Mucker Lake—Border Route	5.4	Difficult-Strenuous

ROUTE-FINDING DIFFICULTY	TIME	USAGE	PERMIT	CAMPGROUND	TRAIL CAMPSITES	CROSS-COUNTRY SKIING	SNOWSHOEING
Easy-Moderate	2:15	Light				x	
Easy-Moderate	8:30	Light			x		x
Easy-Moderate	3:00	Moderate	x	x		x	
Easy-Moderate	3:15	Heavy			x		
Easy	1:45	Moderate	x	x	x	x	
Easy	3:45	Moderate	x	x	x	x	
Moderate	4:00	Moderate			x		x
Easy-Moderate	4:15	Moderate	x	x			x
Easy-Moderate	3:15	Light	x				x
Moderate	3:45	Light	x		x		x
Easy-Moderate	2:30	Light	x		x		x
Easy	0:30	Moderate		x			x
Easy	1:00	Moderate				x	x
Easy	1:30	Moderate		x			x
Easy	1:15	Moderate		x	x		x
Easy	2:00	Moderate		x	x		x
Moderate	2:30	Light		x		x	x
Moderate	2:30	Light	x		x		x
Moderate	3:45	Light		x	x		x
Easy-Moderate	2:15	Moderate			x		x
Easy	1:45	Heavy					x
Moderate	2:00	Moderate	x	x	x	x	x
Moderate	5:00	Moderate	x	x	x		x
Easy	2:30	Moderate				x	x
Moderate-Difficult	3:45	Light	x		x		x

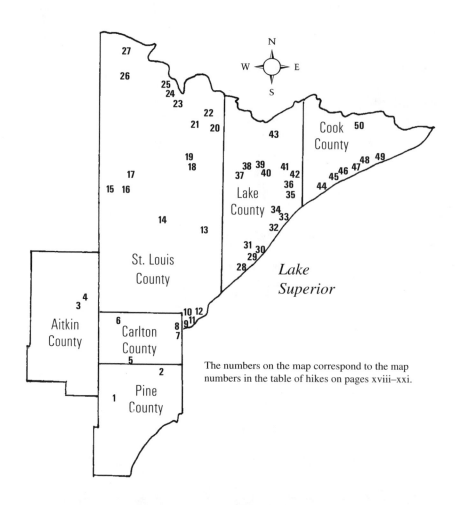

The numbers on the map correspond to the map numbers in the table of hikes on pages xviii–xxi.

KEY TO THE MAPS

U.S. Highway

Minnesota State Road

County Road

U.S. Forest Service Road

P Parking

Park Headquarters

Shelter

Tent site

Scenic Overlook

Quarry Loop Trail E Willow

BANNING STATE PARK

LENGTH	1.8 miles incorporating only the Quarry Loop Trail, 3.6 miles with the addition of the Deadman-High Bluff-Wolf Creek trails loop.
TIME	2:00
DIFFICULTY	Easy-Moderate
ROUTE-FINDING	Easy
MAPS & PERMITS	DNR Banning State Park map. A Minnesota State Park permit is required.
GETTING THERE	Take exit 195 off I-35 (Minnesota State Roads 18 and 23 for Askov and Finlayson); go east on Minnesota State Road 23 for 0.3 mile to the park entrance. Once in the park, follow the signs to the picnic area.

The Quarry Loop Trail combines interesting history with fascinating geology. In addition to the site of a once-active quarry, the trail passes along a section of the Kettle River with notable geology. Banning State Park has ten miles of the Kettle River within its borders, including five sets of rapids that are favorites with kayakers and canoeists, an abandoned sandstone quarry, and the former town site of Banning.

Kettle River Geology

Kettle River got its name from the "kettles" found along its course. Kettles, or potholes, form in soft sedimentary rocks, like the sandstone that makes up a riverbed. The holes begin when grains of sand or tiny pebbles act as grinders powered by swirling water to carve depressions in the rock. The kettles grow larger and larger as successively bigger grinders get caught in them.

The sandstone in this region, known as Hinckley Sandstone, was formed in the bottom of a shallow, mid-continental sea during the Precambrian Era. Silica and sand accumulated in layers on the sea floor, and cemented together to form a sedimentary rock. About 10,000 years ago, meltwaters from receding glaciers flowed south in many streams towards the Mississippi River. One of those streams, the Kettle River, followed a natural depression caused by a fault. Over thousands of years, the river widened and deepened the depression, exposing the underlying sandstone. On this hike you will see evidence of the fault in the form of a horst, a block of the earth's crust that rises on one side of the fault.

At the northernmost section of the park, the Kettle River flows through a narrow valley cut into glacial drift. There the river valley turns into a gorge worn through the Hinckley Sandstone. This is where life for the kayaker and canoeist gets interesting. The rapids, beginning with Blueberry Slide, draw whitewater enthusiasts from all over the Midwest. Between Blueberry Slide and Hell's Gate, where the river flows through 40 foot cliffs that choke the river like a noose, lays Mother's Delight, Dragon's Tooth, and Little Banning. Beyond the rapids, the river valley once again broadens, surrounded by a level, or gently rolling, plain of glacial till.

Before logging, the vegetation in the park area was mainly red and white pine with some aspen and birch. Today aspen and birch predominate with only remnant stands of pine. The rocky terrain along the floor of the river gorge prevents a dense growth of deciduous trees, so one day pines may again dominate this area of the park.

Quarry History

Several books such as *Everyone's Country Estate* by Roy W. Meyer, *Minnesota State Parks* by Rasters Vanderboom, and a DNR brochure available at the park office relate the interesting history of the quarrying years at Banning.

The Water Power Sandstone Company began quarrying sandstone on the banks of the Kettle River in 1892. In the first six months, the company sold 5,000 tons of stone and business grew quickly, along with a village. Operations were temporarily halted by the tragic Hinckley fire of September 1, 1894. This catastrophic fire destroyed the village, claiming many lives, and caused great financial loss for the quarry. Martin Ring and James T. Tobin resumed quarrying operations after the fire, and a new town, named after William L. Banning, president of the St. Paul-Duluth Railroad, was platted on the high ground above the quarry site in 1896. Around 1905, the quarrying boom came to an end, although the Barber Asphalt Company, which had acquired the site from Martin Ring, continued to quarry until 1912. The town of Banning died shortly afterward.

A couple of factors contributed to the end of quarrying at the Kettle River site. One was the lack of quality stone. Second, steel and concrete became popular building materials, thus reducing the demand for stone.

Concrete ruins like the Rock Crusher Building, the Power House, and the Stone Cutting Shed stand among the trees of a second-growth forest, silent reminders of the quarry site. The drip of water seeping from cracks in giant sandstone walls, the wind in the trees, and the roar of rapids have replaced the noise of stream-powered drills, blasting, rock sawing, and hammering.

Trail Highlights

This hike follows the upper and lower grades of the rail line that once served the quarry site. Hiking south along the upper grade, you will pass the quarry sites, large sandstone blocks stacked like cordwood waiting for trains that will never come, and a section of horst. You will also find piles of smaller rocks along the trail. Too small for construction purposes, these were crushed to make cement or road-building material. Mosses, ferns, and liverworts grow on narrow ledges of the sandstone walls, moistened by water seeping from cracks in the rock. Small trees also grow out from the sheer wall where they can find a roothold. Bird's-eye Primrose, which have been found in only one other place in Minnesota, grow in the quarry site.

About halfway along the upper portion of the Quarry Loop Trail, the hike leaves the river gorge on the Deadman Trail. On the higher ground beyond the rim of the river gorge is a northern hardwood forest of maple, oak, basswood, and some aspen, with little pine. This section of the hike contrasts with the landscape of the river gorge. After a 1.9 mile circuit along the Deadman, High Bluff, and Wolf Creek trails, the hike resumes on the Quarry Loop Trail.

You might imagine that the Deadman Trail has a grim story behind its name. That is not the case. In quarry terminology, a deadman refers to an anchoring point on the ground for the cables supporting giant derricks. Workers used the derricks to hoist blocks of stone onto railroad cars that took them to the various work areas around the quarry.

At the southern end of the Quarry Loop Trail, the Hell's Gate Trail branches off and continues downstream. This trail provides a close look at how the river has carved and shaped the rock along its banks. Look for kettles and their grinders along the Hell's Gate Trail. It starts out as an easy trail but becomes difficult as it gets pinched between the river and sandstone bluffs. The trail eventually deadends and does not connect with any other trails beyond its intersection with the Quarry Loop Trail.

Complete the Quarry Loop Trail by hiking north along the lower railroad grade. Here you will find the foundation of the Cutting House, the walls of the Power House, and the Rock Crusher building.

The DNR designed the Quarry Loop Trail as a self-guided hike. An informative brochure that interprets interesting historical and natural sites along the way is available at the park office and at the trailhead.

Stride-by-Stride

MILES	DESCRIPTION
0.0	The hike begins at the south end of the parking lot where three trails meet; the Skunk Cabbage Trail on the left, the Teachers Overlook Trail straight ahead, and the Quarry Loop Trail (QLT) to the right. Turn right on the QLT. This section of trail follows a railroad grade to the quarry site.
0.1	The QLT forks; continue straight ahead on right fork.
0.3	Intersection with the Cartway Trail on the right; continue on the QLT.
0.4	Intersection; continue straight ahead passing trail on the left. In about 120 feet reach intersection with the Spur Trail going right and left; continue on the QLT. The Spur Trail marks the route taken by trains hauling cut stone from the quarry to the main tracks of the St. Paul-Duluth Railroad.
0.5	Site of the earliest quarrying activity begun in 1892.
0.7	Intersection with the Deadman Trail. The southbound railroad grade ended at this point. Piles of scrap rock called spall can be seen in the surrounding area. At this point you have two options: you may bear right on the Deadman Trail if you want to do the entire 3.6 mile hike; or, you may bear left on the Quarry Loop Trail to complete a shorter 1.8 mile hike. If you take the Deadman Trail option you will eventually return to this intersection. This hike description is for the first option. Otherwise, skip to the 2.5 mile point and follow the directions back to the trailhead.
0.9	Trail intersection; bear left on the High Bluff Trail, leaving the Deadman Trail as it continues to the right.
1.6	Trail intersection with the Wolf Creek Trail going left and right; bear right.
2.2	Trail intersection; turn right on the Deadman Trail.

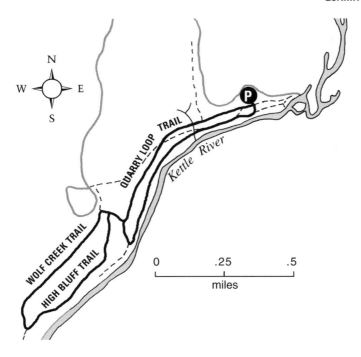

2.3 Trail intersection with the High Bluff Trail; bear left staying on the Deadman Trail and return to the QLT.

2.5 Trail intersection with the QLT; bear right. In about 400 feet come to the horst on right side of trail. Piles of large sandstone blocks, left by the last train to leave the quarry in 1912, sit on either side of the trail.

2.7 Intersection with the Hell's Gate Trail on the right. This trail follows the river downstream. It starts out as an easy trail but gets gradually pinched between the river and sandstone cliffs and becomes more difficult to follow. The circuit hike continues by turning left on the QLT.

2.9 Site of the stone cutting shed about 70 feet off the trail to the left. Look for a small drainage ditch on the right side of the trail.

3.0 Remains of the power house.

3.1 Site of the rock crusher building.

3.3 Intersection with the Spur Trail on the left; continue ahead on the QLT. Note impressions left by crossties along the trail. Excellent views of Dragon's Tooth Rapids on the river below. Swirling currents caused by kettles or potholes in the riverbed have claimed more than a few lives of canoeists and kayakers caught in their grip and pulled under.

3.4 The trail ascends rock steps out of the quarry area. At the top of the steps, turn right following the MCC Trail upriver, passing the QLT on the left.

3.5 Intersection; turn left onto the Teachers Overlook Trail, leaving the MCC Trail which continues upstream. (For a closer look at the river continue on the MCC Trail for about 0.2 miles to the Blueberry Slide Trail which leads down to the river's edge and the head of the series of rapids that finally ends below Hell's Gate.)

3.6 Reach the trailhead after 340 feet on the Teachers Overlook Trail.

National Christmas Tree Trail

2.6 M
EASY

NEMADJI STATE FOREST

LENGTH	2.6 miles
TIME	1:30
DIFFICULTY	Easy
ROUTE-FINDING	Moderate
MAPS & PERMITS	DNR Nemadji State Forest map. USGS quad: Holyoke. No permit is required.
GETTING THERE	*From southern Minnesota:* From I-35 take exit 195 and drive east on Minnesota State Road 23 to Nickerson. At Nickerson, turn right off Minnesota State Road 23, cross the railroad tracks at 0.3 mile and then turn left on Net Lake Road. At 1.1 miles continue straight ahead on County Road 146; at 2.2 miles turn right on Net Lake Forest Road and enter the Nemadji State Forest. Follow the signs to the campground on Pickerel Lake at 4.3 miles. *From northern Minnesota:* Turn left off Minnesota State Road 23 onto County Road 153; continue straight ahead onto County Road 146 following it to Net Lake Forest Road. Turn right and follow the signs to the campground.
TRAILHEAD GPS	46° 24' 20.7" N 92° 26' 22.8" W

The National Christmas Tree Trail got its name for the white spruce that was cut from this forest in 1977 to serve as the National Christmas Tree in Washington, D.C. Five white spruces were planted in its place, along with a sign commemorating the event.

Very little, if any, of the original forest exists along this trail. Heavy logging began at the turn of the century and continues to this day. Initially, the forest provided large pine logs for sawmills in Superior, Wisconsin, and Stillwater, Minnesota. Logging companies transported the logs to mills by floating them down the Nemadji, Willow, and Tamarack rivers. Later, the logs were carried by the railroads. After the larger trees were gone, loggers cut the smaller trees for railroad ties, shingles,

7

barrel staves, pulpwood, and firewood. The vegetation you see along the trail is an example of what replaces a climax forest after logging and after farms have been abandoned.

The Nemadji Forest gets its name from the river that drains the northern part of this state forest. The Native American Indians called the river *Nemadji-tri-guay-och,* meaning *"left hand."* They gave it this name because of its position on the left side of Lake Superior's St. Louis Bay.

As you hike the National Christmas Tree Trail during spring and summer, you may hear what sounds like a squeaky wheel. It's the song of the Black-and-white Warbler. This small bird has a black-and-white head, a gray back streaked with black, and white underparts with black-streaked sides. It inhabits wet or dry deciduous woodlands and brushlands. It's one of the earliest of the warblers to arrive at its summer breeding range each spring. The Black-and-white Warbler creeps with its head either up or down along tree trunks and branches looking for insects. If you don't see this small bird, your ear may let you know it is nearby. The black-and-white's song, a buzzy *wheezy weezy weezy weezy-weet*, is very distinctive, sounding like a turning wheel in need of oiling. Look, and listen, for the Black-and-white Warbler, and other birds, as you hike the National Christmas Tree Trail.

The hike begins on a spur trail from the campground that brings you to the circuit portion of the hike in about 0.6 miles. There are two more spur trails off the circuit. One leads to the slow-moving Net River and the site of an old beaver dam; the other leads to the boggy shore of Cranberry Lake. Bogs make up a good part of the headwaters of the Net River, and many other rivers in northeastern Minnesota. They act as sponges, holding water from melted snow and rainfall and releasing it slowly. This helps create a more even flow of water in streams and rivers throughout the year.

Stride-by-Stride

MILES	DESCRIPTION
0.0	The trailhead, marked with a sign, begins at the north end of the one-way road that loops through the campground.
0.3	Trail intersection; turn right. In about 200 feet, bear right at the next trail intersection. In another 300 feet, continue straight ahead, passing a trail on the left.

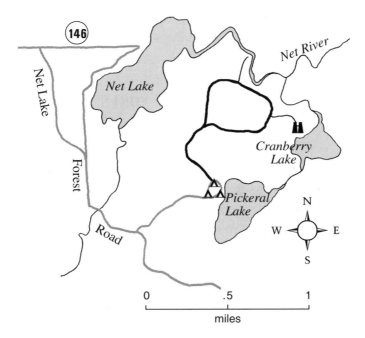

0.6 Trail intersection beginning the circuit portion of this hike. Turn left to begin the loop. You will return to this point in 1.4 miles via the trail on the right.

1.1 Cross a bridge made of split logs.

1.3 Trail intersection; the spur trail to the left leads to the Net River and the site of an old beaver dam in 0.2 miles. Bear right to continue on the main loop.

1.5 Trail intersection; the spur trail to the left leads to the boggy shoreline of Cranberry Lake in 0.2 miles. Bear right to continue on the main loop.

1.8 National Christmas Tree Site.

2.0 Trail intersection completing the circuit portion of this hike. Continue straight ahead, passing the trail on the right, to return to the trailhead.

2.2 Bear left passing a trail on the right. In a short distance, continue straight ahead passing another trail on the right.

2.3 Trail intersection; turn left.

2.6 Trailhead at the campground.

3

5.6 M
MODERATE

Remote Lake
Solitude Area

SAVANNA STATE FOREST

LENGTH	5.6 miles
TIME	3:15
DIFFICULTY	Moderate
ROUTE-FINDING	Moderate
MAPS & PERMITS	DNR Savanna State Forest map. USGS quad: Balsam. No permit is required.
GETTING THERE	Drive west on Minnesota State Road 210 from I-35; right on Minnesota State Road 65 at McGregor; right on County Road 14 for 8.6 miles to a turnoff on the left side of the road leading to a parking lot for the Remote Lake Solitude Area.
TRAILHEAD GPS	46° 48' 13.1" N 93° 11' 45.9" W

The Savanna State Forest, which surrounds much of Savanna Portage State Park and a stretch of the Mississippi River, includes a variety of forest habitats; from hardwood forests covering hilly terrain to low-laying black spruce and tamarack bogs. In between are stands of aspen, birch, balsam fir, and pine.

While the DNR maintains the trails in the Remote Lake Solitude Area for cross-country skiing, they provide, with one exception, excellent hiking in the summer. The exception is the trail along the northwest shore of Glacier Lake; water covers long sections of this trail during warm weather. Otherwise there are about 12 miles of trails suitable for summer hiking. The best time to hike these trails would be in spring, early summer, or late summer and fall, after state forest crews have mowed the trails. Hunting season is not a good time to hike here.

Once past the metal gate at the start of the hike and the first trail intersection, the trail looks like a built-up railroad grade that loggers might have used to haul timber. The ground is lower on both sides of the trail which is wide and grassy as it passes through a mixed forest of maple, oak, aspen, birch, and pines. Continuing north and then northwest past a grassy clearing in the forest, the trail gains elevation and maples and oaks become more predominant. Gradually Remote Lake comes into view through the trees on the right and the trail passes along a narrow ridge separating this large lake from a much smaller, unnamed lake on the left. There is a lean-to shelter on this ridge. Nearby, short trails lead down to the shore of Remote Lake. A small, red pine-covered island sits 70–80 yards off the shore opposite one of these trails. The island looks like a peaceful spot to explore by those hikers up for the short swim over to the island.

The trail continues northwest beyond the shelter for about 0.6 miles before doubling back on a parallel trail. After about a mile on this new trail, it comes upon a large beaver pond; at one point passing just below the dam that holds back water about three to four feet above the level of the trail.

Belted Kingfishers

Belted Kingfishers are likely to use the dead tree snags and stumps standing out in the water to do their fishing. You may become alerted to this unique bird by the rattling call it makes as it flies across the water. The kingfisher ranges over almost the entire continent of North America in one season or another; from northern Mexico in the winter to central Alaska and northern Quebec in the summer, and from the Atlantic to the Pacific.

Both sexes have slate blue colored heads, back, wings, and breast band. Females also sport a rusty belly band that distinguishes them from the males who lack this band. Both sexes have a ragged crest. Their large bills are well adapted for catching small (2.5"–5") fish. They dive for them from perches or from a hovering position. They use their large bills and strong feet to dig nesting burrows in stream and lake banks. In Minnesota, man-made excavations have created more nesting sites for the Belted Kingfisher in a habitat covered with prime fishing locations.

Once it catches a fish, the kingfisher beats it against a branch for a while before swallowing it whole. A young bird, if it doesn't know by instinct, learns quickly that fish don't go down easy when swallowed tail first; the backward pointing scales being an impediment.

William James Davis, writing about the life history of these birds, says that an adult bird needs to eat about ten four-inch fish a day. A pair raising young needs to catch about 90 fish per day to feed themselves and their young. With a success rate of about 40 percent, this means each adult must make over 220 dives a day. During extended periods of bad weather, when fishing conditions are poor due to turbid or ruffled waters, nestlings may starve.

Belted Kingfishers show a role reversal in behavior between the sexes that is uncommon in vertebrates. The female will readily attack both female and male intruders of her and her mate's territory. They spend less time excavating the nest burrow, incubating the eggs, and feeding the young than do the males.

The male takes on more of the female's traditional responsibilities while she regains energy lost during egg laying. Increased parental care and the possibility of a second clutch of eggs helps maximize the number of young produced each summer. This behavior among kingfishers may have evolved for several reasons. First, there is a high possibility that nest sites will be destroyed. Second, the female experiences a substantial amount of stress during egg-laying. Third, there is little time to waste if the female is to lay a second clutch and the young fledged before winter. Finally, there is little chance of the male taking up with a second mate. The female may determine this from the willingness of the male to feed her during courtship. The male who puts out a greater effort to bring her fish is the one she feels will stick by her through the long busy days of summer.

A short way beyond the beaver pond, the trail turns to the southwest passing a lean-to shelter and makes its way through a black spruce-tamarack bog. A boardwalk keeps you high and dry. At the other end of the boardwalk, the trail continues through a forest of balsam fir, aspen, and white pine before reaching a clearing of young red pines beneath scattered white pines, and eventually a mature forest of oaks and maples before returning to the trailhead.

If you don't do this hike early in the spring or early summer, it might be a good idea to call the Savanna State Forest office to find out if they have mowed the trails recently. They usually do the mowing sometime after mid-July, depending on other work requirements.

Stride-by-Stride

MILES	DESCRIPTION
0.0	To begin the hike, walk past the metal gate and along the dirt road.
0.1	Trail intersection beginning the circuit portion of this hike. Turn right, passing the trail to the left. The wide and grassy trail enters a mature mixed forest composed of oaks, maples, aspen, and red pines with occasional white pines.

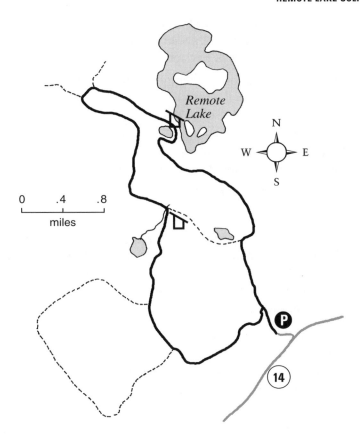

0.7 The trail enters a clearing; continue across the clearing and bear right at its northern end. The trail begins to gradually ascend over a rolling terrain.

1.6 Remote Lake comes into view through the trees on the right.

1.8 The trail approaches a small, unnamed lake on the left and passes around its east side along a narrow ridge that separates it from Remote Lake.

2.0 Trailside shelter (46° 49' 12.5" N 93° 12' 46.5" W). About 100 feet beyond the shelter is a small trail on the right leading to the shore of Remote Lake. From the shore, note the red pine covered island off to the right. A second trail, about 100 feet or so before the shelter, also leads to the lake shore.

2.6 Trail intersection; bear left passing the right trail. In 200 feet, bear left again at the next trail intersection.

3.7 The trail enters a small clearing near a beaver pond that is not on the State Forest map; turn right. Shortly the trail passes just below a long beaver dam. Note the level of the water relative to that of the trail.

3.9 Trail intersection; turn right and come to a shelter in 100 feet (46° 48' 47.2" N 93° 12' 51.0" W). Continue past the shelter to a 645 feet boardwalk through a black spruce bog.

4.1 A small lake can be seen through the trees on the right side of the trail. This is the lake which receives the flowage from the beaver pond passed earlier.

4.3 The trail emerges from the mature forest into a clearing scattered with young white birches, aspens, and red pines under widely scattered towering white pines.

4.6 Trail intersection; turn left passing the trail on the right.

4.7 The trail reenters the forest.

4.8 Pass a slightly overgrown trail on the right that ends at a boggy area in 755 feet. This is a "winter only" trail that skirts the northwestern shore of Glacier Lake. The main trail continues through a forest of towering oaks and maples.

5.1 Trail intersection; bear left passing the trail to the right.

5.4 Intersection with an overgrown road going right and left, continuing straight ahead across the road.

5.5 Intersection on the dirt road completing the circuit portion of this hike. Turn right to return to the trailhead.

5.6 Trailhead.

Continental Divide– Savanna Portage Trails

4
4.9 M
MODERATE

SAVANNA PORTAGE STATE PARK

LENGTH	4.9 miles
TIME	2:45
HIKE RATING	Moderate
ROUTE-FINDING	Easy-Moderate
MAPS & PERMITS	DNR Savanna Portage State Park map. USGS quad: Balsam. A Minnesota State Park permit is required.
GETTING THERE	From I-35 drive west on Minnesota State Road 210. Turn right on Minnesota State Road 65 in McGregor. Turn right again after 6.9 miles onto County Road 14 and drive 10 miles to the park.
TRAILHEAD GPS	46° 49' 42.0" N 93° 9' 3.0" W

Think of a savanna and you're likely to conjure up an image of a vast grassland with clouds of dust kicked up by large herds of wandering animals. This image doesn't fit Savanna Portage State Park. The name savanna, applied to the portage trail by voyageurs and later to the park, refers to an area of marsh grass at the east end of the portage. Blood-sucking insects rather than large herbivores inhabit this savanna.

The Savanna Portage

Canoes once served the purpose that cars and trucks do today, and the many lakes and rivers of northeastern Minnesota served as highways. The Savanna Portage was part of a vital transportation route between Lake Superior and the Mississippi River basin. Chippewa and Sioux were the first to use the portage, followed by fur traders, explorers, and missionaries. Beginning in the east, travelers departed Lake Superior near present-day Fond du Lac in western Duluth by way of the Grand Portage Trail. This portage provided access to navigable waters on the St. Louis River to Cloquet. After a relatively short, one-mile portage, travelers continued on the St. Louis River to Floodwood where they turned up the East Savanna River to its source.

15

At the upper reaches of the East Savanna River, travelers poled their canoes along a narrow stream through nearly twelve miles of tall grass, reeds, and wild rice. A narrow canal was dug to shorten the length of the portage to come. Voyageurs left some goods on wharves when the water level was too low for fully loaded canoes. They could go on in their lightened canoes, deposit their half loads, and return with empty canoes to pick up what they had left behind.

On July 2, 1832, the Reverend William T. Boutwell, traveling with the Schoolcraft expedition, wrote about this part of the Savanna Portage: "…our canoes brought up through the mud and water knee deep,…one (man) at the bow and another at their stern, the latter pushing and the former drawing in mud and water to their middle…The musketoes came in hordes and threatened to carry away a man alive…The rain Saturday evening and the Sabbath, has rendered the portage almost impassable for man and beast. The mud, for the most part of the way, will average ankle deep and from that upwards. In spots it is difficult to find bottom—a perfect quagmire."

Eventually the water route gave out and travelers had to walk the difficult six-mile portage to the West Savanna River. It took voyageurs an average of five days to complete the portage. Each man normally hauled two bundles weighing up to ninety pounds each between rest stops, or pauses, located about a half-mile apart. There were thirteen pauses along the Savanna Portage Trail. After carrying a load from one pause to the next, a voyageur ran back for another load. After everything had been advanced one pause, the voyageurs had time to smoke their pipes and rest before resuming their grueling work.

The first three pauses were located in a tamarack swamp. Poles had been laid across the trail to walk on; but sharp points on the poles hurt their feet, so the voyageurs preferred to struggle through the swamp.

The portage became easier as the trail climbed out of the swamp and ran through hardwood forests and along piney ridges. Once they reached the West Savanna River, travelers moved downstream to the La Prairie River and on to Big Sandy Lake and the Mississippi River.

Another noteworthy feature of the park is the continental divide. On one side of the divide waters flow to the Mississippi River and on to the Gulf of Mexico; on the other side, rivers and streams flow to the Atlantic Ocean by way of the Great Lakes and the St. Lawrence River. Northern hardwoods, such as oak, maple, and basswood dominate the forests of Savanna Portage State Park. There are also birch, aspen, conifers, and tamarack peat bogs in the park. The tamarack bogs formed behind eskers or ridges pushed up by the leading edges of glacial ice sheets.

After passing through a red pine plantation, the route of this hike travels along the continental divide through a mature, northern hardwood forest. A stroll on a lightly used park road brings you to a section of the Savanna Portage. So you don't have to struggle through a wet, mosquito-infested marsh a la the voyageurs, a boardwalk keeps you high and dry. Here you will also find interpretive signs about rivers used as transportation routes in past centuries and the people who used them.

Stride-by Stride

MILES	DESCRIPTION
0.0	The hike starts on the Pine Plantation Trail at the west end of the parking lot.
0.1	Just before entering the pine plantation, turn right on the trail skirting the edge of the plantation.
0.2	Turn left and enter the pine plantation passing a trail on the right.
0.5	Trail intersection beginning the circuit portion of this hike; turn right just after passing a trail on the left.
0.6	Five-way trail intersection; turn left onto the Continental Divide Trail running along a sharp ridge.

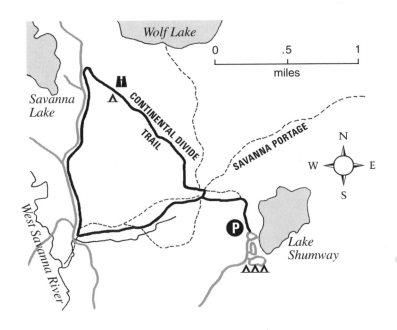

1.2   Continue straight ahead crossing a snowmobile trail.

1.7   Pass a backpack camping site on the left. In 140 feet, come to an overlook providing an excellent view of Wolf Lake to the northeast.

2.2   Intersection with a park road; turn left and hike about 1.1 miles passing three roads on your right.

3.3   Bear left onto a hiking trail leaving the road as it bears slightly to the right.

3.4   Intersection with another park road; turn left and walk along the road for about 100 feet and then left onto the Savanna Portage Trail leading to the East Savanna River. The trail becomes a boardwalk where it crosses a marsh.

3.7   Continue straight ahead passing a trail on the left.

3.8   Four-way trail intersection; bear right passing trails on left. In about 100 yards, pass another trail on the right and then turn left staying on the Portage Trail.

4.2   Trail intersection; bear right passing a trail on the left.

4.4   Trail intersection completing the circuit portion of this hike. To return to the trailhead, continue straight ahead passing trails on the left and right.

4.7   Pass a trail on the left staying on the trail to Lake Shumway. Here the trail emerges from the pine plantation and turns right.

4.9   Trailhead.

MOOSE LAKE STATE PARK

1.4, 2.1, & 2.3 M
EASY

LENGTH	Hikes of 1.4 miles, 2.1 miles, and 2.3 miles are described.
TIME	1:15 for the 2.3 mile hike.
DIFFICULTY	Easy
ROUTE-FINDING	Easy
MAPS & PERMITS	DNR Moose Lake State Park map. USGS quad: Hanging Horn Lake. A Minnesota State Park permit is required.
GETTING THERE	From I-35 take the Moose Lake exit for Minnesota State Road 73. Go east on Minnesota State Road 73 for about 0.4 miles to the park entrance.
TRAILHEAD GPS	46° 26' 5.9" N 92° 44' 3.8" W

Moose Lake State Park was established in 1971 on land originally known as the Moose Lake State Hospital farm. It lies in an area of the state covered with glacial till and outwash deposited about 10,000 years ago. The old growth white and red pines that once covered this area have been logged. In an effort to recreate the original forest, the DNR has planted pine and spruce in some of the fields of abandoned farms. Stands of mature aspen mixed with basswood, birch, and maple cover other parts of the park.

The mix of forest types, some still-open, grassy fields, and the two lakes and two wildlife ponds that are within or border the park provide for a variety of wildlife. Northern pike, walleyed pike, largemouth bass, and panfish populate the lakes and ponds. A pair of Osprey, which feed almost exclusively on fish, nest in the park. You can see the nest in the top of a dead conifer standing in the water on the west side of the largest wildlife pond. Take your binoculars with you on this hike and spend some time watching the Ospreys. The day I hiked the Rolling Hills Trail one was sitting in the nest while the other perched in a nearby tree.

Ospreys

Ospreys typically build large stick nests in the tops of dead trees standing near or in water. They have also made nests on power line support structures and artificial stands built to encourage Osprey nesting. Each year nesting pairs add new material to already existing nests, which can grow to be more than nine feet deep.

Research biologists Michael Barker and Sergei Postupalsky discovered that other birds will build their nests in or beneath occupied Osprey nests in the Great Lakes region. They found Common Grackles, Tree Swallows, European Starlings, and House Sparrows nesting in the large nests. A Northern Flicker nested in a hole in the tree beneath one nest, and a Barn Swallow in a concrete building that was part of the support structure for another nest.

The term *protective nesting* refers to the practice of weaker species nesting in or around the nests of birds of prey or other, more aggressive, species. The smaller birds probably benefit from less risk of predation, because Ospreys fiercely defend their own nests against crows, other raptors, and mammals. Ospreys benefit from this close association by having extra pairs of eyes on the alert for potential predators.

The Rolling Hills Trail travels over gently rolling terrain across open grassy fields, and through young and mature forests. It passes a beaver dam in an aspen forest. There is a shelter about a mile into the hike, and this is a good spot to stop and watch the Ospreys. This hike is not a long one, and so permits more time for viewing wildlife. White-tailed deer frequent the stands of newly planted pines and spruce, and there are plenty of birds.

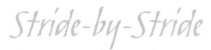
Stride-by-Stride

THIS DESCRIPTION IS FOR THE FULL 2.3 MILE HIKE

MILES   DESCRIPTION

0.0   A sign marks the start of the Rolling Hills Trail approximately 100 feet east of the park headquarters on the road to the campground. Cross Minnesota State Road 73 in about 100 yards, walk past the chain gate, and, in another 100 feet, bear left at the trail intersection.

0.2   Trail intersection; bear right, passing the trail to the left.

0.3   Trail intersection. Bear left; in about 300 feet, at the next intersection, bear right passing a snowmobile trail on the left.

0.4   Come to a beaver pond on the left side of the trail. Just beyond the beaver pond, the trail emerges from the forest into a field surrounding the large wildlife pond on the right.

0.8   Trail intersection and shelter (46° 26' 24.8" N 92° 43' 56.7" W). The trail to the right leads south between the two wildlife

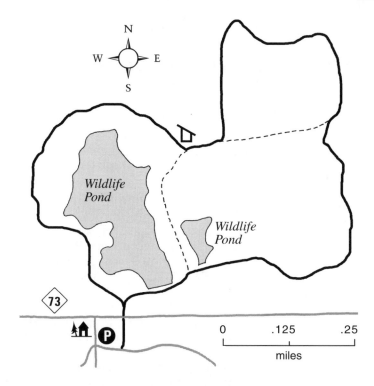

ponds and reaches a trail intersection between their dams in 0.3 miles. From there the trailhead can be reached in 0.4 miles making for a 1.4 mile hike. The trail to the left leads to additional trails and the 2.1 and 2.3 mile-hike options. Bear left at this point to continue on the main circuit.

0.9   Trail intersection. The trail to the right forms a loop around the smaller wildlife pond. Follow it back to the trailhead for a 2.1 mile hike. The left fork forms a separate loop for the 2.3 mile hike. Bear left to continue on the main circuit.

1.4   Trail intersection. Bear left passing the trail to the right which leads back to the shelter. Those doing the 2.1 mile hike will turn right at this point.

1.9   Reach the dam of the smaller wildlife pond. A short way beyond the dam, the trail comes to an intersection where the right trail leads north to the trail shelter. Take the left trail for the dam of the larger pond. Just before reaching the second dam the trail turns sharply to the left .

2.1   Trail intersection near Minnesota State Road 73. Take the trail to the left to return to the trailhead.

2.3   Trailhead.

Rogers Lake

FOND DU LAC STATE FOREST

LENGTH	4.0 and 6.0 miles
TIME	3:30 for the 6.0 mile hike.
DIFFICULTY	Difficult
ROUTE-FINDING	Difficult
MAPS & PERMITS	DNR Fond du Lac State Forest map. USGS quad: Cromwell East. No permit is required.
GETTING THERE	From I-35, take exit 235 for Carlton and Cromwell on Minnesota State Road 210 going east. After 19.3 miles turn right onto County Road 73 going north. In .9 mile turn right on Krough Road; in 2.1 miles turn left on County Road 120 and follow it for about 6.9 miles until you reach Rogers Lake Road on the right. Turn right on Rogers Lake Road and go about 0.5 mile until you reach a gate. There is room on the side of the road here to park your car. I wouldn't encourage driving past the gate and parking further on if the gate is open. No telling who might come along will you're hiking and lock it.
TRAILHEAD GPS	46° 43' 46.1" N 92° 47' 51.8" W

The hike around Rogers Lake is noteworthy for the oak-maple forest and the hilly terrain. The trails in the area are used primarily for cross-country skiing and snowmobiling. Only the trails immediately around the lake and to the east on higher terrain are passable in the summer. Water covers the trail to the west between Rogers Lake and County Road 120.

People in the local area know the region as the "ditchbanks," after the ditches dug in the late 1910s to drain the land and tempt settlers to set up homesteads. The days of cut, burn, and farm lasted until the mid 1920s. Most homesteaders only lasted about three years before giving up and moving on.

Rogers Lake is named after an early settler who homesteaded near the lake. Kenneth and Blanche Kingsley cleared the area around the lake after they moved there in 1931. They farmed until 1940 when they moved to another farm south of Cromwell. In 1956, the DNR planted jack pine in the fields cleared by the Kingsleys. Plantations of white spruce and red pine are located here as well. A shelter was constructed at the east end of Rogers Lake in 1989 from logs of white spruce taken from one of these plantations.

Broad-winged Hawk

You may see a Broad-winged Hawk on your hike around Rogers Lake. It's not difficult to miss if one should scold you from an overhead perch along the trail as you pass through its territory. But you may get only a glimpse as it disappears through the trees. While the Broad-winged Hawk is one of the most numerous birds of prey nesting in North America, it prefers secretive nesting sites within large continuous forests.

Arthur Cleveland Bent, a well-known ornithologist in the early part of this century, writes about the Broad-winged Hawk: "In May, when the tender, freshly opened oak leaves are as big as a crow's foot, when the farmer goes out to sow his corn, and when the hosts of warblers are migrating through the treetops, then may we look for the home secrets of the Broadwings. They are gentle, retiring, quiet birds of the deep forests."

Broadwings belong to the group of raptors known as buteos—large, soaring hawks with rounded wingtips and banded tails. They are among the smallest buteos, with a wingspan of just over three feet. The wings are white to cream underneath with a dark border on the trailing, or back, edges; the tail has broad black and white bands with the last white band being wider than the others. The head, back, and wing-tops are dark brown.

The Broadwing breeds in large, deciduous or mixed deciduous forests east of the plains. Its preference for forests restrict it to the eastern two-thirds of Minnesota. Ornithologists L. J. Goodrich, S. C. Crocoll, and S. E. Senner, writing on the natural history of the Broad-winged Hawk, report that in Wisconsin and Minnesota, Broadwings prefer managed oak-aspen forests at least 35 to 50 years old. Northern red oak tend to dominate in nesting stands. The hawks usually built their nests in the first major crotch of deciduous trees or on a branch against the trunk of a conifer.

Broadwings are complete migrants, leaving the North American continent, except for the southernmost tip of Florida, in winter. They spend their winter months in Central and South America, traveling as far as Chile and Argentina. Broadwings are one of the latest migrants to return in the spring and one of the earliest to leave in the fall, partly because they rely heavily on cold-blooded prey. They take about 40 days to make their twice-a-year trips from one continent to another, traveling anywhere from 60 to 300 miles a day depending on the weather. Their fall migration coincides in some regions with the migration of dragonflies and damselflies, which they prey upon during their long journey.

Broad-winged Hawks feed below the forest canopy near openings, clearings, or bodies of water. They are seldom seen during the breeding season. They eat frogs and toads, insects, small mammals, snakes, and juvenile birds. Broadwings eat small mammals whole, while they skin frogs and snakes, and pluck birds.

A hawk observer described the Broadwing as "one of the most sluggish and indolent of birds, rarely undertaking any vigorous exertion which can well be avoided." The author continues: "After alighting on a low branch or stub overlooking some shallow reach of calm water bespectacled with innumerable floating toads absorbed in the cares and pleasures of procreation, and rending the still air with the ceaseless din of their tremulous voices, the hawk will often gaze down at them long and listlessly, as if undecided which particular one to select from among so many, or dreamily gloat over the wealth of opportunities for such selection." This passage may leave one to wonder whether the writer was attributing to the hawk something of his own nature.

The hike begins at the locked gate on Rogers Lake Road and along a dirt road. The trail soon enters a forest dominated by birch and maple, and passes a red pine plantation. As you continue, the forest becomes dominated by oak, with maple and birch and occasional tree plantations. You will reach the circuit portion of this hike 1.3 miles from the trailhead. It circles Rogers Lake over a terrain of short hills with many small woodland ponds that are attractive to Broad-winged Hawks. This would be a good fall hike when the oaks, maples, and birches are changing colors.

Stride-by-Stride

MILES	DESCRIPTION
0.0	Walk past the large metal gate and along the dirt road.
0.3	The road enters the forest.
0.4	Enter a grove of red pines and bear left passing a trail to the right.

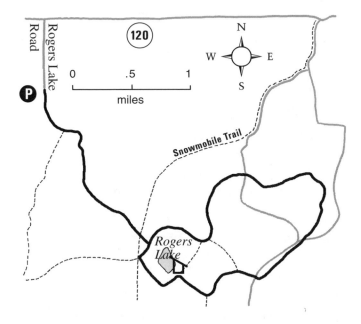

0.8 The trail emerges from the forest, skirts the edge of a clearing, and reenters the forest in 400 feet.

1.1 Continue past a snowmobile trail, marked with an orange diamond, coming in on the left.

1.2 Trail intersection; bear left passing the snowmobile trail on the right.

1.3 Trail intersection beginning the circuit portion of this hike; bear left on the trail marked with blue diamonds.

1.7 Trail intersection. For the 6.0 mile hike bear left at this point and then left again in 150 feet at the next intersection. Turn right for the 4.0 mile hike.

THE REST OF THE 4.0 MILE HIKE

1.9 Trail shelter near the shore of Rogers Lake.

2.1 Trail intersection; turn right to return to the trailhead, passing the trail on the left.

2.5 Five-way trail intersection; take the trail marked with a blue diamond immediately on the right.

2.7 Trail intersection completing the circuit of Rogers Lake. Turn left to return to the trailhead.

2.8 Trail intersection; continue straight ahead passing the trail to the left. In a short while, at the next intersection, bear left.

3.6 Bear right passing te trail to the left.

3.7 The trail emerges from the forest.

4.0 Trailhead.

THE REST OF THE 6.0 MILE HIKE

2.2 Continue straight ahead across the road.

2.9 The trail makes a hard turn to the left immediately after crossing two gullies.

3.3 The trail enters a narrow clearing with a pond on the left and a road coming in on the right; continue straight ahead.

3.5 Trail intersection; bear left following the blue diamond trail.

3.7 Trail intersection; continue straight ahead crossing a snowmobile trail. In 400 feet, at another intersection, continue straight ahead passing a trail to the right.

4.0 Trail intersection; bear right passing the trail to the left.

4.1 Trail intersection; bear left. The trail to the right leads to the Rogers Lake shelter in 0.2 miles.

4.5 Five-way intersection; take the trail immediately on the right marked with a blue diamond.

4.7 Trail intersection completing the circuit of Rogers' Lake. Turn left to return to the trailhead.

4.8 Trail intersection; continue straight ahead passing the trail to the left. In a short while, at the next intersection, bear left.

5.6 Bear right passing the trail to the left.

5.7 The trail emerges from the forest.

6.0 Trailhead.

Silver Creek–
Bear Chase Trails

3.3, 6.6 M
MODERATE-DIFFICULT

JAY COOKE STATE PARK

LENGTH	3.3 and 6.6 miles
TIME	3:45 for the 6.6 mile hike.
DIFFICULTY	Moderate-Difficult
ROUTE-FINDING	Easy
MAPS & PERMITS	DNR Jay Cooke State Park map. USGS quads: Esko and Cloquet. A Minnesota State Park permit is required.
GETTING THERE	From I-35 take Exit 235 for Carlton and Cromwell. Turn east on Minnesota State Road 210 and drive 5.4 miles to the Jay Cooke State Park Headquarters entrance on the right.
TRAILHEAD GPS	46° 39' 17.2" N 92° 22' 14.8" W

Jay Cooke State Park offers 50 miles of hiking trails along both sides of the St. Louis River. Here you will find a rolling terrain where the hiking ranges from easy to challenging and the trails are well maintained and marked. There are plenty of spectacular views of the St. Louis River valley and of tributary valleys.

Jay Cooke Geology

A highlight of Jay Cooke State Park is the extreme age contrast of its geological features: outcrops of ancient Thompson Slate and the more recent deposits of red clay. The slate outcroppings are most prominent along the St. Louis River gorge above and below the swinging bridge behind the park headquarters. According to George Schwartz and George Thiel, in *Minnesota's Rocks and Streams*, the slate beds formed from sediments in a mid-continental Precambrian sea. The weight of accumulated sediments compressed the lower layers to form shale which was later transformed into slate. Underground pressures and movements folded the slate and tilted so that the rock layers now dip at sharp angles. In most places the river flows parallel to the exposed edges of the tilted slate. You can see this clearly from the swinging bridge.

A short distance below the bridge, the slate exposures end and the river valley broadens. Here the river flows between banks of red clay deposited about 10,000 years ago when Glacial Lake Duluth covered much of the lower St. Louis River valley, including Jay Cooke State Park.

In some places there are "dikes" of igneous rock within the Thompson Slate. Dikes form when molten magma intrudes between layers of existing rock. In *Minnesota Underfoot,* an excellent resource for those interested in Minnesota's natural history, author Constance Jefferson Sansome writes that after the folding and tilting of the Thompson Slate had occurred, molten material forced its way into cracks in the slate, cooled, and hardened to form dikes. One such dike is visible from the swinging bridge. It runs from the north end of the bridge in a southwesterly direction across the river channel and ends east of the nearby island.

If you look closely enough, you can see rain prints, mud cracks, and ripple marks in the slate that were present in the sediment layers just before more layers of sediment covered them and they were transformed into shale. The ripple marks show up as elongated dimples. You can see them on the west side of the bridge at its north end.

After crossing the St. Louis River on the swinging bridge, this hike follows the River Trail downstream. Here you will get a close look at the river as it begins to broaden out below the narrow dales and turbulent rapids. Leaving the river, the hike continues on the Silver Creek Trail with more views of the river from higher vantage points. Eventually though, the trail turns away from the river to follow Silver Creek. At a trail shelter high above the creek, you get an idea of the depth of sediment left behind by Glacial Lake Duluth. The shelter sits on about 50–60 feet of red clay.

As you hike along you can't help noticing the openness of the understory in the forested areas. This is because of the high number of white-tailed deer in the park. Protected from regular hunting, and with no other large predators to keep their numbers in check, the deer population has grown unnaturally. Their heavy browsing of young vegetation, including tree seedlings, keeps the undergrowth thin. The Minnesota DNR has plans to allow hunters with muzzle-loaded rifles to shoot deer in an effort to reduce their population.

After crossing Silver Creek, the trail continues along the creek before moving on to the hillier Bear Chase Trails. The steep nature of the terrain is because of the severe erosion of lakebed sediments. Fortunately, the climbs are short, and the ridges provide some excellent views.

After the Bear Chase Trails, the hike returns to the Silver Creek Trail and returns to the trailhead.

From early to mid-June, you are likely to find large numbers of Yellow Lady's Slippers along the upper portion of the Silver Creek Trail near the end of the hike. This wildflower belongs to the orchid family and grows in bogs and swamps and rich forests throughout much of North America. The flowers include the distinctive yellow, inflated, pouch-shaped lip petal. Cherokee Indians of southeastern North America used a drink prepared from the roots of the Lady's Slipper as a treatment for worms.

There are many opportunities for watching wildlife on this hike. Birds, beaver, and deer are abundant in the park, along with black bears. When I did this hike in early June, I saw a black bear sow with two cubs along the river and bear scat in several places along the trails. While you may not see black bears, which are secretive creatures, white-tailed deer are more accustomed to people and are as likely to watch you hike by as you are to watch them.

BEGINNING OF BOTH THE 3.3 AND 6.6 MILE HIKES

MILES   DESCRIPTION

0.0   Both the 3.3 and 6.6 mile hikes begin at the swinging bridge behind the park headquarters. After crossing the bridge, turn left onto the River Trail.

0.2   Trail intersection; continue straight ahead on the trail along the river, passing the trail to the right.

0.6   The trail bears away from the river and comes to a trail intersection. Turn left here onto the Silver Creek Trail.

1.1   The trail bears away from the river.

1.4   Trail shelter overlooking Silver Creek (46° 38' 42.7" N 92° 21' 7.8" W).

1.8   Trail intersection; turn left here for the 6.6 mile hike; go right for the 3.3 mile hike.

THE 3.3 MILE HIKE

2.1   Cross a small bridge. The trail is wet in places beyond the bridge and eventually comes to a second bridge and a beaver pond on the right. Here you can get a good look at a

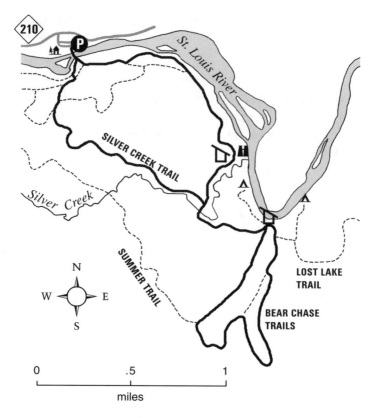

beaver dam and lodge. The trail begins to ascend shortly after the second bridge. It is along this section of the trail that you will find Yellow Lady's Slippers blooming in early to mid-June.

2.9   Trail intersection; bear right.

3.0   Trail intersection; continue straight ahead passing the trail on the right.

3.1   Trail intersection; continue straight passing the trail coming in from the left. From this point on there are a number of trails leading off the main trail. Stay along the edge of the river until you reach the swinging bridge.

3.3   The swinging bridge and trailhead.

THE 6.6 MILE HIKE

1.8   Shortly after turning left onto this trail (in about 100 yards) come to a bridge crossing Silver Creek. The trail bears left after crossing the bridge and follows the creek.

2.2   Trail shelter and intersection (46° 38' 25.1" N 92° 20' 54.3" W); the trail to the left leads to the High Landing Remote

30

Campsite. Continue on the trail leading straight ahead to begin a circuit on the Bear Chase Trails that will return to this point via the trail coming in on the right.

2.4 Trail intersection just before reaching the power lines; the trail to the left leads to the Upper and Lower Lake Trails. Continue straight ahead on the trail passing under the power lines.

2.5 Trail intersection; bear left, cross a small bridge, and begin to ascend.

2.9 Pass along a sharp ridge crest with good views of the valley to the east.

3.1 The trail descends into a ravine.

3.4 Trail intersection; turn sharply to the left and begin a steep ascent from the ravine.

3.9 Trail intersection; continue to the right passing the Summer Trail on the left.

4.5 Trail shelter and intersection; you have been here before. This completes the Bear Chase Trails circuit portion of this 6.6 mile hike. Turn left to return to the trailhead.

4.9 Bridge over Silver Creek.

5.0 Trail intersection; bear left.

5.4 Cross a small bridge. The trail is wet in places beyond the bridge. Pass a beaver pond on the right. Here you get a good look at a beaver dam and lodge.

5.9 Pass a picnic table on the right. Just beyond this point you can see Yellow Lady's Slippers blooming from early to mid-June.

6.2 Trail intersection; bear right.

6.3 Trail intersection; continue straight ahead passing the trail on the right.

6.4 Trail intersection; continue straight passing the trail on the left. From this point on there are a number of trails leading off the main trail. Stay on the main trail until you reach the swinging bridge.

6.6 The bridge and the trailhead.

Organtz Trail

JAY COOKE STATE PARK

LENGTH	2.0 miles
TIME	1:00
DIFFICULTY	Easy
ROUTE-FINDING	Easy
MAPS & PERMITS	DNR Jay Cooke State map. USGS quad: Esko. A Minnesota State Park permit is required.
GETTING THERE	From I-35 take Exit 235 for Carlton and Cromwell. Turn left going east on Minnesota State Road 210 and continue for 6.4 miles to the picnic area on the right side of the road.
TRAILHEAD GPS	46° 39' 18.6" N 92° 21' 9.1" W

Jay Cooke State Park offers 50 miles of hiking trails along sections of the St. Louis River and over the rugged terrain bordering the river. The state initially formed the park from 2,350 acres of land owned by the St. Louis River Power Company. The power company had earlier bought all the land along the river between Fond du Lac and Carlton. Jay Cooke, a wealthy financier, encouraged this effort. His heirs were instrumental in making the land donation to the state, which has purchased additional lands to bring the park to its current size of 8,818 acres.

Before settlers came in the 1800s, Indians, fur traders, and missionaries traveled the region's lakes and rivers. The era of the fur trader began with the French trading with the Dakota. Later, Ojibwa tribes, forced out of their territory by increased settlement in the east, moved into the area driving out the Dakota. The French also had problems as disputes with the British broke out over rights to trade in the area.

An important feature of the fur trading years was the Grand Portage of the St. Louis River, part of which is in Jay Cooke State Park. This trail, used by travelers moving between Lake Superior and the Mississippi River or Rainy Lake regions, was seven miles long. It began above Fond du Lac and ended just below Scanlon. From there, travelers continued up the St. Louis River to Lake Vermilion and the Rainy Lake country; or they could turn west at Floodwood on the Savanna River to get to the Mississippi.

Eventually the demand for furs declined, along with a decline in available fur-bearing animals, and the fur trade came to a halt. It wasn't until railroads reached the area that it experienced a second boom in activity. Settlers rode the rails north to new land and jobs. Loggers came to cut timber, and farmers followed. Loggers cut timber within the area of Jay Cooke State Park in the 1850s, but the land was too rough for farming. Instead, the St. Louis River Power Company developed the river to provide hydroelectric power.

At one time, beginning in 1870, the Lake Superior and Mississippi Railroad, with financial support from Jay Cooke, had a line along the north bank of the St. Louis River connecting Thomson west of the park with Fond du Lac to the east.

The Organtz Trail, passing through forests of aspens, birches, and maples, provides excellent views of the St. Louis River. In this part of the park the river valley broadens between banks of red clay. The clay collected on the floor of Glacial Lake Duluth some 10,000 years ago at the end of the last great ice age. When the retreating continental ice sheet blocked the current outlet of Lake Superior, the water level in the lake basin was much higher then it is today. The high waters of Glacial Lake Duluth reached up the St. Louis River valley to Jay Cooke State Park. The ancient lake drained southward through the Brule and St. Croix rivers. As the ice sheet began its gradual retreat, it exposed successively lower outlets until finally the lake was able to flow into Lake Huron through the St. Mary's River. The drop in the lake's water level unveiled thick accumulations of red clay. The erosion of this clay into steep valleys accounts for some of the rugged topography within the park.

Stride-by-Stride

MILES	DESCRIPTION
0.0	From the parking lot the trail leads south between the two stone buildings. In 340 feet come to a trail intersection where the trail to the right leads 50–60 feet to an observation deck providing panoramic views of the St. Louis River. The main trail bears left.
0.2	Oldenberg Point—an overlook providing views of the St. Louis River to the south and east. Leave the overlook on the Organtz Trail to the left. In about 250 feet, bear right at the trail intersection.

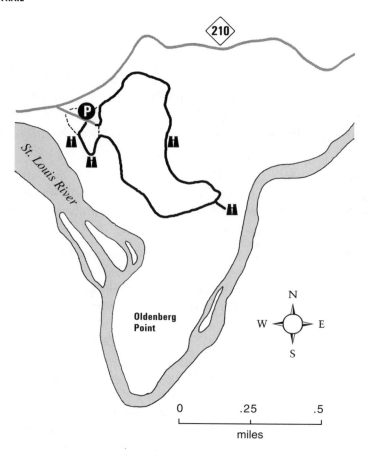

0.3   Trail intersection; bear right, staying on the Organtz Trail, passing the trail to the left.

0.7   A spur trail to the right leads to an overlook and a small bench in 260 feet. The overlook provides a panoramic view downstream along the St. Louis River.

1.1   A spur trail, marked with a sign post, leads to another overlook. A small woodland pond is on the right side of the trail just beyond this point.

1.8   Trail intersection near Minnestoa State Road 210; bear left.

1.9   Trail intersection; turn right onto a small foot trail leading back to the parking lot and the trailhead in 200 feet.

Mission Creek Trail

131st AVENUE WEST, FOND DU LAC, WEST DULUTH

3.9, 5.0 M
MODERATE

LENGTH	There is a 3.9 mile hike and a 5.0 mile hike.
TIME	3:00 for the 5.0 mile hike.
DIFFICULTY	Moderate
ROUTE-FINDING	Moderate
MAPS & PERMITS	An interpretive brochure with a sketch of the longer loop is available from Duluth Public Works–Forestry Division, either by writing them at 110 North 42nd Avenue West, Duluth, MN 55807, or stopping by their office at the same address. USGS quad: Esko. No permit is required.
GETTING THERE	Drive west through Duluth on Minneosta State Route 23 West (or Grand Avenue) and turn right on 131st Avenue West. In 0.4 mile you will come to a gate. Continue past the gate for another 0.4 mile until you come to the end of the road and the trailhead.
TRAILHEAD GPS	46° 40' 19.5" N 92° 16' 43.2" W

Fond du Lac History

The community of Fond du Lac, where the Mission Creek Trail begins, was once a small Native American settlement. In 1783, Jean Baptiste Cadotte, a French fur trader, made the first written record of an Ojibwa village at this site. Historians believe that Daniel Greysolon, Sieur du Lhut, passed here in 1679 on a mission to get Native American tribes to stop fighting each other and to trade with the French rather than the British.

According to some sources, Fond du Lac eventually became the site of the first permanent settlement of non-Native Americans in Minnesota. (Some sources state that Grand Portage, far up the North Shore near Canada, holds that distinction.) The British Northwest Fur Company set up a trading post at Fond du Lac, near the mouth of Mission Creek, in 1792. In 1817, an American Fur Company trading post replaced it.

In 1834, the Reverend Edmund F. Ely began a mission on the site of the present day Fond du Lac Community Church. The creek takes its name from the Ely Mission. The mission and a school closed in 1849 because of unfavorable relations with the employees of the American Fur Company and the Ojibwa residents. Ely eventually left the ministry and went into business in the Duluth-Superior area.

There is an old cemetery about 0.3 miles off the main trail of the 5.0 mile hike. The cemetery is on land that once belonged to Francis Roussain, who worked for a time for the American Fur Company. He offered this site as a replacement when the Lake Superior & Mississippi Railroad forced the villagers to relocate the Fond du Lac cemetery. Today two headstones, three bases, and several sunken plots without markers are all that remain within a wire fence. Francis Roussain and two of his young children are among those buried here.

One of the two headstones marks the final resting place of Vincent Roy, who died in Superior Wisconsin, on February 18, 1872. According to John A. Bardon, a self-proclaimed historian of the Twin Ports area, Vincent Roy was a successful businessman and wealthy property owner of Superior. Vincent Roy's father was French-Chippewa with connections to the American Fur Company both at Superior and Fond du Lac. His mother was Chippewa. Roy was a voyageur and interpreter for the earliest surveyors, missionaries, and explorers. He spoke French and several Indian dialects. He was self-educated and able to write with a "fine hand." He owned and operated a trading post engaged in fur and fishing businesses around Lake Superior. He and a business partner, Antoine Gordon, owned the Schooner Algonquin that was used in his business on Lake Superior.

In the 1880's, a brownstone quarry began operating just north of a dam located on the creek at the trailhead. This brownstone (from the Fond du Lac Sandstone Formation) was used to construct buildings in Duluth, Minneapolis/St. Paul, and Winnipeg, Manitoba.

A major portion of the Mission Creek Trail follows part of the old Skyline Parkway system. The Works Progress Administration built this length of road, along with its bridges, to connect Minnesota Highway 23 and the section of Skyline Parkway that remains in use today. This bit of road fell into disrepair and was eventually abandoned after frequent washouts made it difficult to maintain. Today five bridges remain: four crossing Mission Creek and one over the Willard Munger State Trail.

Mission Creek Geology

The geology of the Mission Creek area varies from ancient slates formed more than 1.7 billion years ago, to deposits of glacial till left by glaciers only tens of thousands of years ago. It differs significantly from most streams and rivers along the North Shore in that its course is a gradual descent. Mission Creek drains a valley with gentle slopes; you won't find any waterfalls or cascades like those along North Shore rivers.

Large-flowered Trillium

The hiker can find huge patches of Large-flowered Trillium blooming in early June along the trail before reaching the Willard Munger State Trail. This flower is a member of the lily family and grows in rich woods and thickets; it is the largest and most showy of the trillium flowers. Native Americans gathered the roots and chewed them for medicinal purposes. They also cooked and ate the greens, a practice that killed the plant, because the rootstock usually dies when the leaves are picked. Late spring, when thousands of trillium paint the forest floor white with their blossoms, is an excellent time to enjoy this hike.

Trail Highlights

The Mission Creek Trail begins at the site of a holding dam built to catch logs and other debris eroded from the creek's banks. The steep banks at the dam site provide an excellent opportunity to see the youngest part of the area's geological record. The bottom of the bank consists of till, a mixture of fine silts, sand, rocks, and boulders deposited by glaciers. Near the top of the bank are fine, silty deposits from the time when Fond du Lac was covered by Glacial Lake Duluth, a giant lake fed by the meltwaters of the shrinking glacier.

The trail passes through a mature forest of white spruce and balsam fir as it heads north along a small tributary stream of Mission Creek. It then ascends gradually, crossing a number of small wooden bridges. Exercise caution as some of the bridge boards are rotted.

As the trail ascends to the Willard Munger State Trail, it passes into a mature forest of northern hardwoods: maple, oak, and basswood. After following the Willard Munger State Trail for a short distance, the trail climbs to the top of a bridge that carried the old road over the railroad. From here the hiker can see Ely's Peak to the southeast. This peak, volcanic in origin, is about 1.1 million years old. From the bridge, the trail descends along Mission Creek on the old road through an aspen and white birch forest. This is a primary or pioneer forest type that will eventually be replaced by northern hardwoods like those seen at nearby Magney-Snively.

While some of the original bridges still cross Mission Creek, there are several places were the trail crosses the creek without the benefit of bridges. Unless there has been a recent heavy rainfall, these shallows can usually be crossed without getting too wet.

Three miles into the hike the trail forks and the hiker can choose between the left fork that returns directly to the trailhead in just under one mile, and the right fork with a longer hike of another 1.8 miles.

Stride-by-Stride

MILES   DESCRIPTION

0.0   Take the trail that ascends the right side of Mission Creek. In about 460 feet, pass a trail descending to the left.

1.4   Pass a trail coming in sharply from the right; continue straight ahead.

1.5   Intersection with the Willard Munger State Trail; turn left.

1.7   Bear left just before reaching the overpass on the Willard Munger State Trail (46° 41' 25.2" N 92° 16' 41.3"W). This trail ascends to Seven Bridges Road in about 250 feet; turn left and follow the road as it descends along Mission Creek.

2.2   Continue straight ahead. passing a trail to the left.

2.3   Come to the first bridge crossing Mission Creek.

2.5   A second bridge crossing Mission Creek.

2.7   Creek crossing with no bridge; after crossing the creek come to another crossing, also without a bridge, in about 190 feet. After this second crossing come to a third bridge over Mission Creek in about 100 feet.

3.0   Trail intersection. The left fork continues along Mission Creek and leads back to the trailhead in 0.9 mile. The right fork leads away from Mission Creek and returns to the trailhead in another 2.0 miles.

TAKING THE LEFT FORK

3.2   Take a short trail to the right into the woods. This will bring you, in about 200 feet, to a creek crossing. After crossing the creek, walk downstream a short way to pick up the main trail once again. If you miss this turn to the right, the main trail will bring you to a deep crossing. Backtrack and look for the short trail leading to the shallower crossing.

3.3   Another creek crossing.

3.4   The fourth bridge crossing Mission Creek.

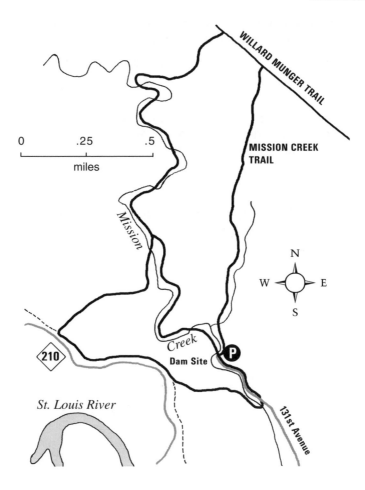

3.8   Yet another creek crossing.

3.9   The next to last creek crossing. In about 200 feet, come to the last creek crossing and the trailhead.

TAKING THE RIGHT FORK

3.0   About 400 feet beyond the Y-intersection, come to a bridge crossing Mission Creek. After crossing the bridge, the trail ascends away from the creek until it reaches Minnesota State Highway 210.

3.6   Trail approaches Minnesota State Highway 210. Just before reaching the highway pass a trail on the right. (This trail leads, in about 0.3 miles, to an old cemetery.) Several more feet on reach a trail to the left. Turn left on this trail and follow it as it parallels Minnesota State Highway 210.

4.1 A short spur trail to the right leads to a small parking area along the highway in about 50 feet.

4.2 The trail turns sharply left and away from the highway. Look for a hiker sign on a tree about 30 feet ahead after making this turn.

4.4 Cross the first of a series of small wooden bridges as the trail descends rather steeply along a narrow ravine with steep slopes on either side.

4.6 The trail gradually approaches Mission Creek on the left.

4.8 Cross Mission Creek. Turn left after the crossing and make your way across the field to the road and back to the trailhead.

5.0 Trailhead.

Magney-Snively

WEST SKYLINE PARKWAY, DULUTH

3.2, 3.8, 5.8, & 7.8 M
MODERATE-DIFFICULT

LENGTHS	Hikes of 3.2, 3.8, 5.8, and 7.8 miles are possible on this trail system.
TIME	4:15 for the 7.8 mile hike
DIFFICULTY	Moderate-Difficult
ROUTE-FINDING	Moderate
MAPS & PERMITS	City of Duluth Public Works–Forestry Division has a rough map of the Magney-Snively Cross-Country Ski Trail. USGS quads: West Duluth and Esko. No permit is required.
GETTING THERE	Take Exit 249 off I-35 (Boundary Avenue exit) and turn east on West Skyline Parkway. At 0.4 mile continue on West Skyline Parkway by turning left at stop sign. Continue on the Parkway for another 2.0 miles to parking lot on the left.
TRAILHEAD GPS	46° 42' 10.6" N 92° 13' 35.3" W

Although the City of Duluth maintains Magney-Snively for cross-country skiing, it is a good place for hiking as well. You will hike through a northern hardwood forest of oak, maple, and basswood, and over many short ridges and shallow swales. Late May is a good time to do this hike, when Marsh Marigolds and Large-flowered Trillium are in bloom, and lush green grass carpets the forest floor. This would also be a good hike to do in the fall after the leaves have turned their brilliant oranges and reds, and the trails are perhaps a little drier.

The Bardon's Peak and Ely's Peak overlooks provide panoramic views of the lower St. Louis River valley and the Duluth-Superior Harbor. The views from the overlooks make them good spots to linger and have a snack or lunch.

Hikers at Magney-Snively have different options for hikes from 3.2 to 7.8 miles long. The main circuit, without the loops to the two overlooks, is 3.8 miles long. The main circuit and both of the overlook loops is 7.8 miles long. A trip just to Bardon Peak Overlook by way of the loop and returning directly to the trailhead without completing the main circuit is 3.2 miles long. Taking the main circuit and either one of the overlook loops is 5.8 miles long.

Duluth Gabbro

The overlooks at Magney-Snively provide some of the largest exposures of Duluth Gabbro along the North Shore. This huge expanse of volcanic rock, exposed in scattered locations like these two overlooks, never made it to the earth's surface in the rock's infancy.

At the time the magma of the Duluth Gabbro was rising through the earth's crust, a thick accumulation of lava from previous eruptions already covered the surface. This thick layer of hardened rock kept the magma from breaking through and reaching the surface.

Millions of years of erosion, caused mostly by glaciers, wore away the overlaying layers of rock, exposing the gabbro in various places, most notably in Duluth. Today the gabbro mass extends at or beneath the surface for about 60–100 miles up the North Shore, and under Lake Superior to the South Shore where it reappears in Wisconsin and Michigan.

Duluth-Superior Harbor

The Duluth-Superior Harbor is a good example of an estuary, or drowned river mouth. This estuary exists because of a difference in the rate at which the earth's crust at the eastern and western ends of the Lake Superior Basin rebounded after the last ice age.

With the advance of glaciers from the north, the earth's crust sank under the tremendous weight of the ice sheets, which were a thousand feet thick in places. As the glacier filling the Superior Basin retreated from the Duluth-Superior end of the basin, the crust began to rebound very slowly. Meanwhile, the eastern end of the basin remained under the weight of the glacier for one thousand years. Only when the glacier had retreated further north did the east end of the basin begin to rebound. By this time, though, the rebounding at the west end of the basin had slowed. The rebounding eastern end, rising faster than the western end, pushed Lake Superior up the mouth of the St. Louis River, "drowning" it. If it were not for this geological event, the Duluth-Superior Harbor would not be the world class harbor it is today.

Stride-by-Stride

THIS DESCRIPTION IS FOR THE FULL 7.8 MILE HIKE, WHICH INCLUDES BOTH OVERLOOKS

MILES   DESCRIPTION

0.0   The trailhead is opposite the parking lot. From West Skyline Parkway, a wide dirt path ascends into the forest. After 150

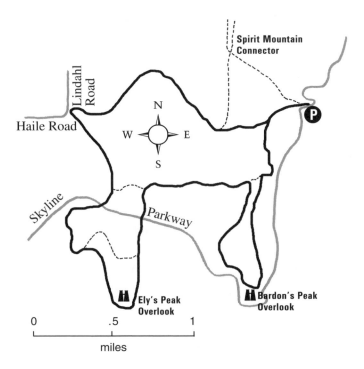

feet the hiking trail, marked with blue diamonds on some trees, bears left.

0.1   The trail crosses a snowmobile trail; continue straight ahead.

0.2   Pass a trail coming in sharply on the right.

0.5   Trail intersection beginning the circuit portion of this hike; continue straight ahead. The circuit will be completed via the trail coming in on the right.

0.6   Trail intersection with the Bardon's Peak Overlook Loop on the left. The trail to Bardon's Peak Overlook is a 2.0 mile loop that eventually brings you back to the main circuit trail about 400 feet further ahead. Turn left.

0.8   Trail intersection; bear left passing a trail on the right.

1.6   Bardon's Peak Overlook. The trail turns sharply to the right here leading away from the overlook and back to the main circuit trail.

2.4   Trail intersection; continue straight passing a trail on the right.

2.6   Trail intersection with the main circuit trail. Turning right at this point takes you back to the trailhead, for a 3.2 mile hike. To continue the full circuit hike, turn left.

3.0 Trail intersection with the beginning of the Ely's Peak Overlook Loop on the left. This is another 2.0 mile loop. The trail to the right is the Cut Off Trail which bypasses Ely's Peak. (If you take the Cut Off Trail, bear right in 0.3 miles at a trail intersection. In 0.4 miles, bear right again and come to the main circuit trail in another 120 feet. Then turn right. At this point you will be 2.3 miles from the trailhead.) Turn left to continue the full circuit.

3.1 Cross Skyline Parkway.

3.3 Trail intersection; bear left towards Ely's Peak Overlook passing a trail on the right.

3.9 Ely's Peak Overlook where the trail bears sharply to the right, leading away from the overlook and back to the main circuit trail.

4.3 Trail intersection; bear left passing a trail on right.

4.8 Reach Skyline Parkway. Bear right on the road for about 300 feet and then left onto the trail.

5.0 Trail intersection; the Cut Off Trail comes in on the right. Bear left on the main circuit trail.

5.3 Cross a wooden bridge and soon pass a beaver pond on the left.

6.9 Trail intersection; continue straight ahead, passing a trail on the left. Cross another trail in 75 feet. In another 200 feet, pass a trail again on the right.

7.2 Trail intersection ending the circuit portion of this hike. Turn left to return to the trailhead.

7.8 Trailhead.

Park Point Nature Trail

4.1 M
MODERATE

MINNESOTA POINT, DULUTH

LENGTH	4.1 miles
TIME	2:30
DIFFICULTY	Moderate
ROUTE-FINDING	Easy
MAPS & PERMITS	A brochure with a diagram of the trail is available from the City of Duluth Public Works. USGS quad: Superior. No permit is required.
GETTING THERE	Take Minnesota Avenue in Canal Park, Duluth, to the parking area next to the Sky Harbor Airport. The trail begins on the road behind the airport buildings.
TRAILHEAD GPS	46° 43' 38.9" N 92° 2' 49.7" W

The Park Point Nature Trail covers two miles of Minnesota Point, a seven mile sand spit at the mouth of the St. Louis River separating the Duluth-Superior Harbor from Lake Superior. Together with the three miles of Wisconsin Point, they form the longest fresh water sand bar in the world. The sandbar is formed from sand eroded from the banks of the St. Louis River and the south shore of Lake Superior by the prevailing wave action and currents of the lake. A natural opening, the Superior Entry, exists where the Nemadji and St. Louis Rivers meet and flow into Lake Superior. The 300 foot-wide ship canal near the base of Minnesota Point was dredged in 1871.

Minnesota Point

Native American Indians often camped on Minnesota Point. The Chippewa Indians called it *Shaga-wa-mik*, meaning "long narrow point of land." A Chippewa legend relates how the Great Spirit created the sand bar to save a young brave from capture by the Sioux. The brave was cornered by the Sioux on the south shore of Lake Superior, and the Great Spirit urged him into the lake's icy waters. As the brave stepped into the water, land began to form in front of him and so he raced ahead. The Great Spirit then made the land sink behind the fleeing brave, forming the Superior Entry.

Because of its location and makeup, Minnesota Point is an important stopping off place for migrating birds. It is not uncommon during spring migration for thousands of birds to spend a day or more at Minnesota Point resting and refueling before resuming their journey northward. While a spring day with light rain or fog on Minnesota Point may find most people staying indoors, birdwatchers will head for Minnesota Point to scope out "grounded" migrants.

Minnesota Point is also noted for its virgin stand of red and white pines. You can distinguish these trees by their appearance at a distance and by differences in their bark and needles. The silhouette of a white pine shows a dark trunk, with spreading, horizontal branches. The red pine silhouette also shows a tall, straight trunk with horizontal branches with ascending tips. Its crown is symmetrical, which is not true of the white pine. The red pine's branch tips, with their long, dark green needles, look like bottle brushes. The bark of white pines is dark, thick, and deeply furrowed. The bark of the red pine is reddish, not as thick, and quite scaly. You can also distinguish the pines by their needles. White pine needles are arranged in bundles of five, while red pine needles occur in bundles of two. An easy way to remember this is to relate the five letters in the word "white" with the five needles per bundle of the White Pine.

Trail Highlights

There are several ruins along the hike that reveal how white people developed the southern end of Minnesota Point. After one mile, the trail passes a lone cottage, one of many that used to exist in the area. You can see the remains of the foundations of former cabins on the left side of the trail.

At 1.6 miles, the trail passes the ruins of an old lighthouse that once housed Duluth's first high-powered navigational light beacon. The light-house, built between 1855 and 1858 at a cost of $15,000, was 50 feet high and built of red bricks from Cleveland, Ohio. It was used only until 1875. Its lens is now used in the lighthouse on the west pierhead of the Superior Entry. The lighthouse served as the zero point for the first marine surveys of Lake Superior. All other points on the lake were located with reference to the lighthouse. The ruins is about two-thirds of the lighthouse's original height.

A tenth of a mile beyond the lighthouse is an abandoned boat house where a company built buoys and small boats. At the southernmost end of Minnesota Point, the trail reaches the Superior Entry, where large boats head to and from the Superior ore docks and grain elevators.

As you hike the sandy Park Point Nature Trail, be aware of poison ivy which grows abundantly on and off the trail. It has shiny or dull leaves arranged in groups of three. The leaves are reddish in the spring, green in the summer; the flowers yellow; and the fruit clusters white and berrylike. Poison ivy can grow as ground cover or a shrub. All parts of the plant contain the volatile oil that can cause a rash upon direct contact or exposure to the smoke of burning plants. If you touch the plant or handle clothing that may have brushed a plant, wash with soapy water to remove the toxic oil. Although humans find the plant harmful, the leaves provide forage for wildlife, and the fruit provide food for birds in winter.

Stride-by-Stride

MILES   DESCRIPTION

0.0   A sign marks the start of the nature trail on the dirt road behind the airport buildings.

0.4   Bear left off the road onto a sandy trail leading into the forest. This trail travels down the middle of the forest.

0.7   A thicket on the right in a break in the pine forest is filled with red osier dogwood and box elder.

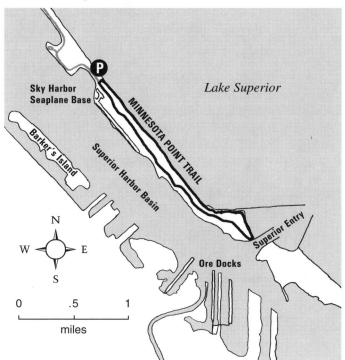

0.8   The trail emerges from the forest at the water pumping stations. Continue straight ahead, reentering the pine forest.

1.0   Pass a lone cottage on the right.

1.1   Pass the remains of an old metal tower.

1.6   Pass the lighthouse ruins (46° 42' 36.2" N 92° 1' 32.1" W).

1.7   Pass the remains of the boat house.

2.0   The Superior Ship Canal, a natural break between Minnesota and Wisconsin points. From here you can return to the trailhead by walking along the lake shore.

2.6   The end of the breakwater.

3.3   Pass the pumping station.

4.1   Come even with the light beacon at the northeast corner of the airport. Turn left here and cross over the dunes to return to the trailhead.

Summit Ledges

HAWK RIDGE NATURE RESERVE, DULUTH

LENGTH	1.4 miles
TIME	1:00
DIFFICULTY	Easy
ROUTE-FINDING	Moderate
MAPS & PERMITS	A Hawk Ridge Nature Reserve brochure provides a map of the trails along Hawk Ridge. USGS quad: Duluth. No permit is required.
GETTING THERE	The trailhead is located on the Skyline Parkway, 1 mile north of Glenwood Avenue in Duluth.
TRAILHEAD GPS	46° 50' 49.3" N 92° 1' 52.7" W

Hawk Ridge is the premier spot in the midwest, and one of the best in the United States, to view hawks during their fall migration. From August to December, bird enthusiasts descend upon Duluth from all over the world to witness thousands of hawks on the move.

Hawk Migration

Hawk Ridge hosts so many birds inpart due to Lake Superior. Hawks don't like to fly over large bodies of water because there aren't any thermal up drafts over cold water. Hawks rely on thermals to get altitude without expending a lot of energy. As hawks meet the lake in their migration south they funnel down the north shore in search of a way around the lake at Duluth, the westernmost tip of Lake Superior. The bluffs overlooking Duluth also create the updrafts hawks need to rise thousands of feet into the air and soar off to the south and warmer weather. Hawks can be seen in greater numbers on days when northwest to westerly winds tend to concentrate the birds along the north shore. Fewer hawks are seen from Hawk Ridge on days with precipitation or east winds.

Fall migration generally starts in mid-August when small raptors, like American Kestrels and Sharp-shinned Hawks, appear. The migration continues until December, when large raptors such as eagles and Red-tailed Hawks fly overhead. Peak migration is from mid-September to late October.

Many different things lure birdwatchers to Hawk Ridge. For some it's a day like September 18, 1994, when hawk counters saw a record 49,552 hawks; or the day 644 Bald Eagles soared overhead, showing that they are well on their way to recovery in the northland. For others, it's not the numbers but the species. The sighting of a Gyrfalcon, Peregrine Falcon, or a Golden Eagle can stir the blood of an avid hawk watcher.

Previous to 1950, anybody who went to Hawk Ridge probably did so to hunt the large birds. In 1950, the Duluth Bird Club (now the Duluth Audubon Society) put a halt to the slaughter by getting the city to enforce a prohibition against shooting within city limits. In 1972, the City of Duluth purchased the 115-acre Hawk Ridge Nature Reserve with funds donated by the Duluth Audubon Society. Today the Society manages the reserve for study and enjoyment under a trust agreement with the city.

Hawk Ridge provides over 2.5 miles of hiking trails. In addition to a good view of hawks from Summit Ledges in the fall, this 1.4 mile hike also provides a chance to see different forest types. Oaks dominate the dryer ridges, with balsams, spruces, and birches in the wetter areas. Paint blazes on trees and rocks indicate the trails, with blazes of different colors and shapes used to indicate the different trails.

Stride-by-Stride

MILES	DESCRIPTION
0.0	The hike begins on Ole's Trail which leaves the Main Overlook in a northerly direction, away from the lake. Ole's Trail is marked with red dots. After 325 feet, reach Ole's Knob. Here the trail makes a turn to the right and descends into the forest.
0.2	Trail intersection with the Amity Trail going right and left. Continue straight ahead following the red dots. In about 300 feet, reach Middle Knob which provides limited views of Duluth. From here the trail bears left.
0.4	Intersection with the Ridge Loop Trail (marked with yellow dots) going left and right; bear left. In 20 feet the trail forks; bear right.
0.5	The trail passes under a power line.
0.6	Summit Ledges; a good vantage point for hawk watching during the fall migration when there's a northwest wind. The Ridge Loop Trail continues across the ledges and begins to

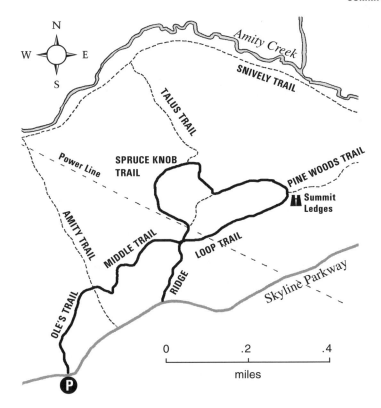

descend. In 150 feet, bear left passing the Pine Woods Trail (marked with blue diamonds) on the right.

0.8   Bear right on the Spruce Knob Trail leaving the Ridge Loop Trail. The Spruce Knob Trail is marked with orange diamonds.

0.9   Spruce Knob; bear left, staying on the Spruce Knob Trail, passing the Talus Trail (marked with red diamonds) on the right.

1.0   The trail emerges from the forest underneath the power line. Bear left staying on the Spruce Trail which ascends the right-of-way for about 100 yards until it intersects the Ridge Loop Trail. Turn right on the Ridge Loop Trail, following the yellow dots once again.

1.1   Pass the right fork of the Ridge Loop Trail (now on your left) and continue straight ahead. In about 20 feet, bear left on the Ridge Loop Trail passing the middle trail on the right.

1.2   Reach Skyline Parkway. Turn right and follow the road back to the trailhead.

1.4   Trailhead.

13

4.2 M
MODERATE

Otto Lake

SUPERIOR NATIONAL FOREST
LAURENTIAN RANGER DISTRICT

LENGTH	4.2 miles
TIME	2:30
DIFFICULTY	Moderate
ROUTE-FINDING	Moderate-Difficult. Moderate if the trail has been recently brushed.
MAPS & PERMITS	USGS quad: Fairbanks. No permit is required.
GETTING THERE	From Minnesota State Road 53 turn right on County Road 16, drive 26.7 miles to Forest Service Road 416, turn right and drive 4.0 miles to parking lot on the left side of the road. From Minnesota State Road 4, turn right on County Road 16 and drive 15.3 miles to Forest Service Road 416.
TRAILHEAD GPS	47° 19' 8.2" N 91° 58' 0.5" W

Otto Lake is at the very headwaters of the south branch of the White-face River, a tributary of the Cloquet River, which flows into the St. Louis River and on to Lake Superior. This is a region of wetlands, spruce bogs, and woodland swamps. While most of the route around Otto Lake is on the dry ground of ridge tops and slopes, there are two wet areas that must be crossed. At the north end of the lake is a spruce bog traversed by a 900 foot boardwalk. At the south end is an alder swamp that is crossed by a 250 foot boardwalk. Both of these board-walks have been in place for quite some time; they are considerably moss covered and partially rotten. However, with some care, and with the aid of a long walking stick for balance, you should be able to navi-gate them and stay fairly dry. Consider it a slight inconvenience for the sake of an otherwise good hike.

From the trailhead, the hike begins on the Otto Lake Portage Trail which crosses a small valley grown over with white birches and balsam firs. The trail descends very gradually at the start, but then ascends to a short ridge just before reaching the east shore of the lake. Here the trail turns north. As the route swings west, the trail climbs a narrow ridge, descends to the lake shore, crosses a small hill, and finally reaches the boardwalk through the spruce bog.

The bog supports black spruce and tamarack growing on a soggy bed of sphagnum moss which is the dominate groundlayer species. This is the typical habitat for the black spruce. What appear to be rather short, young trees, are actually quite old. Habitat conditions do not support the rate of growth for the bog-dwelling black spruce that is exhibited by most of the other trees in the region. Spruces with a diameter of only 2" have been found to be 127 years old.

If you look closely, you may see dense clusters of branches in the spruces. Sometimes referred to as "witches brooms," they are caused by dwarf mistletoe, a parasite of the black spruce. Mistletoe, while they have chlorophyll and can make their own food, have no roots and are partially parasitic on trees. While humans are poisoned by a sticky substance that covers the fruit, birds, such as Cedar Waxwings, love the small berries.

The trail down the west side of the lake is on dry ground, passing among white birches, aspens, and balsam firs. Signs of gnawed tree trunks attest to the presence of beavers. They are especially fond of the aspens. Moose also find the aspens much to their liking, and you'll see plenty of aspen saplings with their tops bent over and broken. The moose do this to reach the tender ends of the branches, which they feed on during the winter. The woody browse accounts for the sawdustlike appearance of their winter droppings.

At the southwest end of the lake, the 2.5 mile trail to Harris Lake branches off to the left. While the trail to Harris Lake is open, passing along a maple-covered ridge most of the way, the trail around Harris Lake is a different story. It is almost impassable in places due to heavy blowdowns. If you think you might like to add the Harris Lake Trail to your outing, call the Forest Service to check whether they have removed the blowdowns. If you decide to hike to Harris Lake you'll come to an intersection shortly after leaving the Otto Lake Trail. One trail forks off to the left, another continues straight ahead, and a third turns to the right. Take the middle trail.

Once past the turnoff to Harris Lake, the route around Otto Lake continues along a ridge, providing views up the length of the lake, and then descends as it comes to the second wetland area crossed by a boardwalk, this one passing through an alder thicket. The speckled alder, a tall, deciduous shrub, is the dominate species. Ruffed Grouse and woodcock prefer this type of vegetation as its dense growth helps to keep predators at bay.

Once across the second boardwalk, the route climbs back onto higher ground and turns north for the trailhead. There are two campsites on

Otto Lake, one on a small peninsula at the north end of the lake, and the other on a peninsula on the east side. Fall would be a good time to plan this hike, but be sure to go before deer season. Signs indicate that this is a very active hunting area.

Despite its relatively small size and lack of an island, the remoteness and sunlight Otto Lake gets makes it a suitable habitat for Common Loons. The dense vegetation along the shoreline, especially on the east side, provides them with the secretive nesting sites they prefer. Walking along the trail in midsummer, you may catch a glimpse of a family slipping away from shore, seeking the protection of open water.

Stride-by-Stride

MILES	DESCRIPTION
0.0	Hike northwest on the Otto Lake Portage Trail opposite the parking lot.
0.4	Trail intersection beginning the circuit portion of the hike; turn right on the Otto Lake Trail.
0.8	Trail bears left and ascends a short, narrow ridge at the northeast corner of Otto Lake.

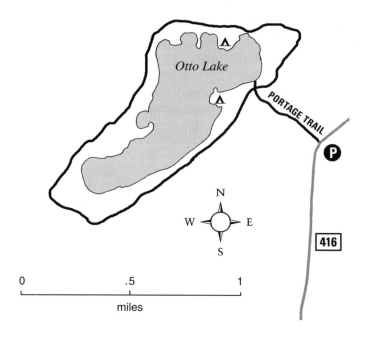

1.1 Trail descends briefly to the lake shore before ascending and moving away from the lake again.

1.3 Reach 900 foot boardwalk through a spruce bog. Use caution when crossing.

1.6 Trail intersection; a trail comes in sharply on the right from behind, continue straight ahead.

2.3 Trail intersection; bear left, passing the trail to the right.

2.4 Trail intersection; bear left passing the trail to Harris Lake on the right.

2.6 A second boardwalk, this one through an alder thicket. The condition of this 250 foot boardwalk is about the same as the first; be careful.

2.9 Trail intersection; continue straight ahead passing a trail to the left (which leads to the lake) and the right. In about 450 feet, pass another trail to the left.

3.6 A spur trail on the left leads to a campsite on the lake.

3.7 Trail intersection with the Otto Lake Portage trail. Turn right to return to the trailhead.

4.2 Trailhead.

14

4.5 M
MODERATE

Laurentian Divide

SUPERIOR NATIONAL FOREST
LAURENTIAN RANGER DISTRICT

LENGTH	4.5 miles
TIME	2:45
DIFFICULTY	Moderate
ROUTE-FINDING	Moderate
MAPS & PERMITS	An information sheet with map is available from the Laurentian District office in Aurora, Minnesota. USGS quad: Virginia. No permit is required.
GETTING THERE	Drive four miles north of Virginia on Minnesota State Highway 53. The parking area is on the right side of the road.
TRAILHEAD GPS	47° 34' 36.5" N 92° 32' 37.8" W

The Lookout Mountain Trails, located on the Laurentian Divide just north of Virginia, are in the heart of the Mesabi Iron Range. Streams and rivers north of the divide flow through Canada to Hudson Bay, while those to the south flow to Lake Superior, the Atlantic Ocean, or the Gulf of Mexico. Lookout Mountain is also a part of the Giants Range Batholith, a large mass of intrusive granite rock that has an igneous origin. Batholiths form the core of some mountain ranges and are associated with the mountain building process. Also in this part of northeastern Minnesota lie some of the world's richest deposits of iron ore: the Mesabi, Cayuna, and Vermillion ranges.

Iron Deposits

Iron formations in the Lake Superior region are about 2.2 billion years old, dating from the Early Proterozoic Era. In *Geology of the Lake Superior Region*, Gene LaBarge writes that similar iron formations occurred in other places around the world about the same time, but that there were no iron formations after the end of the Early Proterozoic, about 2.0 billion years ago. This raised an interesting question for geologists, "What happened that would cause deposits of iron mineral on a massive scale to occur and then never reoccur?"

Some geologists believe it was the advent of our oxygenated atmosphere that led to the iron formations and that has prevented formations since. Prior to the Early Proterozoic Era, iron was dissolved in the seas and oceans. At that time the earth's water and atmosphere were deficient of oxygen. Iron is soluble in oxygen deficient water; it is not, however, soluble in oxygenated water.

With the evolution of photosynthetic organisms and their explosive growth during the Early Proterozoic Era, oxygen gradually became plentiful in the air, and in the water. As oxygen levels increased, iron began to precipitate out of the water and settle in huge quantities on the floor of seas and oceans. Since water became oxygen rich, no more iron has dissolved in the water, hence, no large iron formations have reoccurred.

It's a fascinating story. A major biological event that made possible life as we know it, also formed vast deposits of an element that has played a major role in building modern civilizations. However, the story isn't over yet.

Silicas that were a part of early organisms also precipitated out of the water along with the iron. The rock formations that resulted had an iron content of from 25–35 percent. Much later, geological events occurred that increased the iron concentrations to 55–60 percent. Underground water circulated through the iron-containing rock leaching the silica out of the rock and carring it away. This process occurred in formations along underground water channels, as in the Mesabi range.

European settlers discovered the iron-rich Mesabi Iron Range in 1892, the Vermillion Range to the northeast in 1875, and the Cuyuna Range to the southwest in 1904. Immigrants from Europe came to mine the high-grade ore, and then taconite, a low-grade iron ore. Taconite contains about 65 percent iron after being processed into pellets. According to the Iron Mining Association of Minnesota the Mesabi Iron Range provides about 70 percent of the nation's supply of taconite feeding U.S. steel production. They estimate that 8.8 billion tons of taconite remain on the Mesabi Iron Range, enough for about 200 years of mining at current rates.

Trail Highlights

This 4.5 mile hike crosses rolling terrain through a forest of mostly white birch and maple. At the beginning, the trail passes a number of stations that are part of a 0.5 mile Fitness Trail. Once on the circuit portion of the hike, the forest has an open understory, evidence of the thick canopy overhead that blocks out much of the sunlight. There are a couple of overlooks providing views of the surrounding countryside, including a nearby taconite mine in Virginia.

If you happen to have a map showing the streams and rivers that flow from this area, check it out. You'll find a river that flows north to Canada, another that flows to Lake Superior, and a third flowing to the Mississippi River and the Gulf of Mexico.

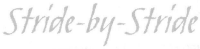

Stride-by-Stride

MILES	DESCRIPTION
0.0	The hike begins by walking through the picnic area, bearing right at a sign for the fitness trails, and passing the trail to the left. In about 300 feet you'll come to an intersection of a number of trails; turn right. Beyond this point, the main trail passes a number of fitness stations.
0.4	Trail intersection; Junction 1. Bear left passing the trail on the right.
0.5	A spur trail on the left ascends to an overlook on a rocky outcropping.
0.7	Cross under the powerline.
1.1	Trail intersection; Junction 4. Continue straight ahead passing a trail on the right.

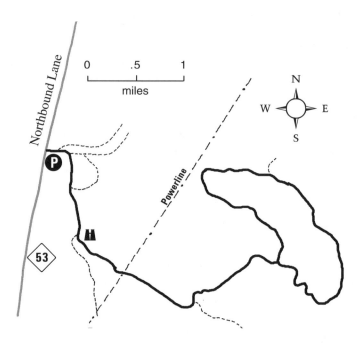

1.3   Trail enters a small clearing and in about 75 feet turns right and reenters the forest.

1.4   Trail intersection; Junction 9. Bear left to begin the circuit portion of this hike passing the trail to the right.

1.8   Trail intersection; bear right passing the trail on the left. This is an unmarked intersection that does not appear on the information sheet.

2.1   Trail intersection; Junction 6. Continue straight ahead passing the trail on the left.

3.1   Trail intersection at Junction 9, completing the circuit portion of this hike. Bear left to return to the trailhead.

4.1   Trail intersection; Junction 1. Bear right.

4.4   Trail intersection; turn left.

4.5   Trailhead.

15 Big Hole & Ridge Trails

3.9 M
MODERATE

MCCARTHY BEACH STATE PARK

LENGTH	3.9 miles
TIME	2:15
DIFFICULTY	Moderate
ROUTE-FINDING	Easy-Moderate
MAPS & PERMITS	DNR McCarthy Beach State Park map. A Minnesota State Park permit is required.
GETTING THERE	Drive north on County Road 5 to an intersection where County Road 65 turns right (east) and County Road 501 left (west). Turn left on County Road 501 and drive 0.9 miles to the parking area on the right side of the road.

Without question, glaciers are one of the most powerful and awe in-spiring forces in the natural world. We may not realize this because they are largely things of the distant past. Today's glaciers are much smaller than the continental ice sheets that once existed, and they tend to be in remote areas far from human habitation. What we do have is the geological evidence of past glaciers and ice sheets, and our imaginations. McCarthy Beach State Park is an excellent place to let your imagination run wild. Here, glacial moraines and kettle lakes testify to the great ice sheets that once covered this area and much of Minnesota.

Glacial Markings

During the Pleistocene Epoch, which began about 2 million years ago, large ice sheets periodically covered much of North America, Europe, and Asia. The ice sheets advanced and retreated several times over thousands of years. The North American ice sheets covered an area greater than the present day Antarctic ice sheet. There were three centers in Canada from which ice sheets moved outward in all directions: the Labradorian sheet centered in northern Quebec and Labrador; the Keewatin center northwest of Hudson Bay; and the Patrician center southwest of Hudson Bay. Lobes from the Keewatin and Patrician centers flowed into Minnesota.

While glaciers often make their mark by carrying away material and creating U-shaped fjords and valleys or turning mountains into sharp pinnacles, they also create new landforms by depositing materials. Moraines and kettles are just two of these landforms. A moraine is composed of rock debris picked up and transported by the moving ice and laid down in ridges during both the advance and the retreat of the ice. This rock debris may range in size from clay and sand to large boulders. A kettle lake forms when a huge chunk of ice breaks off the bottom of an ice sheet and becomes buried by glacial till or moraine deposits. Over time the ice melts, leaving a small depression filled with water. Kettle lakes are usually very small, more like ponds than lakes.

The Ridge Trail and the Big Hole Trail, both of which are a part of this 3.9 mile circuit hike, traverse a moraine and encircle a kettle lake. They provide a unique opportunity to view the handy work of a continental glacier, and the forests and animals that have followed in its wake.

McCarthy Beach's 135 acres of virgin red and white pine originally belonged to a reclusive homesteader, John A. McCarthy—"Old Man McCarthy." Evidently Old Man McCarthy allowed the local people to picnic and tent beneath the swaying branches of the tall pines. After his death, and the sale of the land by McCarthy's heirs to a timberman, the locals became concerned about the fate of the trees, and the pleasure they took in them. They began a fund-raising effort and, with additional funds from the state, purchased the land from the timberman giving him a 233 percent profit.

Today the virgin red and white pines in the area of the campground, located between Side Lake and Sturgeon Lake, is about all there is of the old forest. When mining turned nearby Hibbing into a boom town, there was a big demand for timber and two men, Hibbing and Trimble, started the first sawmill in the area. In 1895, the Swan River Logging Company, owned by a couple of businessmen from Saginaw, Michigan, built a railroad to Sturgeon Lake. The company hauled timber on the railroad to the town of Swan River and on to the Mississippi River where they floated the logs to sawmills in Minneapolis.

Trail Highlights

From the parking lot on County Road 501, the hike begins on the Big Hole Trail. As you make your way around a kettle lake you will hike over a rolling terrain with several short steep ascents and descents. Aspens, birches, maples, and red pines shade the wide grassy trail. On the Red Top Trail the forest alternates between one dominated by red pine with aspen, birch, maple, and oak, to one similar to that found around Big Hole. There are more "big holes" in this area, although not all of them have ponds in them.

From the Red Top Trail the hike takes you up the steep side of a moraine to the Ridge Trail which passes along its crest. Hiking along the Ridge Trail under towering red pines, you can begin to imagine something of the immensity of glaciers. Looking up through the branches of the tall trees, consider that ice sheets over 1,000 feet thick, at least six or seven times the height of the pines, once covered this region. The green world you are walking through doesn't begin to match the scale of the ice that once overrode much of Minnesota and North America.

Stride-by-Stride

MILES	DESCRIPTION
0.0	The hike begins at the east end of the parking lot. In about 50 feet you'll reach an intersection beginning the circuit portion of this hike. Continue ahead on the Big Hole Trail passing the trail to the left.
0.1	Trail intersection; turn right passing the trail to the left.
0.3	Trail intersection; turn left, staying on the Big Hole Trail, passing the trail to the right leading to County Road 501.
0.6	Trail intersection; turn left passing an overgrown trail bearing to the right. The "Big Hole" soon appears on the left side of the trail.
0.8	The trail turns left. At this point there are two small turn-arounds used by cross-country skiers in winter.
1.0	A spur trail on the left descends into the "Big Hole."
1.3	Trail intersection; turn right on the Red Top Trail passing the Big Hole Trail which continues to the left.
1.6	Cross County Road 501.
1.9	Trail intersection; bear right passing the trail to the left.
2.0	Trail intersection; turn left passing a trail to the right and one continuing straight ahead.
2.2	Trail intersection; make a sharp turn to the left leaving the trail that continues straight ahead.
2.4	Trail intersection; take the right fork and ascend steeply.
2.5	Trail intersection at the top of the ascent; turn right passing the trail to the left. In about 500 feet, reach another trail intersection among tall red pines. Continue straight ahead passing the trail on the left.

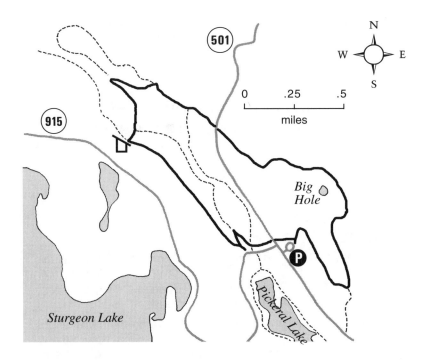

2.6 Trail intersection with the Ridge Trail; turn left. In about 250 feet, you will come to a shelter.

3.2 Trail intersection with road; continue ahead on the road.

3.3 Trail intersection; leave the road and turn left onto the Red Top Trail.

3.4 Trail intersection; turn right leaving the Red Top Trail which continues straight ahead.

3.6 Trail intersection; continue straight ahead passing the trail that comes in sharply on the left. In about 10 feet, bear left passing the trail to the right. In another 200 feet, come to another intersection; continue straight ahead passing the trail on right.

3.7 Cross County Road 105.

3.9 Trail intersection; turn right and reach the trailhead parking area in 50 feet.

16

8.1 M
STRENUOUS

Sturgeon River Trail— South Loop

SUPERIOR NATIONAL FOREST
LAURENTIAN RANGER DISTRICT

LENGTH	8.1 miles
TIME	4:30
DIFFICULTY	Strenuous
ROUTE-FINDING	Difficult
MAPS & PERMITS	An information sheet with map is available from the Laurentian District office in Aurora, Minnesota. USGS quad: Dewey Lake NW. No permit is required.
GETTING THERE	From Chisholm, drive north on Minnesota State Highway 73 to County Road 65 and turn left. Go about 1.25 miles to the trailhead parking area on the right just prior to crossing the Sturgeon River.
TRAILHEAD GPS	47° 40' 29.0" N 92° 53' 44.5" W

This 8.1 mile hike utilizes a part of the 20-mile Sturgeon River Trail system that lies to the north and south of County Road 65. This hike circles a portion of the Sturgeon River, one of the larger rivers in St. Louis County. From its headwaters at Sturgeon Lake and a vast wetland area northeast of Chisholm, this river flows north to the Little Fork River, a tributary of Rainy River. Ultimately the waters of the Sturgeon River flow into Hudson Bay.

The route crosses a variety of terrain from river banks to steep ridges. It wanders through stands of mature red pines, dense growths of deciduous trees along the river's edge, recent clearcuts, and grassy openings. Along much of the route, the evidence of clearcutting is quite obvious.

Logging Operations

In *The Boundary Waters Wilderness Ecosystem,* author Miron Heinselman contrasts the effects on forest ecosystems of two major logging eras: the big-pine logging era, which lasted from about 1895 to 1930; and the pulpwood logging era, which began around 1935 and continues to this day. Heinselman, a forest ecologist who spent a lifetime studying the woods of northern Minnesota, writes that current logging practices have had a greater effect on forest ecosystems than did earlier logging operations. The result of modern logging has been "damage to the natural landscape and ecosystem substantially exceeding that of the early big-pine logging."

In the early years, there was "virtually no disturbance of the natural soil profile and little direct effect of logging on the ground vegetation" according to Heinselman. Companies built few, if any, year-round roads, used no tractors to haul logs out of the woods, did not use mechanical ground preparation for planting replacement seedlings, and used no herbicides to control early vegetation growth afterwards. The use of sluiceways and dams on streams also had, with a few exceptions, minimal lasting effect. The water levels of most lakes and streams that were raised by dams have now returned to normal.

In some circumstances, aspen and birch have replaced mature pine forests because of the work of early loggers. Loggers ignited fires after an area had been cleared of all mature pines, destroying the remaining pine saplings and seedlings. Often, where high-intensity fires did not follow on the heels of clear-cutting, pine replaced pine.

Also, because early loggers concentrated on stands of large red and white pines, stands of other tree types were less effected by cutting. Loggers usually ignored stands of jack pine, black and white spruces, aspen, and the birches. While their saws may not have directly affected forests of these other trees, these stands often felt the sting of fires that got their start in the slash of the cut pines. But, these fires were little different from the natural ones ignited by lightning that have swept the forests of northeastern Minnesota for thousands of years.

In contrast, Heinselman lists a number of factors that were instrumental in making the pulpwood logging era such a powerful negative influence on today's forest ecosystems. With the creation of the US Forest Service and its emphasis on fire control, there was a coming of age for many of the young forests that grew up after the early logging operations. About this time there was also a shift in interest from the giant sawmills of the big-pine era to wood pulp and paper. This, and the start of World War II, produced a demand for spruce, jack pine, aspens, and other trees that had been largely ignored in the past.

This time period also saw the development of powerful logging equipment. Loggers now operated machines capable of cutting trees and dragging them out of the woods to a central area where they loaded the timber onto trucks and hauled it to any one of the new pulpwood or paper mills that had sprung up across the region. An extensive all-weather road system linked the forests with the industry users just hours away, completing the forests demise. Anticipating the public outcry over the extent to which northern Minnesota forests were being logged, Heinselman writes that the Forest Service did not reveal this road system on any of the recreational maps prepared for the public.

The result of logging in the pulpwood era has been a considerable shift from conifer forests to aspen-birch-fir or other communities with a decreased percentage of conifers. And, as more and more of the tree is put to use for some purpose other than being recycled back into the ground and made available for future growth, the already nutrient-taxed soils are slowly becoming depleted.

Trail Highlights

From the trailhead on County Road 65, the route leads south through mainly balsam fir, aspen, and white birch, with scattered spruce and jack pine and a plantation of young jack pine, red pine, and spruce. As it turns to the west, the trail enters a stand of aspen that shortly changes to balsam fir and jack pine. From there it enters a forest of immature pines, then spruces, and finally reaches the bridge over the Sturgeon River. In some years spring floods may wash this bridge off its foundation; call the Forest Service to make sure the bridge is in place before setting out on this hike.

On the west side of the river, after crossing the bridge, the trail continues south through balsam fir and white birch, and tall pine forests, and clearings overgrown with the saplings of birches and conifers that are about 15 feet tall. Eventually the trail comes to an area that was logged in 1996, followed by plantations of red pine. After a mile on the logging road, the route once again becomes a hiking and skiing trail that crosses a bridge over a small stream and then another over the Sturgeon River at the southern end of the loop. Exercise caution crossing bridges as they may have boards weakened by weathering and age.

The bridge over the Sturgeon River is a good spot to stop for lunch or a snack while you enjoy the sights and sounds of the rushing water. On the east side of the river, the route turns north to begin closing the circuit. After following the river for about 0.4 miles, the trail turns east away from the river and crosses a recently logged area and wanders through mature, mixed forests of aspen and balsam fir and stands of red pines. The trail crosses five small bridges in the last mile or so before completing the circuit at the northern bridge over the Sturgeon River. From there it's 1.4 miles back to the trailhead.

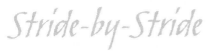

Stride-by-Stride

MILES   **DESCRIPTION**

0.0   The south loop of the Sturgeon River Trail begins on the south side of County Road 65 opposite the parking area. The trail crosses a small bridge about 60 feet from the road.

0.1   Trail intersection; turn right passing the trail to the left.

1.2   Pass an unmarked trail on the left.

1.4   Trail intersection beginning the circuit portion of this hike; turn right and cross the bridge over the East Branch of the Sturgeon River, passing the trail continuing straight ahead on the east side of the river. After crossing the bridge, the trail follows the river downstream for about 100 yards before moving away from the river and ascending a ridge.

1.8   Trail intersection; cross an unmarked trail going left and right.

2.4   Trail intersection with road; turn left and follow the road.

2.7   Road intersection; bear right passing the road which continues straight ahead.

2.8   Road intersection; bear left at fork in the road.

3.0   Road turns right, passing a grassy trail on the left.

3.4   Trail intersection; turn left off the road onto the trail just before the road exits the red pine plantation.

3.6   Cross a bridge over a small stream.

3.9   Trail intersection; turn left passing the trail straight ahead leading to County Road 279.

4.0   Bridge crossing the East Branch of the Sturgeon River. From here the trail turns north along the east side of the river.

4.4   The trail bears right away from the river by ascending a short bank to a shrubby field. Across this field the trail takes a bearing of about 50° heading for a mature forest.

4.6   Trail intersection; turn left passing the trail continuing straight ahead.

4.8   Cross a stream.

5.8   Bridge over small stream.

6.0   Bridge over small stream.

6.6   Bridge over small stream.

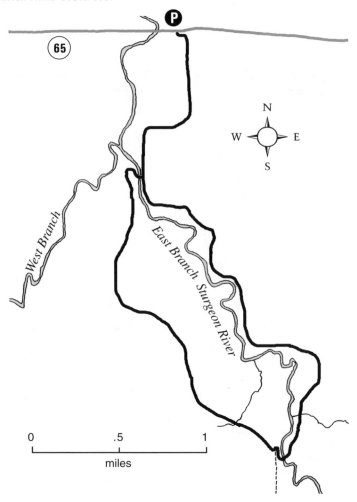

6.7 Bridge over small stream. In about 200 feet reach the trail intersection at the first bridge crossing the East Branch of the Sturgeon River completing the circuit portion of this hike. Continue straight ahead to return to the trailhead.

6.9 Trail intersection; continue straight ahead and enter jack pine forest, passing the trail on the right.

7.9 Trail intersection; turn left passing the trail which continues straight ahead.

8.1 Reach the trailhead on County Road 65.

North Dark River

17

1.8 M
EASY

SUPERIOR NATIONAL FOREST
LAURENTIAN RANGER DISTRICT

LENGTH	1.8 miles
TIME	1:00
DIFFICULTY	Easy
ROUTE-FINDING	Easy
MAPS & PERMITS	A recreational opportunity sheet with information on the trail is available from the Laurentian District office in Aurora, Minnesota. USGS quad: Dark Lake. No permit is required.
GETTING THERE	Drive 14 miles north from Chisholm on Minnesota State Highway 73 to County Road 688. Turn right on County Road 688 and go east 1 mile. Park by pulling off onto the shoulder at the top of the hill after crossing the Dark River.
TRAILHEAD GPS	47° 42' 13.9" N 92° 50' 55.1" W

The North Dark River Hiking Trail follows the eastern rim of a small valley carved by the Dark River. It starts out as a foot trail and returns to the trailhead on the Old Woods Road, a former logging road. The trail passes through a jack pine plantation planted in 1939. In late spring and early summer, the hiker can find moccasin flowers, also known as Pink Lady's Slippers, along the trail. At several points along the rim, hikers can look out over the small valley and see the twists and turns of the Dark River as it makes its crooked way past willowed banks.

Jack pine is a gnarly-looking tree with short, twisted needles bundled in pairs. The distinctive cones are strongly curved with their tips pointing toward the ends of the branches, which they closely hug. No other pine in our region has such short needles and characteristic cones. Jack pines produce poor quality wood, but are grown in plantations like this one because they grow better in poor soils than other pines.

Red-tailed Hawk

If you hike the North Dark River Hiking Trail on a sunny summer day, keep an eye out for a large hawk circling overhead. You may be alerted to it by a sudden outburst of alarm calls from small birds among the trees.

The Red-tailed Hawk is a common buteo in our region. Its summer range takes in much of Canada and the northern border states. The Red-tail's range has increased in the east as widespread deforestation has created open country where these birds of prey prefer to hunt, in the west where fire suppression has created small forested areas, and where telephone poles provide convenient perches from which to hunt.

Buteos are high-soaring hawks with wide tails and broad, rounded wings. Red-tailed Hawks are among the largest buteos, with a wing-span of over four feet. While Red-tails can search for prey as they soar high overhead, this is not their primary reason for soaring. They use soaring mainly to defend their territories. From their high vantage points, soaring Red-tails can survey a wider area and advertise to other Red-tails that the area is occupied. Soaring at great heights also allows the hawk to dive from above on intruders, which is probably more intimidating to the other bird than a defender flying up from the ground.

Red-tailed Hawks prefer to search for prey from perches. This sit-and-wait hunting method provides the highest success-to-cost ratio. Red-tails feed on a variety of animals including snakes, frogs, rodents, crayfish, and sometimes young birds. They will also feed on insects while walking along the ground.

Because of its habit of soaring, the Red-tailed Hawk is one of the easiest raptors to spot. Look to the tail for help in identifying this hawk. On adults it will be reddish above and light pink below. There is usually a dark band across the light belly of both sexes.

John James Audubon, the famous American naturalist and painter of birds, noted that adult Red-tails, after raising their young, often become hostile toward each other as they fight over prey. However, this behavior could merely be a variation of the aerial display put on by courting pairs of Red-tails that normally form lifelong bonds. One observer noted how a male Red-tailed Hawk attempted to pass a snake dangling from its talons to a female who turned over to meet him as he swooped by.

In typical courting flights, the male Red-tail dives at speeds of up to 120 mph. Coming up from the ground, the female rolls over onto her back and presents her talons to the male, who checks his flight at the last second in order to avoid a collision. The female rights herself and the pair fly off together, executing a series of swoops and dives.

Stride-by-Stride

MILES   **DESCRIPTION**

0.0   The trail begins at a large sign set back about 30 feet from the edge of the road. Here the trail enters a jack pine plantation and travels southeast along the east rim of the Dark River valley.

0.3   Trail makes a U-turn at a point along the ridge. Seventy-five feet beyond this point, the main trail crosses a small wet weather stream. After the trail ascends back onto the rim and into the jack pine plantation, there are views of the meandering river below.

0.4   Trail comes to a point providing a good view of river bends and the bottomlands.

0.5   Trail intersection. The main trail turns sharply left and a faint trail descends to the right. The latter is heavily overgrown on the valley floor.

0.6   Point providing more views of the Dark River.

0.9   Trail intersection. The main trail turns left while a faint spur trail on the right descends to the riverbank in about 100 yards.

1.0   Trail intersection with the Old Woods Road. Turn left and return to County Road 688 and the trailhead via the Old Woods Road.

1.7   Trail intersection; bear left passing the trail on the right.

1.8   Trailhead on County Road 688.

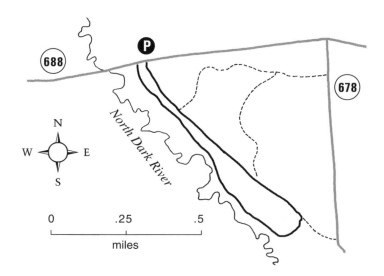

East Bay–
Norberg Lake

BEAR HEAD LAKE STATE PARK

LENGTH	3.0 miles
TIME	1:30
DIFFICULTY	Easy
ROUTE-FINDING	Easy
MAPS & PERMITS	DNR Bear Head Lake State Park map. USGS quad: Eagles Nest. A Minnesota State Park permit is required.
GETTING THERE	The park is located 18 miles east of Tower on County Road 128, 6 miles off Minnesota State Highway 169. Drive to the picnic area parking lot.
TRAILHEAD GPS	47° 47' 13.6" N 92° 4' 48.4" W

White pines once dominated the region around Bear Head Lake, as well as much of northeastern Minnesota. They were heavily logged around the turn of the century and only a few of the original trees remain. Within their range, white pines may exist in almost pure stands or as scattered individuals in communities of other trees; the latter is more likely today, due to heavy logging. These scattered white pines add diversity to stands of aspen, birch, spruce, and fir trees that would not exist otherwise. Tall white pines reach above the canopy to add a vertical aspect to the forest and opportunities for nesting and foraging for a greater range of species. Of particular interest is how black bears, Bald Eagles, and Ospreys use white pines.

In the spring, when the black bear sow brings her cubs out of the den for the first time, she will often leave them near white pines while she wanders off to forage. The deeply furrowed bark of mature white pines makes them easier to climb if the cubs need the safety of a tree. Sows with cubs also select white pines for their day beds more often than females without cubs. Compare the rough bark of the white pine with the smooth, scaly bark of the red pine or the smooth bark of most other trees. Imagine yourself a bear cub needing to climb a tree. Which one would you prefer?

White pines have large, horizontal branches with delicate foliage that makes them good nesting places for eagles and Ospreys. The tops of white pines, rising like mountains above the lower canopy, provide a perfect place for unobstructed landings and take-offs for the large-winged birds. A study revealed white pines as the tree species of choice for 81 percent of nesting eagles and 77 percent of nesting Ospreys. In recent years, a pair of Bald Eagles has successfully nested in one of the old-growth white pines near the picnic area.

Beginning at the picnic area, this hike passes along the north side of the East Bay of Bear Head Lake, at one point ascending a narrow ridge between the bay and Norberg Lake. From the ridge there are views of the two lakes through the trees. After a short walk along a park road, the hike continues through a lovely stand of red and white pines that hugs the north shore of Norberg Lake. This is a perfect spot to rest, listen to the music the wind plays on the pines, and watch how it ruffles the surface of the lake. Beyond the lake, the hike makes its way back to the picnic area through a forest of white birch and aspen, with scattered red and white pines.

Stride-by-Stride

MILES   **DESCRIPTION**

0.0   From the parking lot hike east on a wide hiking and skiing trail.

0.2   Trail intersection beginning the circuit portion of this hike; leave the wide trail and bear right on the narrow trail.

0.9   Trail intersection; continue straight ahead passing the trail on the left. From here the trail ascends a ridge separating Norberg and Bear Head lakes.

1.1   Intersection with a dirt road to the Primitive Group Camp to the right. Turn left and walk along the road.

1.2   Road intersection; bear left, continuing to walk along the road, passing road on right leading to parking area for Backpack Camping sites on Becky and Blueberry lakes.

1.6   Trail intersection; turn left off the road onto the hiking trail. This section of the trail is pleasant as it passes through a stand of tall red pines along the north shore of Norberg Lake.

1.7   Trail intersection; continue straight ahead passing a trail to the right which leads to a parking lot on County Road 128 in

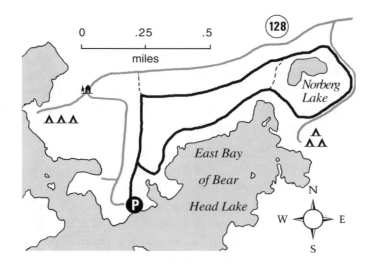

325 feet. By starting from this parking lot, it is possible to complete a short 1.1 mile hike around Norberg Lake.

1.8 Trail intersection; continue straight passing the trail on the left which leads in 0.2 mile to the trail earlier hiked between East Bay and Norberg Lake. Use this cutoff trail to complete the 1.1 mile loop of Norberg Lake.

2.4 Trail intersection; turn left passing the trail which continues straight ahead. In 45 feet, turn left again at the intersection with the wide hiking and skiing trail.

2.8 Trail intersection completing the circuit portion of this hike; bear right to return to the trailhead.

3.0 Trailhead.

4.2 M
MODERATE-DIFFICULT

BEAR HEAD LAKE STATE PARK

LENGTH	4.2 miles
TIME	2:30
DIFFICULTY	Moderate-Difficult
ROUTE-FINDING	Easy-Moderate
MAPS & PERMITS	DNR Bear Head Lake State Park map. USGS quad: Eagles Nest. A Minnesota State Park permit is required.
GETTING THERE	Turn left off County Road 128, 6 miles from Minnesota State Highway 169. Drive 0.3 mile to the Backpack Camping parking lot.
TRAILHEAD GPS	47° 47' 39.7" N 92° 3' 33.6" W

The forest in Bear Head Lake State Park is second growth with some old-growth pines scattered here and there. In 1899, the Tower Logging Railroad purchased an old sawmill and moved it from Wisconsin to Bear Head Lake. Tower Logging Railroad, incorporated in 1895, was the earliest small logging railroads to operate east of Virginia in the iron mining region. Initially the company did contract logging for other companies and moved the logs on its railroad line. With the purchase of the sawmill, Tower Logging got into the logging business for itself.

Tower Logging cut an average of about 30 million board feet per year, and by 1905 had depleted the forest in the Bear Head Lake area. Today logging continues in the Bear Island State Forest that surrounds the park to the east, south, and west. You can see some evidence of this where the trail passes around the east side of Blueberry Lake.

While this hike at 4.2 miles is moderate in length, there are stretches of short, steep ascents that make it somewhat strenuous. The hiking trail is rugged in places but easy to follow overall. After a short walk along a road closed to motorized traffic, you will head east for Bear Head Lake covering one of the stretches of steep ascents and descents. Just beyond a shelter overlooking the East Bay of Bear Head Lake, the trail turns east for Becky Lake, passing through a fine stand of red and jack pines. At Becky Lake, you have two options: you may continue on the circuit around Blueberry Lake before heading back to the trailhead for a 4.2 mile hike, or you can bypass Blueberry Lake and return directly to the trailhead for a 2.4 mile hike.

The trail to East Bay and around Becky Lake back to the trailhead is a cross-country skiing and hiking trail. The Blueberry Lake circuit is a hiking-only trail, and is narrower and more rugged, but a reward awaits you for your effort. An elegant stand of red pines, towering above moss and pine needle-covered boulders, shades a portion of the east shore of the lake and is an idyllic spot for lunch and perhaps a nap. Once back at Becky Lake, the trail heads north and over a second series of steep ascents and descents.

Stride-by-Stride

MILES	DESCRIPTION
0.0	Begin the hike by walking south along the road, past the wooden posts that block access to motor vehicles.
0.1	Trail intersection on the right side of the road beginning the circuit portion of this hike. Take the trail on the right. You will return to this point via the left trail.
1.1	Spur trail on the right leads to Backpack Camping site #5. In about 150 feet you will come to a shelter on the right side of the trail. A short trail past the shelter leads to the shore of Bear Head Lake. Just beyond this point the main trail turns east through tall stands of red and jack pines and heads for Becky Lake.
1.6	Trail intersection with Becky Lake on the left. The trail to the left leads back to the trailhead in 0.8 mile allowing for a 2.4 mile hike. To continue the longer hike turn right and in 200 feet reach another trail intersection that begins a circuit of Blueberry Lake. Turn right at this second intersection.
2.2	Spur trail on the left leads to Backpack Camping site #4.
2.6	Evidence of recent logging in the Bear Island State Forest on the right side of the trail. The trail, marked by blue diamonds, soon passes through a very nice stand of red pines.
3.1	Spur trail on left leads to Backpack Camping site #3.
3.2	Spur trail on left leads to Backpack Camping site #2.
3.3	Trail intersection completing the circuit of Blueberry Lake; turn right to return to Becky Lake. In 200 feet, turn right again at the trail intersection.

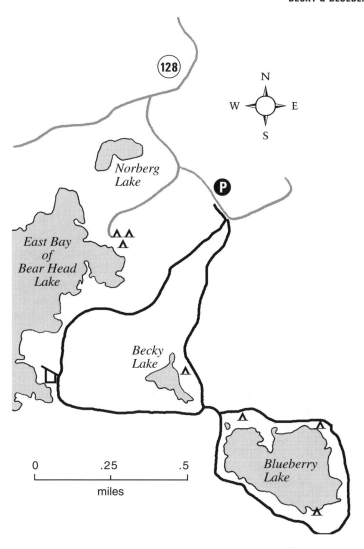

3.5 Spur trail on the left leads to Backpack Camping site #1. The main trail now becomes quite hilly with short steep ascents and descents.

4.1 Trail intersection completing the circuit portion of this hike; turn left on the road to return to the trailhead.

4.2 Trailhead.

20

5.9 M
MODERATE

Bass Lake Trail

SUPERIOR NATIONAL FOREST
KAWISHIWI RANGER DISTRICT

LENGTH	5.9 miles
TIME	3:30
DIFFICULTY	Moderate
ROUTE-FINDING	Moderate
MAPS & PERMITS	Fisher Map F-9. USGS quad: Ely. No permit is required.
GETTING THERE	From Ely, drive east on Minnesota State Highway 169 to County Road 88 and turn left. Drive 2 miles to County Road 116 (Echo Trail), turn right, and continue 3 miles to the Bass Lake parking area on the right side of the road.
TRAILHEAD GPS	47° 56' 58.6" N 91° 52' 14.6" W

On May 18, 1925, the *Hibbing Daily Tribune* carried a story with the following lead-in: "The famous 10,000 lakes of Minnesota today number but 9,999 if reports that Bass Lake, a body of water located about 3 miles northeast of Ely and covering about 550 acres, has almost completely disappeared are considered to be reliable." While the report proved unreliable, during the previous month Bass Lake had lost about 250 acres in size, and, where there used to be one lake, there were three.

Formation of Bass Lake

Bass Lake and neighboring Low Lake occupy a long narrow basin formed from a fault in the Precambrian bedrock that covers much of northeastern Minnesota. A fault is a fracture in the earth's crust where rocks split and move apart; one of the best known is the San Andreas Fault in California. Minnesota also has its share of faults, although they have long been dormant. A fault was responsible for forming the Lake Superior Basin. Another, known as the Vermilion Fault, runs across the northern part of the state. It enters Minnesota in the northwest near the Red River and leaves northeastern Minnesota near Basswood Lake. A number of smaller faults are part of the Vermilion Fault, one of which eventually became the basin occupied by Bass and Low lakes.

A ridge of glacial gravel once separated Bass and Low lakes. The ridge acted as a dam, holding back the waters of Bass Lake at a level about 60 feet higher than Low Lake. Loggers built a sluiceway to facilitate the movement of logs across the ridge and into Low Lake. One account claims that seepage weakened the sluiceway and eventually led to a washout that carried away the sluice and gravel ridge one night in April. Imagine the surprise of loggers the next morning when they found Bass Lake "gone!"

The washout left a gorge 250 feet wide between the two lakes. With the ridge gone and Bass Lake's water level 55 feet lower, water now flows calmly into Low Lake. This catastrophe also formed two new lakes, Dry and Little Dry lakes, in the old Bass Lake basin. This natural event, rather than resulting in one less lake as suggested by the *Hibbing Daily Tribune*, actually added two to the long list of lakes in Minnesota.

The washout of the gravel ridge and the lowering of Bass Lake exposed about 250 acres of the old lake bed. What is happening on the newly exposed land, mainly to the southwest and north of today's lake, is a case study in how pioneer plant species take hold and replicates what happened when glaciers retreated from this region about 10,000 years ago. This newly formed ecosystem is very fragile; hikers should stay on the trail when crossing the old lake bed.

Trail Highlights

The hike passes through three regions of old lake bed that differ considerably in appearance. At the very beginning and end of this hike, the trail passes along a thin narrow band of the old lake bed. Hikers get an excellent view of this area after climbing a ridge about a half-mile into the hike. Where lake waters once lay, a small stream now meanders through a narrow valley. Aspen trees grow in the wetter areas of the valley floor and its lower sides, while pines and oak grow on the drier ridges.

As the trail continues northeast along the north side of Bass Lake, it passes Dry Falls, where a small stream flowing from Dry Lake plunges 20-30 feet into Bass Lake. Beyond the falls, the trail moves away from the lake, passes behind a ridge and through a small stand of red pine, before coming to the second area of exposed lake bed. Here the soil is sandy in places with mixed stands of white and jack pines, balsam fir, and aspen. The forest is more open and rock cairns mark the route as it gradually descends toward the west end of Bass Lake. At the very end of Bass Lake where it joins Low Lake is the site of the 1925 washout.

Once around the west end of Bass Lake and on its south side, the trail passes through the third distinct region of the old lake bed. Large cedars slanting toward the lake mark the old shoreline. Looking at them, it's easy to imagine when these trees grew out from a wave splashed, rocky shore. A high rock ledge provides a broad vista of Bass Lake about half-way down the lake. River otters occasionally play in the water below the ledge. At the very eastern end of the lake, you will get an excellent view of Dry Falls across the lake before returning to the trailhead.

Stride-by-Stride

MILES	DESCRIPTION
0.0	The trail begins at the western end of the parking lot.
0.1	Trail intersection beginning the circuit portion of this hike; turn left on the trail to Dry Falls passing the portage trail which continues to Bass Lake. In about 225 feet, cross a small bridge over a wet weather stream. Then it's over a short ridge and into a narrow valley once part of the old lake bed.
0.2	Bridge crossing over a stream flowing to Bass Lake. The trail then ascends steeply to the ridge and continues along it providing overlooks of the valley below. The ridge top supports red pines and cedars. Aspens fill the valley sides.
0.8	A short spur trail on the right leads to an overlook providing views of the old lakebed occupied now by a meandering stream. Shortly beyond this point, Bass Lake comes into view.
1.0	Trail descends steeply from the ridge to a rocky bluff overlooking Bass Lake and Dry Falls.
1.1	Cross bridge just above Dry Falls (47° 56' 29.1" N 91° 51' 50.3" W). The stream flows from Dry Lake to Bass Lake. Beyond the bridge the trail ascends steeply and comes to an intersection in about 75 feet. The left fork leads to Dry Lake in 100 yards. Bear right at this intersection to continue on the main trail as it bears away from the lake and passes behind a ridge putting the lake out of sight for the next 0.9 mile.
1.2	Spur trail on the right leads to a campsite on the lake shore. Beyond this point, the trail ascends before leveling out and crossing rock outcroppings. Rock cairns mark the way.
2.0	Overlook with views of the north end of Bass Lake. From here the trail begins a gradual descent.

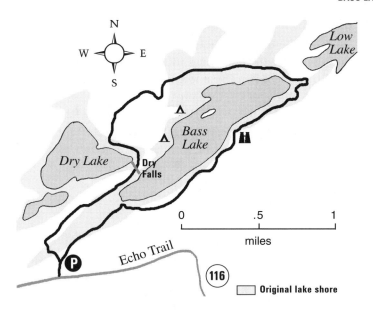

3.1 Reach remnant of the glacial ridge at the north end of Bass Lake. Walk along the sandbar to where the trail bears right and comes to the stream flowing from Bass Lake to Low Lake.

3.4 Cross small bridge. In 155 feet cross a second bridge. The trail then ascends through white birches, balsam firs, and stands of red pines. The trail stays just above the old lake shoreline which is marked by leaning cedar trees.

4.3 Overlook with views of the lake through a screen of jack pines. From here the trail descends and occasionally dips below the old shoreline. The trail is very rocky along this stretch.

4.8 Bridge over a wet weather stream. The trail begins to descend until it reaches the portage trail at the south end of Bass Lake.

5.2 Trail intersection with the portage trail. Bear left on the portage trail to return to the trailhead.

5.8 Trail intersection completing the circuit portion of this hike; continue straight ahead.

5.9 Trailhead.

Ole Lake– North Star Run

SUPERIOR NATIONAL FOREST
KAWISHIWI RANGER DISTRICT

LENGTH	8.0 miles
TIME	4:45
DIFFICULTY	Difficult
ROUTE-FINDING	Moderate
MAPS & PERMIT	Fisher Map F-9. USGS quads: Shagawa Lake and Crab Lake. A day permit is required to enter the BWCAW. There is a self-registration station at the trailhead.
GETTING THERE	Drive east from Ely on Minnesota State Highway 169 to County Road 88 and turn left. Drive 2 miles to St. Louis County Road 116 (Echo Trail), turn right, and continue 8.7 miles to County Road 644 (North Arm Road). Turn left and drive 3.5 miles to the parking lot on the left side of the road.
TRAILHEAD GPS	47° 58' 48.7" N 91° 58' 54.4" W

Hikers entering this enchanted land of pine forests and blue-watered lakes nestled among granite ridges, must tread a path guarded by giant twin sentinels, that leads over the Troll's Bridge and through the realm of The Griz. Your reward is Ole Lake. Lest you should worry about how to get back home, fear not for the North Star Run shall be your way in the end.

While all of this may sound like fantasy, there is more truth than fiction. Near the start of the hike, the path passes between two 300-year-old white pines. They stand close on either side of the trail as if guarding it from unwanted intruders. Slightly to the northwest, as the trail gradually ascends a ridge, is the Troll's Bridge, attended by majestic red and white pines, maples, and aspens. The image conjured up by the name is infinitely more ominous than the setting.

Beyond the Troll's Bridge, the route follows the trail with the peace-loving name of Hug-a-Tree before coming to the more threatening sounding The Griz. Beyond The Griz, the route wanders west on the

Ole Lake Trail. For a short distance, the trail follows an old logging road passing through dense stands of young trees before entering the Boundary Waters Canoe Area Wilderness (BWCAW) and returning to the older, more impressive forests of old pines.

At Ole Lake you will want to rest under the large pines on a bluff 20–30 feet above the water. With a wide view of the lake and its border of bogs and forest, nature seems to be on display. Belted Kingfishers sound their rattling cries as they fly up and down the shoreline protecting their fishing territories or carrying food to hungry nestlings. The alarming calls of Blue Jays rise from the trees and echo across the water. Red squirrels voice their disapproval of intruders from the safety of high branches. All the while, the wind writes graceful calligraphy on the waters below, and gently whispers through the branches overhead.

From Ole Lake the route heads north, crossing the top of an old beaver dam at the northeast end of the lake and passing along ridges grown up with jack pine, oak, and maple. Rock cairns mark the way across bare outcroppings of lichen covered granite. An overlook near the end of the Ole Lake Trail provides distant views of Silica Lake and Coxey Pond from the edge of a large granite outcropping that ends in a shear cliff. Just beyond the overlook, the trail heads east, and briefly exits the BWCAW before turning onto the North Star Run, a 2 mile trail through more majestic pines, that leads back to the Sentinels and the trailhead.

This hike presents in reality what most people imagine northeastern Minnesota's forests must have looked like long ago. For mile after mile, the route lies through towering red and white pines, and along dry rocky ridges where gnarled oaks and weather-beaten jack pines predominate. Considering the age of the white pines, up to 300 hundred years in some cases, it's hard to imagine that in geological terms they are only recent immigrants to Minnesota.

White Pine Migration

Like birds and large herds of mammals, plants also make migrations. However, rather than coming and going in annual cycles, the movement of a tree species from one region to another requires thousands of years.

To study the changes in plant ecosystems over very long periods of time, scientists rely on the presence or absence of pollen in core samples taken from the muddy bottoms of large lakes. Every year millions of pollen grains, released from all the plants in a region, end up on the waters of lakes where they eventually settle to the bottom. Over time, the layers of sediment produce a chronological record of the species of plants present in an area, and their relative abundance. Relying on such information, G. L. Jacobson, in his article "A 7,000 Year History of White Pine," tells the story of white pine migration to Minnesota. He writes that the earliest record of white pine in the postglacial period is from the Shenandoah Valley in Virginia. About 13,000 years ago, white pines were riding out the waning centuries of the last great ice age. It is believed that the species survived on the land exposed off the east coast during the maximum extent of the great ice sheets, when ocean levels dropped hundreds of feet.

From Virginia, the white pines gradually spread north into New England and then west through the Great Lake States. Pollen records indicate that while white pine was concentrated mainly in the eastern Great Lakes region and New England around 6,000 years ago, white pine made its appearance in Minnesota about 7,000 years ago.

For about 2,500 years, white pine was restricted to the area north of Lake Superior. Its advance westward into the central part of the state was stalled during an interval known as the "prairie period." During this time, a warmer and drier climate led to the eastward expansion of western prairies, and jack pines and oaks, and forest fires, were more prevalent. Then, about 4,000 years ago, the prairie/forest border began to shift westward. When it did, the white pine followed at a rate of about 65 miles per one thousand years. Since about 2,500 years ago, changes in the distribution of white pines have occurred more slowly. Prior to settlement by European immigrants, as Minnesota's climate slowly became cooler and more moist, the range of the white pine had been decreasing.

Stride-by-Stride

MILES   **DESCRIPTION**

0.0   Follow the trail at the northwest corner of the parking lot and in 195 feet reach a three-way intersection. Take the left trail to the Sentinels, passing the Moose Horn Trail to the right, and the Slim Lake Trail which continues straight ahead.

0.2   Pass a trail coming in sharply on the left.

0.3   The Sentinels. The circuit begins at the trail intersection 80 feet beyond the twin white pines; turn left, passing the trail that continues straight ahead.

0.5   Cross the Troll's Bridge.

0.6   Trail intersection; continue on the Hug-A-Tree Trail, passing the trail to the right.

0.9   Cross a private road and continue on The Griz.

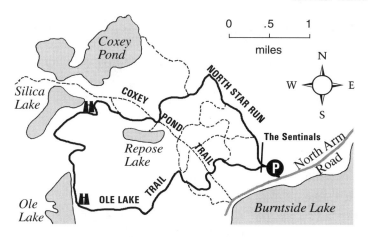

1.3 Intersection with a road; turn right.

1.4 Trail intersection; turn left on the Ole Lake Trail, passing trails that continue straight ahead and to the right.

2.1 Enter the BWCAW.

2.5 Turn right off the road onto a footpath.

3.0 Ridge overlooking Ole Lake (47° 58' 28.9" N 92° 1' 33.4" W).

3.5 The trail enters a narrow stream valley and continues across the top of an old beaver dam and climbs the bank on the other side.

4.7 Overlook of Silica Lake and Coxey Pond from a rock outcropping on the left.

5.0 Junction with a road going right and left; turn right.

5.3 Exit the BWCAW.

5.6 Junction with a road going right and left; turn right. In about 0.10 mile, leave the road by turning left on the North Star Run, passing the trail to Repose Lake on the right. The trail shortly reenters the BWCAW.

6.1 Trail intersection; pass Lost Lake Trail on the left.

6.6 Trail intersection; pass Barren Ridge Trail on the left.

6.8 Trail intersection; pass trails to the right and left.

7.1 Exit the BWCAW.

7.4 Trail intersection; pass Thor's Trail on the right.

7.7 Trail intersection at the Sentinels, completing the circuit. Continue straight ahead to return to the trailhead.

7.9 Bear right as the trail forks.

8.0 Trailhead.

22

13.6 M
STRENUOUS

Angleworm Trail

SUPERIOR NATIONAL FOREST
KAWISHIWI RANGER DISTRICT

LENGTH	13.6 miles
TIME	8:15
DIFFICULTY	Strenuous
ROUTE-FINDING	Moderate
MAPS & PERMITS	Fisher Map F-9. USGS quads: Angleworm Lake and Fourteen Lake. A day permit is required as part of this hike is in the BWCAW. There is a self-registration box at the trailhead.
GETTING THERE	From Ely, take Minnesota State Highway 169 east to County Road 88 and turn left. Drive 2 miles to County Road 116 (Echo Trail), turn right, and continue 14 miles to Angleworm Lake parking area on the right side of the road.
TRAILHEAD GPS	48° 3' 52.8" N 91° 55' 50.4" W

At various overlooks along the trail around Angleworm Lake, the hiker can imagine how the lake might have gotten its name. Looking along the narrow, gentle twisting length of the lake from a high ridge, it is easy to picture a giant angling worm crawling across the Precambrian bedrock of the Boundary Waters Canoe Area Wilderness (BWCAW).

Angleworm Lake is one of a number of long, narrow lakes that are connected along major stream systems draining large watersheds. Such lakes, located in granite bedrock, get their shape from the joints in the rock. The topography around Angleworm Lake consists of low bedrock ridges, alternating with narrow valleys containing small streams, ponds, and bogs. The shoreline varies from gentle slopes in shallow bays to steep slopes of bedrock jutting out of the water.

The mixed conifer forest surrounding Angleworm and Home lakes grew after an 1822 forest fire that burned an area of 75 square miles (48,000 acres). Scattered stands of mature pines escaped the deadly effects of the fire.

Logging History

While the Wilderness Act of 1964 defines wilderness in part as "land retaining its primeval character and influence without permanent improvements…with the imprint of man's work substantially unnoticeable," the BWCAW has seen its days of human impact. As early as 1922, logging companies began to move in on the forests around Angleworm and Home lakes. The Cloquet Lumber Company, after acquiring the logging operations of the Swallow and Hopkins Company, built spurs off the Duluth, Mesabi, and Iron Range Railroad to the east of Angleworm and Home lakes. They cut some big timber in the area, but because most of it originated after the 1822 fire and was too small to be of economic interest, they left tracts of forest uncut. Also, the fact that the federal government owned the land prevented the large scale logging of mature pines that companies conducted in other parts of the region.

The United States Forest Service used the spur line to Angleworm Lake until the late 1930s for access to a lookout tower on a ridge along the west side of the lake. The rails were finally removed around 1940. The 1940s also saw the arrival of small-scale logging on the east side of Angleworm Lake. With the conversion of the old railroad grade into a roadbed, trucks could haul the cut timber. At one time, there was a temporary sawmill on the east shore of the lake. Today, large fuel tanks, fuel pumps, fuel cans, and other debris sit alongside the trail to the campsite located about 3.7 miles into this hike. Small-scale logging continued in the area into the 1970s.

Trail Highlights

From the trailhead, the trail runs northeast, crossing Spring Creek, to the south end of Angleworm Lake. Here, at a trail intersection, a portage trail leads south to Trease Lake, while the two trails that make this circuit hike possible head for the east and west sides of the lake. From this junction, the hike continues up the east side of the lake along ridges, occasionally dipping down to cross narrow valleys that often contain beaver ponds. The trail eventually leaves the east shore of Angleworm Lake to pass around Whisky Jack and Home lakes. Once again the hiking is along narrow ridges with occasional panoramic views of valleys. At its northern limit, the Angleworm Trail crosses the portage trail between Home and Gull lakes. Then it passes through old growth stands of white pine around Home Lake and turns south to continue down the west side of Angleworm Lake along scenic ridges to the Trease Lake Portage junction and back to the trailhead.

Hikers can complete this hike in a day with an early start. Plan on about eight to ten hours to complete it, plus or minus depending on your speed and number of rest stops. There are several campsites along the route for a good two-day backpacking trip. If you do backpack overnight, you must register for a permit at one of the district offices (not at the self-registration station at the trailhead).

Stride-by-Stride

MILES	DESCRIPTION
0.0	Trailhead.
0.5	Cross a boardwalk. The trail begins to descend gradually to a stream crossing.
0.9	Enter the Boundary Waters Canoe Area Wilderness (BWCAW).
1.0	Cross boardwalk and bridge over Spring Creek.
1.3	Trail forks; the hiker may take either fork as they rejoin in about 100 yards. Ponds appear on either side of the trail.
1.8	Four-way trail intersection beginning the circuit portion of this hike. The Trease Lake portage leads off to the right. The portage to Angleworm Lake continues on the left trail. To continue this hike take the middle trail which descends to cross a small stream and then continues level.
2.1	Cross a boardwalk and bridge over a stream flowing to Angleworm Lake from Trease Lake. Once across the bridge, the trail ascends gradually through spruces, red and white pines, and balsam firs as Angleworm Lake comes into view on the left.
2.5	Overlook with views of the lake from a rock outcrop (48° 4' 47.3" N 91° 53' 27.8" W).
3.0	The trail descends from the ridge to a beaver pond at the mouth of a narrow valley. Cross two beaver dams before reaching higher ground. Eventually the trail returns to a ridge, passes through a stand of white pines, and comes to an overlook with views of the beaver pond in the valley just crossed. Beyond the overlook, the trail continues along the ridge with views of the valley on the right. Large rock cairns mark the trail.
3.7	The trail forks in a small clearing. The left fork leads to a campsite on Angleworm Lake in 845 feet, passing two large,

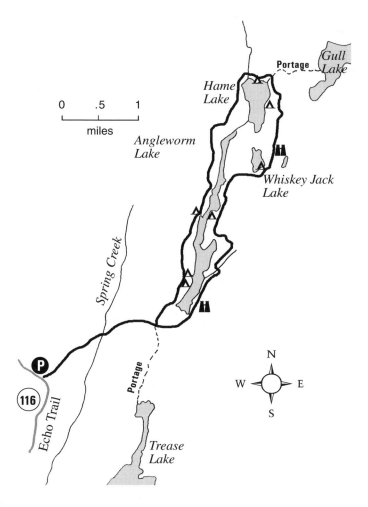

old fuel storage tanks, a fuel pump, and various large cans scattered through the trees along the trail. The main trail continues on the right fork.

3.9 Trail intersection; turn right passing the trail on the left which leads to the campsite on the lake that is reached via the left fork at the last intersection.

4.5 Spur trail on the left leads to a campsite on the lake shore.

4.8 The trail turns east towards Whiskey Jack Lake.

5.4 Spur trail on the left leads to a campsite on Whiskey Jack Lake. The main trail ascends a short steep slope to an overlook with views of the lake. Further on, the trail passes along a ridge with panoramic views of a narrow valley on the right. Mature white pines line the trail.

6.5   Overlook with a view of a small pond in the valley on the right. Gull Lake can be seen in the distance to the northeast.

6.9   Trail intersection; spur trail on the left leads to a campsite on the east shore of Home Lake.

7.1   Intersection with the portage trail between Home and Gull lakes. Continue straight passing a campsite on the left side of the trail just beyond the portage. Making its way through jack pine around Home Lake, the trail heads west and then south along ridges before descending to Angleworm Lake.

9.5   The trail descends steeply to Angleworm Lake. In 50 feet the trail passes a spur trail on the right leading to a campsite.

10.8 Overlook; looking north from here it is possible to get an excellent view of Angleworm Lake gently winding its way into the distance.

11.3 Spur trail on the left leads to a campsite.

11.4 Spur trail on the left leads to a campsite. In 175 feet, pass the portage trail descending to the lake on the left.

11.7 Trail intersection completing the circuit portion of this hike; turn right to return to the trailhead.

13.6 Trailhead.

Astrid Lake Trail

6.4, 7.3 M
DIFFICULT

SUPERIOR NATIONAL FOREST
LACROIX RANGER DISTRICT

LENGTH	7.3 miles, with a shorter 6.4 mile option.
TIME	4:30
DIFFICULTY	Difficult
ROUTE-FINDING	Moderate
Maps & Permits	Fisher Map F-8 and Map F-15. USGS quads: Lake Jeanette and Astrid Lake. No permit is required.
GETTING THERE	From Orr, drive 16 miles on County Road 23 to Buyck, where County Road 23 turns into County Road 24. Continue on County Road 24 for 3.5 miles to the Echo Trail (County Road 116). Turn left off the Echo Trail onto Forest Road 360 and drive 0.1 mile to the trailhead parking lot on the right opposite the trailhead.
TRAILHEAD GPS	48° 7' 49.2" N 92° 17' 45.4" W

Standing on a bit of sandy beach on Astrid Lake, gazing across the calm water reflecting the forest that hugs the shoreline like a child clutching the hem of her mother's skirt, a Bald Eagle flies over the water from a hidden perch to the right. Its white head and tail flash brilliant in the sunlight. Quickly, with a few beats of its powerful wings, the eagle turns downshore and into an unseen cove. Suddenly the cries of several loons rise in alarm filling the once still air. The Astrid Lake Trail is a lightly used trail that holds moments like this in store for its visitors.

Its highlights include two campsites on Astrid and Pauline lakes that are picturesque spots for lunch or a swim. Each site has a small sandy beach. Along the way, the trail passes through forest types ranging from a spruce bog to jack pine and oak-covered ridges, along with mixed stands of towering red and white pines, aspens, and white birches. Huge moss-covered boulders, remnants of the last Ice Age, lay scattered about some sections of the trail. Wildlife and their signs abound: Bald Eagles, loons, and mergansers on the lakes; Broad-winged Hawks in the forest; and the scat of moose along the trail. Moose pellets that look like small ovals of compressed sawdust indicate this area is part of their winter range, while fresh tracks indicate they spend their summers here as well. This isn't surprising considering the number of lakes that offer succulent food and refuge from swarming insects.

Labrador Tea

Perhaps the place that presents the most interesting features is the small spruce bog about 0.5 mile into the trek. Here you will find two unique plants of the northland: the Labrador tea and the purple pitcher plant. The Labrador tea is a medium-sized shrub growing to four feet tall. It is easily identified by the woolly undersides of its leaves. The wool is white when the leaves are new and gradually turns rusty with age. Labrador tea is indicative of peaty soils, especially bogs like this one where it grows in a soft thick carpet of sphagnum moss and cottongrass. As its name indicates, people have used the leaves to make a tea. Canadians know the plant as Hudson's Bay Tea. To make the tea pick the leaves when their wool has turned rusty and dry them in the sun or an oven. Pour a cup of boiled water over one tablespoon of dried, crumpled leaves and let it steep for ten minutes. Don't boil the leaves in the water as they contain a harmful alkaloid.

Pitcher Plants

The second denizen of the spruce bog is the purple pitcher plant. As its name implies, this wildflower has specially adapted leaves shaped like pitchers that catch and hold rainwater. The water is part of an elaborate trap designed to snare insects and other prey which the plant needs for nutrients.

One overwhelming characteristic of bogs is that they are very acidic, sometimes as acidic as the vinegar in a pickle jar. Because of the preservative nature of bogs, dead organisms decay very slowly. The remains of animals and people dating back 2,000 years or more have been recovered from peat bogs in Europe. Due to the slow decay of organic matter, very little free nutrients are available for living plants. Some, like the pitcher plant, have devised ways of getting nitrogen and other nutrients in the animallike fashion of carnivores.

The pitcher plant exudes a sugary excretion which attracts prey species including ants, flies, snails, and slugs. Part way into the pitcher, the inner surface of the leaves is smooth. Below that are stiff downward-pointing hairs. Once in the pitcher, prey, unable to struggle past the stiff bristles, fall into the water and drown. But, there are a variety of organisms that have found a way to make a home in the lion's mouth so to speak. They include bacteria and protozoa, rotifers, mites, and the larvae of three flies. One of them is the pitcher plant mosquito

(*Wyeomyia smithii*). Rather than becoming the pitcher plant's prey, the adult female is able to fly into the trap, deposit her eggs, and leave by the way she came in through the long narrow tube.

Stephen B. Heard, writing in the journal *Ecology*, describes the association between the pitcher plant mosquito and the pitcher plant. They have a relationship that is mutually beneficial, although neither is in a position of having to rely on the other. The plant releases oxygen into the water for the animals that live in it, while the tiny creatures give off carbon dioxide and create nitrogen-rich ammonia which the plant just loves since the soil has so little to offer.

After the female has laid her eggs in newly opened leaves, the eggs hatch and the larvae feed on the bodies of trapped prey. Eventually, the shortening day length signals the larvae to empty their guts in preparation for spending the winter frozen in the pitcher plant's water. The next spring the larvae resume feeding, soon pupate and new adults emerge to start another round in the daring life of the pitcher plant mosquito.

Before you think bad thoughts about these mosquitoes despite the risks they take to reproduce, consider the fact that the female does not need a blood meal to provide energy for the development of her eggs. Her ovary development is mostly completed while she was in the pupal stage and feeding as an adult does not affect the number of her offspring. So don't worry about doing the pitcher plant a disservice by slapping that biting mosquito. It won't be a *Wyeomyia smithii*.

Trail Highlights

The route of this hike follows several different trails. The first is the trail from Lake Jeanette to Maude Lake. Between Jeanette Lake and Nigh Lake this trail is also a portage route. The second trail is the northern section of the Astrid Lake Loop; and the third is the Nigh-Pauline Lakes Loop. All of the intersections along the way have a sign post indicating trail directions.

Once on the south side of the Echo Trail, the route follows the well-groomed portage trail, passing through the spruce bog and traversing a small hill before reaching Nigh Lake. Beyond Nigh Lake, the path is narrower and more rugged. It gradually ascends to a jack pine-oak capped ridge where you will find the intersection that is the start of the circuit portion of the hike. Following the trail leading southwest to Maude Lake by way of Astrid Lake, the route continues along a series of ridges often crossing rock outcroppings that force openings in the canopy overhead. At one point the trail passes fire-scarred stumps and snags, evidence of a fire that swept the area almost 100 years ago. The forest is constantly shifting from one type to another, much like a day when the weather seems unsettled and the clouds come and go, alternating with the sunshine.

At Astrid Lake, the route turns north up the east side of Astrid Lake and passes the first of the two campsites. They both have a picnic table, fire grate, toilet, and small sandy beach just right for swimming. At the northeast corner of Astrid Lake, the route intersects the 0.9 mile Nigh-Pauline Lakes Loop which continues north to a short portage trail between the two lakes. At the portage you will find the second campsite. After making a short jog to the east, the loop turns south, passes a small waterfall, and ascends to rejoin the Astrid Lake Trail at a point 0.25 miles east of where it left it.

Continuing to ascend, the route now heads east and then north to complete the circuit. But before the circuit is closed you will come to an overlook. From here you will get views to the north of the Superior National Forest stretching into the distance ridge after ridge, and of Nigh Lake nestled in the trees below the overlook ridge. It's a perfect spot to sit and catch the breeze and munch on some blueberries if they happen to be in season before starting the return leg of your journey back to the trailhead.

Stride-by-Stride

MILES	DESCRIPTION
0.0	From the trailhead parking lot, walk about 100 feet toward Lake Jeanette to the start of the trail on the left side of the road.
0.2	Trail intersection with the road leading to the boat ramp providing access to Lake Jeanette. Bear left, walk along the road a short distance, and reenter the woods on the right.
0.4	Intersection with the Echo Trail; pick up the trail on the other side of the road. In about 125 feet, reach the intersection with the Lake Jeanette-Nigh Lake portage trail and turn left. The portage soon enters a spruce bog.
0.6	Reach a boardwalk crossing the wettest section of the bog. Immediately after the boardwalk, the trail crosses a small hill. It passes first through spruce and white birch and then moves gradually into jack pine and large aspens.

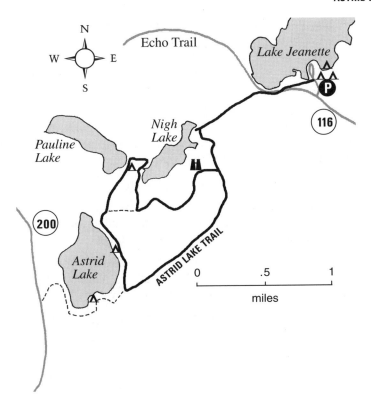

1.1 Trail intersection at Nigh Lake; turn left onto the trail leading to Astrid Lake, passing the portage which continues on to Nigh Lake.

1.3 The trail skirts the edge of a large clearing with a beaver pond and ascends a ridge passing very large boulders and tall white and red pines. Jack pine and oak begin to dominate the forest as the trail reaches the ridge top.

1.9 Trail intersection beginning the circuit portion of this hike. Bear left on the trail to Astrid Lake passing the trail to the right. Cairns mark the way over occasional rock outcroppings.

2.3 Cross a small stream and come to a pond where the trail continues briefly along a rock outcropping at the water's edge before veering into the woods once again.

2.7 The trail crosses an area of fire-scarred tree stumps and snags scattered amongst jack and red pines, and an occasional white pine.

3.0 Trail intersection at Astrid Lake; turn right passing the trail to the left.

3.2   A spur trail to the left leads to a campsite on Astrid Lake (48° 6' 44.3" N 92° 19' 30.4" W). Beyond the spur, the trail approaches the lake shore before veering away again and passing some large red and white pines, some with fire scars on their trunks.

3.5   Trail intersection with the Lake Pauline-Nigh Lake Loop; continue straight ahead to hike this loop, or turn right to skip it for the shorter 6.4 mile option. The directions that follow are for the 7.3 mile circuit hike. Otherwise, jump to mile 4.6.

3.9   Cross a stream flowing west to Pauline Lake.

4.0   Reach the campsite on Pauline Lake (48° 7' 20.3" N 92° 19' 28.1" W). In 85 feet, come to an intersection with the portage trail to Nigh Lake; turn right on the portage.

4.1   One hundred sixty feet short of Nigh Lake the portage trail intersects the loop trail leading south; turn right. In about 450 feet, cross a stream just above a small waterfall.

4.6   Trail intersection completing the Pauline-Nigh Lakes Loop. Continue straight ahead, passing the trail to the right.

5.3   An overlook from a rock outcropping on the left side of the trail provides views to the north of the Echo Trail and Superior National Forest, and of Nigh Lake partially hidden in the foreground.

5.4   Trail intersection completing the circuit portion of this hike. Turn left, passing the trail to the right, to return to the trailhead.

6.2   Trail intersection with the portage trail at Nigh Lake; turn right.

6.9   Reach the Echo Trail. Here you have the option of continuing the hike on the trail, or of walking along the road back to the parking lot.

7.3   Trailhead.

Echo River & Herriman Lake

24

6.0, 9.7 M
DIFFICULT-STRENUOUS

SUPERIOR NATIONAL FOREST
LACROIX RANGER DISTRICT

LENGTH	9.7 miles (6.0 miles without going to the end of the Echo River Trail).
TIME	6:15
DIFFICULTY	Difficult-Strenuous
ROUTE-FINDING	Moderate-Difficult
MAPS & PERMITS	Fisher Map F-15. USGS quads: Echo Lake and Crane Lake. This hike enters the Boundary Waters Canoe Area Wilderness. Permits for day-users only are available at a self-serve permit station 425 feet into the hike.
GETTING THERE	From Orr, drive 16 miles on County Road 23 to Buyck, where County Road 23 turns into County Road 24. Continue on County Road 24 for 8.7 miles to County Road 424. Turn right on County Road 424 and drive 1.5 miles to the trailhead.
TRAILHEAD GPS	48° 14' 57.4" N 92° 27' 33.3" W

The trek along the Echo River and around Herriman Lake has much to offer: panoramic views of the snaking Echo River; oak and pine dominated ridges; easy access to two lakes; and beaver ponds nestled in narrow valleys.

Beaver Ecology

Despite their relatively small size, beaver have a tremendous impact on their environment. Ecologists refer to them as a keynote species for this reason. In their article, "Browse selection by beaver: effects on riparian forest composition," Carol A. Johnston and Robert J. Naiman write that beaver affect the structure and the dynamics of an ecosystem beyond their immediate needs for survival. While animals like moose and snowshoe hares can influence forest succession and the nutrient cycle, only the beaver has the ability to cut down mature trees and cause dramatic changes in the overstory.

Johnston and Naiman report that a single beaver may cut down about 2,866 pounds of woody material per 2.5 acres of territory in a year. By way of comparison, a moose browses only about 200 pounds per 2.5 acres. A second comparison is even more revealing: a colony of six beavers harvests twice as much biomass per area as a herd of ungulates on the Serengeti plain; over 4.8 tons. A beaver doesn't need all that it harvests for food. In captivity beaver eat only about 660 pounds of food per year.

Over the short term, beaver can cause a shift in the composition of the forest around their pond. Through their influence, beaver activity can change an aspen-dominated forest area to show an increase in balsam poplars and birches, which beaver prefer less. In the long run, beaver harvesting can change a stand of deciduous trees into a tangle of shrubs, alder, and beaked hazel giving slower growing conifers, which beaver find unappetizing, an advantage. Thus, beaver have a diversifying effect on the forest. When you hike by a beaver pond, notice the types of trees beaver have gnawed on, and the ones they have left alone.

Trail Highlights

The Echo River Trail leaves the Little Vermilion Lake Trail just east of the bridge over the Echo River. The trail leads south following the river over gently rolling terrain for about 1.5 miles before veering away from the river and taking to ridges. Aspen and balsam fir, with scattered pines and birches, comprise the forest at lower elevations. On the drier ridges jack and white pines, and oaks predominate.

About a mile past the intersection with the Herriman Lake Trail, the Echo River Trail turns away from the river and traverses a series of ridges that provide excellent overlooks of the serpentine Echo River far below. After crossing a very narrow valley the trail climbs to an open hilltop intermittently covered with weather beaten jack pine and oak. There are more fine views of the surrounding forest and Echo River along the 0.7 mile loop of the summit.

The Herriman Lake Trail, heading east from the Echo River Trail, descends into a valley and passes a beaver pond. From the valley, the trail ascends to a ridge just south of Herriman Lake. The path crosses occasional rock outcroppings amid jack pines, oaks, and maples with views of the lake. Past the lake, the trail descends steeply to a stream crossing, turns north, and climbs one last white pine and oak-covered hill.

From here, the trail descends to Knute Lake where a short spur leads to a campsite on the lake shore that makes a good rest stop. Just beyond Knute Lake, the trail returns to the Little Vermilion Lake Trail.

Stride-by-Stride

MILES	DESCRIPTION
0.0	This hike begins on the Little Vermilion Lake Trail on the east side of County Road 424, opposite the parking area. The trail ascends a short distance along the south edge of a recently logged area. In 425 feet, you come to the self-serve permit station.
0.5	Bridge over the Echo River. A hundred feet beyond the bridge is the intersection with the Echo River Trail on the right and the start of the circuit portion of this hike. Turn right onto the Echo River Trail and ascend a ridge along the east side of the river.
1.6	Trail intersection with the Herriman Lake Loop Trail. After a short, moderately steep ascent away from the river, the south end of the Herriman Lake Loop Trail bears off to the left. Continue on the Echo River Trail to the right.
1.7	The trail enters a clearing and continues just below the beaver dam. On the other side of the clearing, the trail bears left and ascends a ridge via switchbacks. Pay close attention to the rock cairns that mark the way across rock outcroppings.
2.5	Overlook with views of the meandering Echo River.
2.6	Overlook with view of horseshoe-bend in the river. From here the trail ascends gradually along a ridge dotted with jack and white pines. Again, rock cairns mark the way.
3.1	The trail reaches the summit of a knob covered with scattered oaks and jack pines. A short 0.7 mile trail circling the knob, and beginning at this point, provides frequent views of the surrounding countryside. One end of the loop bears off to the right at about 150°, and the other to the left at about 60°. It is good idea to mark a rock cairn at the start of this loop with something easily visible because the cairns leading you around the summit will begin to look alike and you might end up walking in circles looking for the way off the knob.
3.8	End of the loop circling the knob. Back track along the Echo River Trail to its intersection with the Herriman Lake Loop.

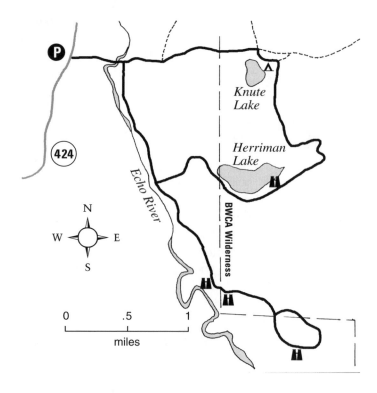

5.3 Trail intersection with the south end of the Herriman Lake Loop Trail; leave the Echo River Trail by bearing right onto the Herriman Lake Loop. The trail ascends, crosses a ridge, and descends into a narrow valley.

5.4 The trail enters a clearing and crosses a beaver dam. Once past the clearing, the trail ascends a ridge via switchbacks. Rock outcroppings, and jack pines and oaks are encountered once again. Cairns mark the way.

6.0 Herriman Lake comes into view through the trees on the left side of the trail.

6.2 Overlook of Herriman Lake.

6.7 Cross a small stream at the east end of the lake. Beyond this stream the trail continues to descend gradually.

7.0 The trail turns north, descends steeply via switchbacks, and crosses a stream flowing northeast in about 425 feet. On the other side of the stream, the trail ascends steeply and crosses a knob.

7.9 Trail intersection with the Knute Lake Loop Trail that is not clearly marked, so close attention is necessary. There is a rock cairn at the intersection where the trail bears left, as well as a line of cairns straight ahead where the trail continues along contour. Turn left at this intersection. If you miss this intersection you will shortly come to the Little Vermilion Lake Trail where you can turn left to return to the trailhead.

8.1 Spur trail on the left leads to a campsite on Knute Lake in about 225 feet.

8.2 Trail intersection with the Little Vermilion Lake Trail. Turn left to return to the trailhead.

8.2 Trail intersection with the east end of the Dovre Lake Loop Trail. Continue straight ahead on the Little Vermilion Lake Trail.

8.4 Cross a small stream on narrow logs laid out lengthwise.

8.6 The trail descends to the shore of a beaver pond on the right.

8.9 Trail intersection with the west end of the Dovre Lake Loop Trail. Continue straight ahead as the trail gradually descends to the Echo River.

9.2 Trail intersection with the Echo River Trail completing the circuit portion of this hike. Cross the Echo River bridge in about 100 feet.

9.7 Trailhead.

25

7.1 M
DIFFICULT

Dovre Lake Trail

SUPERIOR NATIONAL FOREST
LACROIX RANGER DISTRICT

LENGTH	7.1 miles
TIME	4:15
DIFFICULTY	Difficult
ROUTE-FINDING	Moderate
MAPS & PERMITS	Fisher Map F-15. USGS quads: Echo Lake and Crane Lake. This hike enters the Boundary Waters Canoe Area Wilderness. Permits for day-users only are available at a self-serve permit station 425 feet into the hike.
GETTING THERE	From Orr, drive 16 miles on County Road 23 to Buyck, where County Road 23 turns into County Road 24. Continue on County Road 24 for 8.7 miles to County Road 424. Turn right on County Road 424 and drive 1.5 miles to trailhead.
TRAILHEAD GPS	48° 14' 57.4" N 92° 27' 33.3" W

Hikes in the Boundary Waters Canoe Area Wilderness (BWCAW) have a feeling about them that is difficult to get anywhere else in northeastern Minnesota. Once I step across that boundary, it is like entering another world. Something in the air seems to awaken and heighten the senses. The strangely mysterious and powerful nature of the BWCAW transmits a charge that becomes an electric current running up and down my spine. Perhaps it's nothing more than a trick of the mind playing off our myths about wilderness, but the feeling is addicting, drawing me back time and time again.

Woodland Caribou

Despite all the wildness northeastern Minnesota has to offer today, it is less than it was, and more than what the future likely holds in store. Take, for example, the woodland caribou. This magnificent creature once roamed the forests of northern Minnesota. Now they are only a memory floating like wisps of smoke through the trees along long forgotten trails. Along with the caribou, buffalo, elk, and cougars have entirely or almost entirely vanished from Minnesota. Without these, and other animals, our world is slowly becoming something tragically less than it once was. Imagine an orchestra playing a Beethoven symphony without the regal notes of the French horns, or the embellishments of the violins. With the loss of each section, the power of the orchestra to move the spirit diminishes; the score loses a bit of its magic. So it is with the natural world. We lose a piece of the grand symphony each time a species vanishes from our region.

Lichen-covered trees and rocks reminded me of the woodland caribou as I hiked the trail to Dovre Lake. Lichen is an important food that helped the caribou survive the cold months of winter. The woodland caribou, a cousin of the barren caribou of the far north, once inhabited the northern Rocky Mountains, the Great Lakes region, and New England. Fossil records indicate they have inhabited North America for about 1 million years. Today they survive only in northern Idaho, as well as Canada, where they are widespread.

In his book, *The Boundary Waters Wilderness Ecosystem*, Miron Heinselman writes that around 1800 the woodland caribou ranged as far south as Mille Lacs and Kanabec counties. Woodland caribou were still fairly common in parts of Lake County and much of Cook County as late as 1885 according to Thaddeus Surber. Heinselman added that the caribou infrequently sighted today along the North Shore in these counties are probably wanderers from a herd in the Lake Nipigon region, about 150 miles to the north.

In addition to hunting, the loss of habitat is an important reason for the elimination of the woodland caribou from this region. They require large, stable, old-growth forests to survive. Forests disturbed by catastrophic fires or logging are not suitable habitat. We must protect remaining old-growth forests if there is ever to be a hope of reintroducing caribou into Minnesota.

But there is another change in our ecosystem that stands in the way of bringing the caribou back: the increased range of the white-tailed deer. In all of North America, the ranges of these two members of the deer family seldom overlap. The reason is *Parelaphostringylus tenais*, a brainworm that attacks the nervous system of the caribou and the moose. The white-tailed deer carries the worm's larvae with little or no consequence. Snails pick up the larvae when they travel over deer feces; caribou eat the snails and the larvae while grazing. Heinselman identified the Little Saganaga Lake region in the eastern BWCAW as having suitable habitat for the reintroduction of the woodland caribou because of its low deer density and the very low infestation of the brainworm larvae in deer feces. Until such time as the woodland caribou returns to wander the ridges and bogs of northeastern Minnesota, we will have to rely on our mind's eye to imagine them slowly picking their way through the trees.

Trail Highlights

The trail to Dovre Lake passes through a mature mixed forest of pines and deciduous trees. The abundance of jack and white pines, along with maples and oaks, offers a pleasant contrast to the mostly aspen, birch, balsam fir forests of much of northeastern Minnesota. Soon after crossing the Echo River, the trail to Dovre Lake turns north passing along dry ridges and over numerous rock outcroppings. Pines, maples, and oaks dominate the forest here, while aspen and spruce remain confined mostly to the wetter areas. Lichens and mosses are everywhere. Cairns mark the way across some of the longer expanses of outcroppings and there are occasional views of the large tracts of forests to the north.

On the early autumn day that I made this trek, with the sun shining and the air pleasantly cool, Sharp-shinned and Broad-winged Hawks were on the move. The cries of Blue Jays filled the woods, while occasional flocks of slate-colored juncos cheerfully escorted me for short stretches of the way. Purple asters, still in bloom on the trailside, held the fading glory of summer.

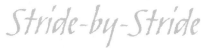
Stride-by-Stride

MILES	DESCRIPTION
0.0	This hike starts on the Little Vermilion Lake Trail on the east side of County Road 424, opposite the parking area. The trail ascends a short distance along the south edge of a recently logged area. In 425 feet, you come to a self-serve permit registration box.
0.5	Cross the bridge over the Echo River. About 100 feet beyond the bridge pass the Echo River Trail on the right by continuing straight ahead on the Little Vermilion Lake Trail.
0.8	Trail intersection beginning the circuit portion of this hike; leave the Little Vermilion Lake Trail and turn left onto the Dovre Lake Loop. In about 300 feet, cross a small stream on boulders and ascend through aspens, white birches, and maples.

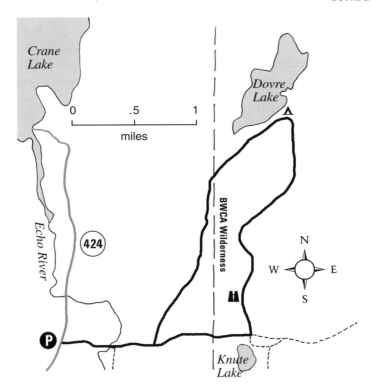

0.9 Overlook of beaver pond. The stream flowing from this pond is a tributary of the Echo River. Jack and red pines occupy the overlook. Just beyond the overlook is a stand of red pines with scattered jack pines. Oaks gradually become more frequent and cairns mark the trail where it crosses rock outcroppings.

3.3 Dovre Lake can be seen through the trees on the left side of the trail.

3.4 A view of the lake through the trees where the trail turns right, away from the lake, and heads south back to the Little Vermilion Lake Trail.

4.0 Pass a meadow bog on the left side of the trail. Water from this bog flows north to Little Vermilion Lake.

5.1 An unnamed lake comes into view on the right side of the trail as it ascends a ridge through jack pine and oak. There are plenty of opportunities to view the lake from this ridge. Knute Lake can be seen in the distance off to the south at one point. From the ridge summit the trail descends to the Little Vermilion Lake Trail.

5.6 Trail intersection with the Little Vermilion Lake Trail under a towering red pine. Turn right to return to the trailhead.

5.7 Cross a cattail marsh and a slow moving stream flowing from the unnamed lake recently passed to Knute Lake just south of this point.

6.0 Reach the shore of the beaver pond passed at the start of the Dovre Lake Loop Trail.

6.3 Trail intersection completing the circuit portion of this hike; continue straight ahead. The trail gradually descends to the Echo River.

6.6 Pass the Echo River Trail on the left and cross the Echo River bridge in about 100 feet.

7.1 Trailhead.

Ash River Falls— Loop B

ASH RIVER RECREATIONAL TRAIL
KABETOGAMA STATE FOREST

LENGTH	4.1 miles
TIME	2:15
DIFFICULTY	Moderate
ROUTE-FINDING	Easy-Moderate
MAPS & PERMITS	DNR Kabetogama State Forest map. USGS quads: Baley Bay and Ash River SW. No permit is required.
GETTING THERE	Drive east from Minnesota State Highway 53 on County Road 129 for 5.8 miles to the parking area on the right side of the road.
TRAILHEAD GPS	48° 23' 10.3" N 92° 52' 31.5" W

There are times when a hike has no panoramic views to revel in, when the forest presents no windows to the outside world. Instead it confines you to a world within walls of trees. So often we want the big experience, like a spectacular view, in order to get the corresponding rush of emotion. We do this to the point that all else is seemingly insignificant. In these cases, hiking may become a series of blind walks from one vista to the next with little attention given to what lies in between. This hike, like several others in this book, has something different from what hikers might ordinarily demand of a good hike. While there are brief glimpses of the expansive coniferous forest from ridges along the way, I didn't find the views to be as dramatic as those on other hikes. What I did discover was a splendor within the forest.

While walking a wide trail through a stand of towering aspens, with white birches and maples forming a devout congregation, the path suddenly became an aisle arcade. Like sunshine pouring through clerestory windows, beams of sunlight poured through breaks in the canopy overhead dappling the path. The lofty woods became a cathedral. Tree branches wove a delicate tracery for its walls. Puffs of wind lightly chanted psalms in the rustling aspen leaves, the music filling every corner of the lofty interior.

Aspen-White Birch-Maple Forest Community

The aspen-white birch-maple forest is one of a number of different types of forest communities found in northeastern Minnesota. In 1971, Lewis F. Ohmann and Robert R. Ream described thirteen upland plant communities in the Boundary Waters Canoe Area Wilderness (BWCAW) based on the relative importance of certain tree species. While the route of this hike is not in the BWCAW, the plant communities Ohmann and Ream identified do not restrict themselves to that wilderness area. The aspen-white birch-maple community is characterized by an overstory of aspen and birch with a strong presence of maples in the understory. It is found anywhere from valleys to the upper slopes of ridges, as is the case on this hike. The community indicates a rich moist soil with a depth of from 20–40 inches to bedrock. With the suppression of forest fires, this community type will probably see an increase in dominance of the more shade-tolerant maples and spruces.

Jack Pine-Oak Community

A second community very much in evidence on this hike is the jack pine-oak forest. While the presence of jack pines and oaks characterize this community, a striking feature is geological rather than biological. Bald rock ridges and rock outcroppings are distinguishing features. Glaciers have scoured the ridges clean of any soil, and forest fires have consumed much of any soil that has tried to accumulate on these slow weathering granite ridges. As a result, the soils are very thin; from only 6 to 20 inches deep.

Stands of jack pine-oak communities tend to be among the youngest, being from 60–105 years old on average, as they develop in the wake of major forest fires. Jack pine is a tree of the pioneer stage of succession following significant forest fires. Jack pines are sun-loving trees. Their seedlings do not do well in shade. To ensure that its seeds will germinate only when conditions are right for the seedlings, saplings, and trees they will produce, this plant has adapted its cone to withstand forest fires. In fact, the cones not only withstand the fires, they need them if they are ever to see the light of day. The tightly shut cones need the heat of fires to melt the resin that would otherwise keep the seeds locked up forever. Without the disturbance of forest fires, this community type will gradually shift to black and white spruces, balsam firs, and paper birch. In other areas, maples and oaks may succeed, or red and white pines.

While jack pine is the dominant tree species, red maples, red oak, and black spruce are next in importance. They tend to occupy the understory, waiting to take over when the jack pine fall to the ravages of old age and are unable to reproduce without the aid of fire. Bush honeysuckle, juneberry, and beaked hazel are important tall shrubs in this community, while late sweet blueberry, wintergreen, and velvet-leaf blueberry are the major low shrubs. The presence of these later shrubs indicates relatively open, dry conditions. On the ground, false lily-of-the-valley, large leaf northern aster, and mosses are common.

Lichen Community

Interspersed within the jack pine-oak community are often found small lichen communities. Much like the jack pine-oak communities, they are restricted to rock outcroppings on ridge tops where the ground surface is up to 30 percent bare rock. Conditions here are xeric, being extremely dry. While it receives rain and snowfall, water runs quickly off the bare rock and cannot be soaked up by the impermeable stone.

Lichen communities are early succeeders of major fire disturbances. Repeated forest fires consume organic materials leaving bare rock where woody plants have difficulty getting established. Instead, lichens have the task of beginning the soil building process. With the suppression of fires, lichen communities will do just that and a woody plant community will eventually succeed them.

As you make the 4.1 mile trek through the different forest communities along this hike, see how many differences you can identify between them. There aren't but one or two vistas to distract you, so you should be able to come up with quite a list as you focus your attention on the close-at-hand rather than the distant.

Trail Highlights

At the start of the route, the wide grassy trail passes through a thin stand of balm of gilead and white birches. Soon, however, balsam firs and white pines appear and the trail begins a very gradual ascent that will continue for the next 2.1 miles to the ridge summit. As the trail heads north and then east, it continues climbing and rock outcroppings become more common. It is along these ridges that you will find the jack pine-oak and lichen communities. The best views of the hike are at the end of a short spur trail at the second trail intersection 1.3 miles from the trailhead.

At the approach to the ridge summit, the forest begins to open up. The trees stand further apart, and more sunlight pours through the fractured canopy of jack pines, oaks, and scattered white pines. Descending from the summit, the trail leaves the ridge tops for their slopes. Here you will find the aspen-white birch-maple community growing in deeper, moister soils. Giant aspen trees, their trunks disappearing through a subcanopy of shorter trees, seem like columns holding up the sky. As the ascent was long and gradual, so to is the descent back to the trailhead. The trail is wide and easy to follow throughout, and while there were probably better views 20–30 years ago when the ridge trees were shorter, the woods are very nice and a spectacular sight in their own right.

Stride-by-Stride

MILES   DESCRIPTION

0.0   The trail heads east from the parking area through scattered white birches, balm of gillead (balsam poplar), and white birch. In about 100 yards, the trail enters a denser forest of aspen and balsam fir and begins to climb gradually.

0.2   Trail intersection beginning the circuit portion of this hike. Turn left, passing the trail on the right. The trail continues to ascend along the north side of a ridge passing occasional white pines. In 0.4 miles, the trail begins crossing rock outcroppings among red, white, and jack pines.

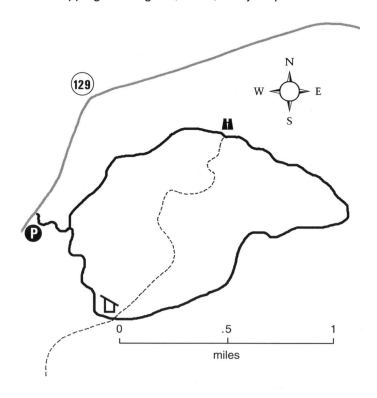

1.3   Trail intersection; continue straight ahead, passing the trail on the right which is a 1.2 mile cutoff allowing for an shorter 3.2 mile hike. A very short spur to the left at this point leads to an overlook with views of the dense coniferous forest to the north.

2.0   The trail approaches the ridge summit where the canopy of jack pines and oaks, with scattered white pines, opens up.

2.1   Beyond the ridge summit, the trail begins a gradual descent through a forest of large aspens, maples, and white birches.

3.4   Trail intersection with a shelter; the cutoff trail, the other end of which was passed 2.1 miles back, comes in sharply from the right just before reaching the shelter. Just past the shelter bear right, passing the trail to the left which connects with Loop A of this ski trail system in 1.4 miles.

3.9   Trail intersection completing the circuit portion of this hike. Bear left to return to the trailhead.

4.1   Trailhead.

Agnes, Ek, & Cruiser Lakes

KABETOGAMA PENINSULA
VOYAGEURS NATIONAL PARK

LENGTH	9.9 miles
TIME	8:30
DIFFICULTY	Strenuous
ROUTE-FINDING	Easy-Moderate. There are trail maps at most intersections, and rock cairns to mark the way across rock outcroppings.
MAPS & PERMITS	MacKenzie K1-Kabetogama. USGS quad: Ash River NE. No permit is required.
GETTING THERE	From the Ash River Ranger Station, paddle due north and enter the small channel leading to Lost Lake. Make the quarter-mile portage to Long Slu and paddle to Lost Bay. Turn right and continue to the head of the bay where you will find a dock and the trailhead.
TRAILHEAD GPS	48° 27' 56.9" N 92° 49' 13.4" W

The Kabetogama Peninsula offers limited hiking opportunities, but what is lacking in quantity is more than made up in quality. This hike offers extensive panoramic views of lakes, beaver ponds, stream valleys, and a major bay on Kabetogama Lake. Well-constructed bridges and board-walks keep hikers dry where the route crosses streams and low-lying wetlands. Although the almost ten miles of hiking and ten miles of paddling sounds challenging, experienced hikers and canoeists should be able to easily finish it in a day. If hiked in the summer, when the days are longest, there should even be enough time to relax at Cruiser Lake or one or more of the many overlooks. If you think the full 9.9 mile hike is too long, consider doing the shorter 3.4 mile hike without the walk to Cruiser Lake. The circuit alone is still an excellent hike.

The canoe route to the trailhead from the Ash River Ranger Station lies across protected waters for the most part. However, there are some stretches of open water where the wind can kick up rough waves. Paddling these stretches after completing a strenuous ten-mile hike will make the going that much more difficult. A motor boat would make the trip to and from the trailhead quicker and easier. But, the slow, quiet pace of the canoe sets a good mood for the hike, and is a unique vantage point from which to reflect on the beauty of Voyageurs National Park.

The Kabetogama Peninsula is 75,000 acres of ridges, lakes, streams, beaver ponds, bogs, meadows, and not a single road. Surrounded by Rainy Lake to the north, Kabetogama Lake to the south, and Namakan Lake to the east, the peninsula has seen many changes. The pink vermilion granite bedrock that forms many of the ridges is over 2.5 billion years old, and dates from a time when the North American continent was formed. This granite is part of a giant batholith that was once the core of a mountain range. Erosion has worn the mountains down over time, and glaciers have scoured the bedrock. Grooves in the hard rock made by the boulder-wielding ice sheet give an indication of the tremendous erosive power of glaciers.

Human Migration in Northeastern Minnesota

Like the glaciers, waves of people have washed over northeastern Minnesota and the peninsula bringing their own changes. The earliest signs of humans living in the Kabetogama Peninsula area date from 7,000–3,000 years ago. During this period, a seminomadic group of Native Americans referred to as the Archaic Tradition occupied the region. They used copper implements and pine log canoes. Beginning about 200 B.C., people of the Woodland Tradition were developing a complex lifestyle that involved gathering and storing plant foods, hunting, and fishing. They made clay pottery for food storage and burial mounds for their dead. By the time French explorers arrived in the mid-1600s, Sioux Indians occupied the region and were fighting a losing battle with the Ojibwa over its control.

On the heels of early white explorers came missionaries, fur traders, loggers, fishermen, miners, and farmers. No changes were more significant than those made by fur traders and loggers. By 1925 the peninsula was almost devoid of beaver, and loggers, cutting until 1972, left practically none of the original forest.

Beaver Ecology

While the forest has been slow to return to its former glory, the beaver have made a dramatic recovery, but it's a recovery they cannot sustain. Their history provides an excellent lesson in the intricate interactions of predator, prey, flora, and geography. In the 1920s, conditions were ideal for the return of beaver to the peninsula. Logging and fires had created an abundant food supply, namely trembling aspen and willows. At the same time, the population of wolves, a major predator of the beaver, was greatly reduced. Researchers determined that in 1927 there were only 64 beaver ponds on the peninsula. With a density of about 0.2 ponds per square kilometer, these ponds occupied less than 1 percent of the peninsula area. By 1988, there were 835 beaver ponds, at a density of 3.0 ponds per square kilometer, occupying about 13 percent of the peninsula.

The scientists also learned that the ponds created before 1961 were significantly larger than those established after 1972. The average area of new ponds until 1961 was about 8.9 acres. New ponds after 1972 were an average of only 3.0 acres in size, almost two-thirds smaller. Researchers Carol A. Johnston and Robert J. Naiman also found that initially, from 1940 to 1961, beavers created new ponds at the rate of 25 ponds per year. From 1961 to 1986, this rate dropped to 10 ponds per year. The findings indicate that initially, when beaver were impounding new ponds at a rapid pace, average pond size was also quite large. Later, the rate of new pond creation decreased, while at the same time the average size of new ponds got smaller. As beaver have used up the most favorable sites for building large ponds, they have been forced to build in less desirable sites.

Since 1961, the peninsula's topography has limited the creation of new beaver ponds. Young beaver leave home and strike out on their own when they are about two years old. They have the difficult task of creating new ponds in areas that are less favorable than the ones they grew up in. This factor is affecting the beaver population. The number of beaver colonies on the Kabetogama Peninsula peaked in 1981 at 398 and has gone down since then. There were 334 colonies in 1987, and 330 in 1988.

Another limiting factor for beaver is food supply. Beaver tend to harvest food within 100 yards of their ponds. They select and cut down aspens and willows, leaving the undesirable trees to mature. After a time, the beaver eat themselves out of lodge and pond and they must move on to find a new food supply. Beaver cannot go back and reoccupy old abandoned sites if new food supplies have not grown back. Forests need a catastrophic event like forest fires to bring back the aspen and willows. It seems that easy times have just about come to an end for the beaver of Kabetogama Peninsula.

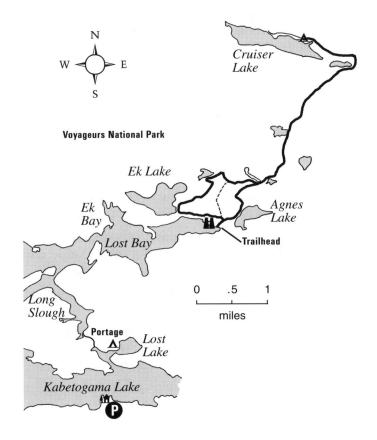

N
W E
S

Voyageurs National Park

Cruiser
Lake

Ek Lake

Ek
Bay

Agnes
Lake

Lost Bay

Trailhead

0   .5   1

miles

Long
Slough

Portage
Lost
Lake

Kabetogama Lake

Stride-by-Stride

MILES	DESCRIPTION

0.0   From the dock, the Cruiser Lake Trail heads northeast, away from the bay.

0.2   Trail intersection beginning the circuit; bear right towards Agnes Lake, passing the south trail to Ek Lake on the left.

0.3   The first of several Agnes Lake overlooks.

0.4   Pass a spur trail on the right to Agnes Lake campsite.

1.1   Trail intersection. The circuit continues to the left on the north trail to Ek Lake. The Cruiser Lake Trail continues straight ahead. The following description includes the hike to Cruiser Lake. If you are only doing the circuit, pick up the description at mile 7.6.

1.2   Bridge over stream flowing from a beaver pond on the left. On the other side of the bridge, quietly walk to the top of the dam. You may see a beaver.

2.1   Intersection with the abandoned Overlook Trail; the Cruiser Lake Trail continues straight ahead crossing a bridge over a stream flowing from the lake on the left.

3.5   Cross a small stream. Just on the other side, a trail to the right leads to the top of a 15–20 foot waterfall. Beyond the stream, the main trail turns to the northwest and ascends a ridge near Cruiser Lake.

4.3   Spur trail to the left leads to the Cruiser Lake campsite in about 500 feet. Backtrack from here to resume the circuit hike.

7.6   Back at the intersection north of Agnes Lake. Continue the circuit by turning west on the north trail to Ek Lake.

8.1   Trail intersection; turn right, passing the closed trail on the left. The trail descends steeply into a narrow valley, crosses a boardwalk, and climbs steeply up the other side.

9.0   The trail descends from a ridge and turns south along the east shore of Ek Lake.

9.2   Trail intersection; turn left, passing the trail heading west to join the Jorgens Lake Trail. The circuit trail now heads east along a ridge providing panoramic views of Lost Bay.

9.7   Trail intersection with the south end of the closed trail; turn right.

9.8   Trail intersection completing the circuit; continue straight ahead to return to the trailhead.

9.9   Trailhead.

Gooseberry River

GOOSEBERRY FALLS STATE PARK

28

5.2 M
MODERATE

LENGTH	5.2 miles
TIME	3:00
DIFFICULTY	Moderate
ROUTE-FINDING	Easy-Moderate
MAPS & PERMITS	DNR Gooseberry Falls State Park map. USGS quads: Split Rock Point and Two Harbors NE. A Minnesota State Park permit is required.
GETTING THERE	The park is about 12 miles northeast of Two Harbors on U.S. Highway 61. The trailhead is located at the new Visitors Center.
TRAILHEAD GPS	47° 8' 29.1" N 91° 28' 9.9" W

Gooseberry River Falls is the most popular state park on the North Shore. One look at the waterfalls located above and below the highway bridge and you will understand what the big attraction is that draws large crowds of tourists. There is the 25 foot high Upper Falls above the bridge, and the two Lower Falls totaling 75 feet below the bridge. Walk about a quarter of a mile upriver from the highway though and you'll most likely have the river all to yourself.

On this hike you will journey from the roar of Lower and Upper falls inland to where the river flows quietly but with purpose. Above the falls, the river seems to be gathering itself, like a spring being slowly wound, for the wild plunge it's about to make through the rocky gorge before emptying lazily into Lake Superior. As the route winds its way upstream, it crosses two footbridges over the river. The second one crosses the river just below the Fifth Falls. On the return leg of the trek, the trail leaves the river to climb a ridge and travel over flat to gently rolling terrain, depositing you along the river once again just above Upper Falls. The trails are wide and grassy, making the trek an enjoyable one for small groups—you'll be able to walk side-by-side much of the time, chatting and sharing. Or you may want to try it on your own. There are many places just right for sitting quietly and letting your mind wander where it will.

Lake Superior Lava Flows

Gooseberry Falls State Park is one of the best places on the North Shore to see some of the lava flows that cover this region. About one billion years ago, lava ran out of fissures in the ground. For hundreds of thousands of years the flows poured forth covering an area about 150 miles wide, from the North Shore to Michigan's Upper Peninsula, and south along the St. Croix River valley. Flows varied from one to more than 60 feet thick and eventually totaled more than 23,000 feet. In Gooseberry Falls, no less than 30 separate lava flows have been identified. When you stop to view the Lower Falls, see if you can pick out the three different flows visible there.

As a result of varying rates of cooling within a lava flow the upper portion is softer than the lower. At the top of each fall is the resistant bottom part of a lava flow. As falling water wears away the softer top layer of the underlying lava flow, it undercuts the overlaying resistant layer which eventually collapses. The waterfall slowly works its way upstream as this process is repeated over and over again. Imagine, one day the Lower Falls will be above the bridge.

Gooseberry River History

While Gooseberry Falls is today a focal point for tourists, in the past it attracted fishermen and loggers. In the 1870s, commercial fishermen began operating near the mouth of Gooseberry River. By the 1890s, loggers were transporting timber from the surrounding countryside to the mouth of the river. According to Frank King, in *Minnesota Logging Railroads*, the Estate of Thomas Nestor, owners of a large Michigan lumber company, purchased the timber in the Gooseberry River area in 1900 which they logged until 1909.

Railroads helped loggers move the timber to the mouth of the river. There, from a ledge along the west bank, the logs were dumped into the river 70 feet below and formed into giant booms. The largest boom ever towed across Lake Superior was owned by the Nestor Company. The boom contained 6 million board feet of timber and was towed 230 miles to a Nestor Company sawmill in Baraga, Michigan. The next winter, there were 800 men working in five camps on the North Shore cutting timber so that by the spring of 1902, 50 million board feet of timber lay at the mouth of Gooseberry River waiting to be towed to sawmills. As a result of heavy logging and large fires in 1903 and 1910, there were no pines left 30 years after logging began. Today the forests of the park consist mainly of white birches, balsam firs, white cedars, and aspens.

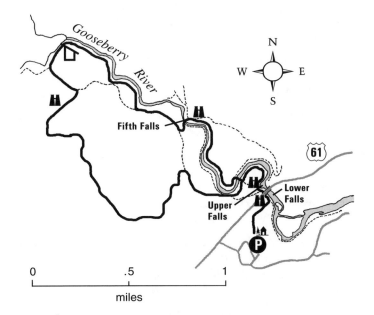

Stride-by-Stride

MILES   DESCRIPTION

0.0   Begin at the north end of the Visitors Center. Follow the blacktop walkway toward the river, descend a flight of cement stairs, and bear left at the bottom.

0.1   Trail intersection at an observation platform that provides a view of the Lower Falls. Turn left here and ascend the stairs and walk under the highway bridge.

0.2   Upper Falls. Continue past a memorial plaque and bear right staying near the edge of the river.

0.6   Trail intersection at the southeast end of a footbridge and the beginning of the circuit portion of this hike. Cross the bridge and turn left onto the Superior Hiking Trail (SHT) and ascend the east side of the river.

1.2   Trail intersection at the east end of the second footbridge. Cross it and turn left staying on the SHT.

1.3   Trail intersection; continue straight ahead passing the trail on the left. In about 400 feet, come to another intersection. Turn right staying on the SHT, passing a trail to the left.

1.5   Trail intersection; continue straight ahead, passing a trail to the left.

1.7   Trail intersection; stay on the SHT as it turns right and descends to the river bank.

2.3   Trail shelter (47° 9' 16.4" N 91° 29' 24.1" W). The hike continues past the shelter and soon begins a steep ascent as it veers away from the river.

2.5   Trail intersection; continue the steep ascent, passing the SHT which turns to the right for Nestor Grade and Castle Danger Parking in 2.7 and 6.7 miles respectively.

2.7   Trail intersection at the top of the steep ascent; turn right, passing the trail to the left. There are good views to the northwest of the Gooseberry River drainage and Lake Superior to the southeast.

3.0   The trail turns sharply to the left and descends the ridge through a stand of immature aspen. Beyond that, the forest, mainly white birch, with occasional cedar and balsam fir, is open with tall grass undergrowth.

4.4   Trail intersection; turn right passing the trail to the left.

4.5   Trail intersection; bear left passing the trail to the right. In 350 feet, at the next intersection, continue straight ahead, passing a trail that descends steeply on the left.

4.6   Trail intersection; bear left and descend steeply to the river bank. Follow the trail along the bank.

4.7   Trail intersection at the southeast end of the first footbridge completing the circuit portion of the hike. Retrace your steps down river, passing the memorial, Upper Falls, and under the bridge to return to the Visitors Center.

5.2   Trailhead.

Split Rock River

SPLIT ROCK LIGHTHOUSE STATE PARK

LENGTH	4.6 miles
TIME	3:15
DIFFICULTY	Moderate-Difficult
ROUTE-FINDING	Easy-Moderate
MAPS & PERMITS	DNR Split Rock Lighthouse State Park map. USGS quad: Split Rock Point. A permit is not required.
GETTING THERE	The trailhead is located at the wayside on the north side of Minnesota State Road 61 0.3 mile beyond the 43 mile marker just prior to crossing the Split Rock River.
TRAILHEAD GPS	47° 10' 56.1"N 91° 24' 31.0"W

The Split Rock River Trail is one of the most popular hikes on the North Shore. It offers spectacular views of the lake as well as the excitement of a river leaping and tumbling over rock ledges and slides. Pines and cedars soften the rugged walls of the narrow river gorge.

By North Shore standards, the Split Rock River drains a relatively small area of about 40 square miles. Other rivers, such as the Manitou, Cross, Temperance, Cascade, Baptism, and Pigeon, drain areas that range from 91 to 610 square miles. Two branches of the Split Rock River join about four miles upstream from Lake Superior. For the next two miles the river drops 110 feet in elevation. In the third mile, amid the roar of water contending with gravity and rock, the river plummets over 350 feet. Finally, the valley opens up and the floor levels out. Here, in its last mile, the river slackens its pace before emptying into Lake Superior.

Logging History

In *Minnesota Logging Roads*, Frank King writes that the mouth of the Split Rock River was once the terminus of a logging railroad built by the Split Rock Lumber Company, a subsidiary of the Merrill & Ring Company. Construction of a 10 mile railroad, known as the Merrill Grade, began in 1899. The railroad was used to haul about 200 million board feet of timber out of the Split Rock River area.

Once in the water, crews formed the logs into giant rafts that were taken by the tug *Gladiator* to a sawmill in Duluth. A novel practice, for Minnesota anyway, was the use by the tug's crew of carrier pigeons to send distress messages.

Logging operations by the Split Rock Lumber Company lasted seven years, ending in 1906. During this time, the company earned a profit of $863,454. By the next year the rails had been taken up. The pilings at the mouth of the river are a small reminder of those logging years.

Trail Highlights

From the wayside parking area, the Split Rock River Trail ascends the west side of the river valley. This portion of the hike is rather strenuous as the trail is steep in places. Your reward is dramatic views of the river descending in torrents of whitewater between cliffs topped with cedars, pines, and white birch.

Shortly after starting out, the trail crosses an unnamed stream. A small waterfall lies just above the bridge in the shade of large cedar trees. This is a cool place even on the hottest summer days. Once past the stream the trail begins to climb in earnest with occasional very steep ascents; but there are several places to rest and enjoy the river.

Near the top of the falls, the trail passes an area known as The Pillars. These chimney-like formations are made of rhyolite, an red igneous rock. As rhyolite cools, it develops vertical cracks that make it susceptible to weathering into sheer cliffs. This weathering pattern accounts for the dramatic cliffs at Palisade Head and Shovel Point further up the North Shore. In the area of the Pillars, shingle-like pieces of rhyolite litter the trail.

At its highest point, the trail crosses the river on a bridge and descends the east side of the river valley. Hikers often linger around the bridge to soak their feet in the cool water and eat lunch. The Superior Hiking Trail Association maintains two backpacking campsites at this spot. They have also placed a guest book at the bridge for campers and hikers to record their thoughts. Some of the entries are amusing, and, who knows, you may feel the urge to add your own reflections.

The descending portion of the Split Rock River Trail is gradual and a relief from the arduous trek up the other side. Initially, the trail stays on the rim of the river gorge, providing views of the river far below. Eventually though, it turns away from the river and passes through a forest of white birch and aspen before reaching a panoramic overlook. Here you get views of the river mouth and the broad valley where the Split Rock River seems to be resting from its quick dash through the falls.

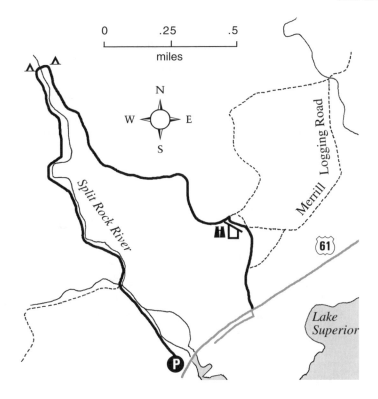

The vast expanse of Lake Superior lies on the horizon. From the over-look it is a short mile to Highway 61 and the parking area.

Stride-by-Stride

MILES	DESCRIPTION
0.0	The trail begins at northwest corner of the parking lot and is one of the access points to the Superior Hiking Trail (SHT).
0.5	Trail intersection with the SHT. The trail to the left goes to Gooseberry State Park in 4.3 miles. To continue this hike, turn right and descend to a bridge just below a waterfall on the left.
0.8	Landslide area; continue on the trail up and around rather than cutting across it.
1.3	Cross a split-log bridge over a small wet-weather stream and climb a steep set of stone steps.
1.7	The trail makes a sharp turn at the river's edge and ascends a steep rocky trail. Exercise increased caution at this point.

2.0   Pass the rock formations known as the Pillars.

2.1   Spur trail on the left leads to a campsite.

2.3   Split Rock River crossing. The trail continuing straight ahead, just before crossing the bridge, leads to a campsite. On the other side of the bridge is a trail to another campsite. The Split Rock River Trail continues to the right after crossing the bridge and begins a gradual descent down the east side of the river.

3.0   The trail turns away from the river gorge.

3.7   The trail emerges from the forest and passes along the edge of a ridge providing panoramic views of the river valley below and of Lake Superior. Reach a trail shelter in a short distance, a good place to rest and enjoy the view (47° 11' 29.1" N 91° 24' 23.2" W).

3.9   Trail intersection; turn right and descend a wide grassy trail leading to "Highway 61 parking." The SHT continues straight ahead at this point reaching Beaver Bay in 10.8 miles.

4.3   Highway 61; cross the highway and walk, facing traffic, back to the trailhead.

4.6   Trailhead.

Corundum Mine Trail 30

SPLIT ROCK LIGHTHOUSE STATE PARK

3.1 M
MODERATE

LENGTH	3.1 miles
TIME	1:45
DIFFICULTY	Moderate
ROUTE-FINDING	Easy
MAPS & PERMITS	DNR Split Rock Lighthouse State Park map. USGS quad: Split Rock Point. A Minnesota State Park permit is required.
GETTING THERE	The trailhead is located at the parking lot on the east side of Split Rock River on the lake side of U.S. Highway 61. The access road to this parking area is at milepost 43.7 miles. Turn right off U.S. Highway 61 and then right again. Drive 0.2 miles to the parking area.
TRAILHEAD GPS	47° 10' 58.7" N 91° 24' 26.8" W

The highlight of this short hike on the shore of Lake Superior is the Corundum Mine Site, or, more correctly, the Oops-We-Thought-It-Was-Corundum Mine Site. The old mine site is on a point high above the lake. According to a state park brochure, Duluth prospector Ed Lewis claimed discovery of corundum at this location in 1901. Corundum is a mineral with a hardness next to diamonds that was used by grinding wheel manufacturers and the makers of sandpaper. In 1904, the North Shore Abrasives Company began mining this site. However, the mineral was not corundum but a softer mineral called anorthosite which is useless as an abrasive. The mine operated only until 1908.

Anorthosite Outcroppings

North Shore Abrasives wasn't the only company to mistake anorthosite for corundum. The Minnesota Abrasives Company (MAC), now known as 3M, had "corundum" mine sites further up the North Shore in what are now Tettegouche and Temperance River state parks. In *Two Harbors 100 Years,* the story is that they made only one sale of their product. In March 1904, MAC sold one ton of "corundum" to Champion Corundum Wheel Company for $20. When MAC learned that what they really had was anorthosite, they kept it a secret from their investors long enough to turn to making sandpaper in Duluth in 1913. The rest is history as they say for this small company was able to recover from its false start.

125

The anorthosite outcropping at Corundum Point is a miniature version of the massive outcropping known as Carlton Peak in Temperance River State Park. While not the hard corundum many thought it to be, this rock is resistant to erosion. All glaciers have been able to do after repeated passes is shape the outcroppings with smooth curves. Take care on the summit of Corundum Point as the smooth rock slopes steeply towards cliffs on Lake Superior.

North Shore Abrasives Company built a crushing house high above the lake shore on Corundum Point. Large concrete footings are still present along the Corundum Mine Site Trail. In *Historical Sites and Place Names of Minnesota's North Shore*, John Fritzen writes that forest fires destroyed the building in May 1910.

From the summit of Corundum Point you can see the lighthouse in the distance across Little Two Harbors. From this distance it looks quite small sitting on top of the distant cliff. If you hike this trail in the fall you may also see a family of Peregrine Falcons. They have recently started nesting on waterside cliffs on the North Shore. By late summer the young are flying, but still rely on their parents for most of their food. The youngsters make quite of fuss, encouraging the parents to get them something to eat.

Another point of interest on this hike is at the mouth of the Split Rock River where the route begins. Here you will see the jagged remains of pilings, remnants of a wharf and dam that was once part of a logging operation conducted by the Split Rock Lumber Company from 1899 to 1906. In addition to the wharf and dam, there was also a store, post office, warehouse, and living quarters for the men at the mouth of the river.

Trail Highlights

From the trailhead at the mouth of the river, the path heads towards the lake. Soon you come to Split Rock Point, a sharp, narrow strip of rocks making a jab into the lake. From here you will be able to see Corundum Point, looking like the bow of a gigantic ore boat. The image comes to life on windy days when waves crash against the base of the sea cliffs—the bow seems to be plunging through the cold waters.

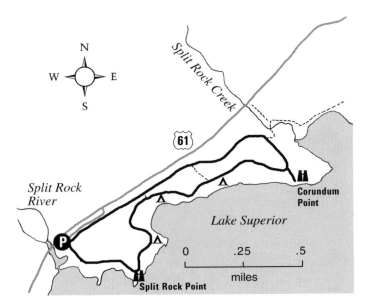

Stride-by-Stride

MILES	DESCRIPTION
0.0	Walk past the metal gate and along the mouth of the Split Rock River towards the lake.
0.4	A trail behind the bench leads out to a point of rocks in 150 feet. To the northeast is an excellent view of Corundum Point.
0.5	Pass Backpack Campsite #4 on the right.
0.9	Trail intersection; continue straight ahead passing a cutoff trail on the left and Backpack Campsite #3 on the right.
1.2	Trail intersection; continue straight ahead, passing the trail to the left.
1.4	Pass Backpack Campsite #2 on the right.
1.5	Trail intersection; turn right on the Corundum Mine Site Trail leaving, for the moment, the circuit trail. In 400 feet, the trail ends at the base of a large rock outcropping high above the lake. Turn to the left and follow a narrow path leading around the back of the large rock and to the summit. Along the way you will pass a trail ascending from the left. (You will take this trail when leaving the summit.) Near the summit the trail forks; take the left fork out to the rock edge. Be careful of the steep slope (47° 11' 16.1" N 91° 23' 10.3" W).

When leaving the summit take the right fork back to the Corundum Mine Site Trail; turn right and reach the circuit trail in 210 feet.

1.9   Back from the summit continue on the circuit trail to the right.

2.0   Trail intersection; continue straight ahead passing the trail to the right.

2.4   Trail intersection; bear right passing the trail to the left. In 90 feet reach old U.S. Highway 61 and turn left to return to the trailhead.

3.1   Trailhead.

Split Rock Creek

SPLIT ROCK LIGHTHOUSE STATE PARK

6.2 M
MODERATE-DIFFICULT

LENGTH	6.2 miles
TIME	3:45
DIFFICULTY	Moderate-Difficult
ROUTE-FINDING	Easy
MAPS & PERMITS	DNR Split Rock Lighthouse State Park map. USGS quads: Split Rock Point NE and Split Rock Point. A Minnesota State Park permit is required.
GETTING THERE	The trailhead is the Trail Center at Split Rock Lighthouse State Park located 20 miles north of Two Harbors on U.S. Highway 61.
TRAILHEAD GPS	47° 11' 56.7" N 91° 22' 33.1" W

Stories of commercial fishermen, loggers, miners, and unrequited love bring to life the history of Little Two Harbors, the forested hills above Lake Superior, Corundum Point, and Day Hill. The pebble beach just south of the trail center is the former site of Little Two Harbors, a commercial fishing village from the turn of the century until the 1940s. Further on is Day Hill, an excellent vantage point from which to watch the lake. In the hills overlooking Lake Superior, the trail follows a section of the railroad grade lumbermen used to haul logs out of the woods. Finally, there's Corundum Point, site of a failed mining venture. While this is not a strenuous hike, there is some elevation gain, and it is moderately long at just over 6 miles.

Near the trail center is the site of the small fishing village, Little Two Harbors. The commercial fishermen, mainly Norwegians, who lived here were the first white people to live in the Split Rock area. During fall and winter, the men went out onto the vast and unpredictable Lake Superior in 16–18 foot skiffs. Using 200–400 foot nets, they went in quest of trout, whitefish, and herring. It must have been a harsh way to make a living, working on a lake that even in summer can be deadly with its sudden storms and bone-chilling temperatures. The cement foundations along the trail and elsewhere mark the locations of their homes and fish cleaning and storage buildings.

Further to the south is Day Hill with its excellent views of the lighthouse in one direction, and Corundum and Split Rock points in the other. The lighthouse stands poised at the edge of a bold, 124-foot-high diabase cliff capped with anorthosite, the same rock that forms Day Hill and nearby Corundum Point. Diabase is a lava formation that is, along with anorthosite, very resistant to erosion. This resistance to erosion accounts for the prominence of the cliff, and the lighthouse, along the North Shore.

Probably the first thing that catches your eye as you reach the top of Day Hill is a fireplace. After gazing at the vistas, you might turn your attention back to the fireplace and wonder how it came to be. While there is no conclusive story about its origin, one possibility is a love story.

Frank Day was once a partner in a real estate firm that owned Day Hill and some of the surrounding land. He loved a woman with whom he was engaged to be married. In anticipation of the blessed event and the happy life to follow, Frank began constructing their dream house. But, it was not to be. She called off the marriage, leaving Frank with a heavy heart that must have made his climbs of Day Hill afterwards all the more difficult.

Beyond Day Hill, the route crosses U.S. Highway 61 and ascends into the hills above Lake Superior along Split Rock Creek. A bench has been perfectly positioned part way up the trail. It provides an opportunity to rest and enjoy the sights and sounds of a waterfall on the creek.

At the intersection with the Superior Hiking Trail you come to the Merrill Grade. The Merrill and Ring Company conducted logging operations in the Split Rock River area from 1899-1906. The forest at that time was mainly Norway spruce and white pine. Today white birch is the dominant species. The Merrill Grade is the route of the railroad line on which locomotives brought logs to the mouth of the Split Rock River. While the hike continues to the left at this intersection, if you hike a short distance on the trail to the right, you will see the remains of old railroad ties, now covered in moss.

Turning west and then south, the Superior Hiking Trail crosses Split Rock Creek and ascends a series of ridges with views of the lake. After 1.2 miles, the trail reaches the intersection where the route turns left and descends to cross U.S. Highway 61 again. However, consider following the Superior Hiking Trail for just another tenth of a mile to a panoramic overlook of the lower valley and mouth of the Split Rock River, and of the lake.

Once back on the lake-side of U.S. Highway 61, the trail heads northeast to return to the trailhead. Along the way it passes Corundum Point, the site of a failed mining venture. There is a description of the Corundum Mine Trail in the circuit hike starting on page 125.

Stride-by-Stride

MILES	DESCRIPTION
0.0	From the Trail Center, walk towards the lake and turn right on the Little Two Harbors Trail which follows the shore of the small pebble-beach cove.
0.4	Where the trail turns sharply to the right and away from the lake, look for an old building foundation on your right. In 150 feet, bear left passing a trail on the right to Campsite #1.
0.6	Trail intersection beginning the circuit portion of this hike; turn right on the Day Hill Trail.
0.9	Intersection with the spur trail to the top of Day Hill (in 0.2 mile) on the left. It is a steep but short climb with great views of Lake Superior (47° 11' 35.9" N 91° 23' 1.7" W).
1.3	Back on the main circuit trail from the summit.
1.4	Trail intersection; bear right leaving the Day Hill Trail as it continues to the left.
1.6	Trail intersection; bear right, cross U.S. Highway 61, and pick up the trail on the other side of the road. The trail ascends along the east side of Split Rock Creek.
1.8	A small bench provides a pleasant resting spot from which to view a waterfall on the creek.
2.3	Trail intersection with the Superior Hiking Trail (SHT); bear left. This section of the hike follows a portion of the old Merrill Logging Road.
2.4	Bridge over Split Rock Creek; bear right on the SHT immediately after crossing the bridge, leaving the Merrill Logging Road Trail as it continues to the left. The trail now becomes a narrow footpath.
3.1	Trail emerges from the forest at an overlook with views of the North Shore.
3.5	Trail intersection; the trail to the right leads to a shelter in 500 feet and an excellent overlook of Split Rock River valley and Lake Superior. The main loop continues to the left at this

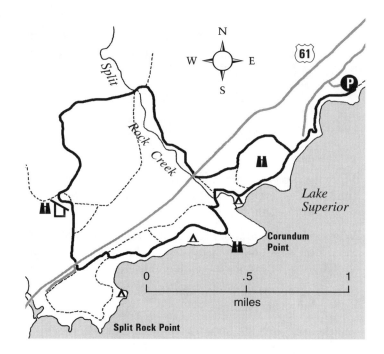

point. Pass two trails on your left before reaching U.S. Highway 61.

3.8 U.S. Highway 61; cross the road and bear right towards an access road. Turn left on the old blacktop paralleling U.S. Highway 61.

4.1 Trail intersection; turn right leaving the old road. At the next intersection, in 100 feet, turn left.

4.5 Bear right passing a trail to the left.

4.7 Spur trail on the right leads to a backpack campsite.

4.8 Trail intersection; bear left passing the Corundum Mine Trail to the right. This spur reaches an old mine site in 0.1 mile.

4.9 Trail intersection; bear right passing the trail to the left.

5.0 Bridge crossing Split Rock Creek. Immediately after crossing the bridge bear right passing the trail to the left.

5.2 Spur trail to the right leads to another backpack campsite.

5.3 Intersection with the Day Hill Trail; bear right.

5.6 Trail intersection completing the circuit portion of this hike; bear right to return to the trailhead.

6.2 Trail Center.

Bean & Bear Lakes

TETTEGOUCHE STATE PARK

6.4 M
DIFFICULT-STRENUOUS

LENGTH	6.4 miles
TIME	4:00
DIFFICULTY	Difficult-Strenuous
ROUTE-FINDING	Moderate
MAPS & PERMITS	DNR Tettegouche State Park map. McKenzie Map 104 (Beaver Bay/Tettegouche). USGS quad: Silver Bay. No permit is required.
GETTING THERE	Turn left off U.S. Highway 61 onto Outer Road in Silver Bay. Continue on Outer Road; it eventually becomes Penn Boulevard which you want to stay on. Parking lot for Superior Hiking Trail is on the right just past where the trail crosses Penn Boulevard.
TRAILHEAD GPS	47° 17' 31.6" N 91° 17' 56.8" W

While there are many dramatic views from overlooks in Northeastern Minnesota, the views on this hike have to be among the best. Standing on top of an exposed ridge, a sheer cliff plummets 300 feet to the shores of Bean and Bear lakes. These "Twin Lakes" are confined to a narrow, steep-walled valley among the Sawtooth Mountains. Adding to the drama each fall, the abundant maples, oaks, aspens, and birches growing along the ridges, paint the landscape with their vibrant yellows, reds, and oranges. In an unrestrained eruption of color, the deciduous trees end the growing season in a flourish before winter catches the land in the tight grip of its icy fist.

Bean and Bear lakes lie end-to-end in a narrow valley that runs northeast-southwest. The steep walls form an almost complete barrier on all sides. Bear Lake fits snugly into the northeastern tip of the valley. A small stream flows to nearby Bean Lake which is about 40 feet lower and at the southwestern end of the valley. A small opening permits a stream from Bean Lake to sneak out of the valley and into a nearby wetland.

Facing northwest, the ridge overlooking the lakes stands about 1,480 feet above sea level at its highest point. This puts it about 250 feet above Bear Lake and almost 300 feet above Bean Lake. According to John Green, geologist and author of *Geology on Display,* the precipice consists of a diabase dike. Diabase is an ingenious rock resistant to erosion. In geological terms, dikes form when molten material is injected into a vertical crack in preexisting rock. While the surrounding basalt, a softer form of igneous rock, has eroded over time, the diabase wall endures making it an excellent vantage point for spectacular views.

The route to Bean and Bear lakes is on the Superior Hiking Trail which continues beyond Bear Lake to Round Mountain and Mount Trudy. From the trailhead on Penn Boulevard, the Superior Hiking Trail climbs moderately at first and then more steeply through an immature mixed-forest of aspens, birches, spruces, and firs. Farther on, maples and oaks dominate the forest with the maples growing in wetter soils and the oaks on drier ground.

The 2.7 mile circuit in the middle of this hike is made possible by two spurs of the Twin Lakes Trail. Near the far end of Bear Lake, the first spur heads south descending from the ridge into a small valley where the trail is softer, a pleasant change from the hard and rocky Superior Hiking Trail. Six-tenths of a mile from the Superior Hiking Trail, the route turns right on the second spur of the Twin Lakes Trail and intersects the Superior Hiking Trail in 0.4 miles. From here it's 1.8 miles back to the trailhead.

Stride-by-Stride

MILES	DESCRIPTION
0.0	From the trailhead a short trail leads to the Superior Hiking Trail (SHT). In about 300 feet turn left on the SHT heading for Bean Lake and Mount Trudy.
0.1	Trail intersection; continue straight ahead.
0.4	Road intersection; continue straight ahead.
0.7	Reach a log walk. Be careful, the logs are slippery when wet.
0.8	Cross another road.
1.1	Spur trail to the right leads to an overlook with views of Silver Bay and Northshore Mining Company.
1.6	Spur trail to the left leads to another overlook with views to the south.
1.8	Trail intersection beginning the circuit portion of this hike. Start by bearing left, staying on the SHT. You will be completing the circuit by returning to this point via the West Spur of the Twin Lakes Trail on the right.

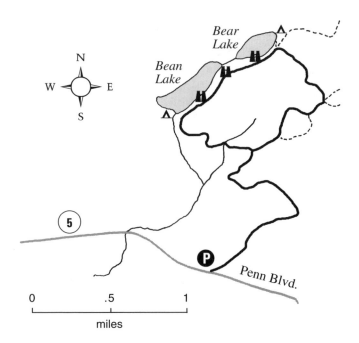

2.2 Spur trail on the left leads to Penn Creek Campsite in 500 feet.

2.4 Spur trail to Bean Lake Campsite. Bear right on the SHT.

2.7 View of Bean Lake from the ridge high above the lake.

2.8 Impressive view of Bean Lake from an exposed rocky ledge. An excellent lunch spot (47° 18' 28.1" N 91° 17' 53.8" W).

3.2 Another impressive overlook with views of Bear Lake.

3.5 Trail intersection; a spur trail on the left leads to the Bear Lake Campsite while the SHT continues straight ahead. To the right is the Twin Lakes Trail. Turn right at this point and bear left when the trail forks in about 100 feet.

4.1 Trail intersection; turn right on the West Spur of the Twin Lakes Trail, passing trails to the left and straight ahead.

4.2 Trail intersection; continue straight ahead passing a trail to the left.

4.5 Intersection with the SHT completing the circuit portion of this hike; turn left to return to the trailhead.

5.6 Cross the road.

6.0 Cross the road.

6.3   Cross trail going left and right. In about 200 feet, the SHT emerges from the forest along Penn Boulevard. Turn right to return to the parking lot.

6.4   Trailhead.

Mic Mac &
Nipisiquit Lakes

6.8 M
DIFFICULT-STRENUOUS

TETTEGOUCHE STATE PARK

LENGTH	6.8 miles
TIME	4:15
DIFFICULTY	Difficult-Strenuous
ROUTE-FINDING	Easy-Moderate
MAPS & PERMITS	DNR Tettegouch State Park map. USGS quads: Illgen City and Silver Bay. A Minnesota State Park permit is required.
GETTING THERE	The trailhead is located at the trail center parking lot and picnic area near the campground.

The interior portion of Tettegouche State Park is a landscape of rugged ridges surrounding four lakes. You can find evidence of this in the waterfalls on the Baptism River, one of which is the highest in Minnesota, and the anorthosite overlooks that provide excellent views of the surrounding country. Along the North Shore, Tettegouche is unique for the lakes within its boundaries, six in all. The largest, Mic Mac Lake, was site of an Alger-Smith Company logging camp.

Before Alger-Smith began logging this area in 1895, Tettegouche contained several types of forest communities: red and white pines, northern hardwoods, aspen-birch, spruce-fir, and cedars in wetland areas. Today, aspen-birch communities are predominate, with maple-yellow birch and cedar communities next in importance. A stop to see the Conservancy Pines along the route of this hike will help you to imagine what once was more common among these hills and lakes. This stand of red pines is just a remnant of the great pines that once grew in this area. The red pine, also known as the Norway pine, although this species is native only to North America, is Minnesota's state tree.

Trail Highlights

From the trailhead just west of the campground, the route heads north and intersects the Superior Hiking Trail. Going west the route passes along ridges through aspen, white and yellow birches, and balsam fir. Cedars grow in scattered areas where the ground is more moist. One such area is at the bottom of the Drainpipe, where the trail ascends a 150 foot crevice in a rock wall.

Next along the route is Raven Rock, an outcropping of anorthosite. This is the same rock that makes up Carlton Peak in Temperance River State Park, and Day Hill in Split Rock Lighthouse State Park. Anorthosite is resistant to erosion making it an excellent rock for overlooks. Raven Rock provides a panoramic view of the North Shore peaks to the southwest, and Lake Superior.

After passing the Conservancy Pines, the trail descends near the south end of Mic Mac Lake to a trail intersection where the route turns north for Tettegouche Camp, the site of the Alger-Smith logging camp. You may want to take some time to wander around the camp and perhaps rest on the lake shore, but be aware that the cabins may be occupied.

From the camp, the route continues north along the west side of Mic Mac Lake. An interesting feature to look for on this portion of the hike is the rock cliffs where the trail crosses Mosquito Creek. Beyond Mosquito Creek, the trail passes Nipisiquit Lake. A spur trail to a campsite provides an access route to the lake. At the north end of Nipisiquit, the route turns east and ascends Papasay Ridge where there is an overlook to the northeast of an open bog with a stream meandering through it, and of the Sawtooth Mountains in the distance.

Near the east end of Nipisiquit Lake, the route turns southward for the trailhead. Aspen and birch grow in dense stands along the trail—ideal habitat for ruffed grouse. The female brings her brood of young chicks to such stands for the protection they provide against predators. Here the birds search the ground for insects and earthworms in relative security. If a potential predator threatens the brood, the hen may try to bluff the enemy with a show of force accompanied by loud cries of alarm that send the young scurrying for cover. Then the hen usually acts injured, luring the would-be predator away from the chicks. Such a display seems out of character for a bird that has been called the "Fool Hen." It earned this name during early settlement years when the bird did not yet know that it should fear people.

Stride-by-Stride

MILES   DESCRIPTION

0.0   Begin on the High Falls Trail at the north end of the parking lot. In 300 feet, pass a trail to the left.

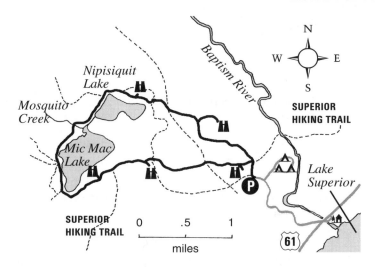

0.3   Trail intersection with the Superior Hiking Trail (SHT) beginning the circuit portion of this hike; turn left.

0.5   Spur trail on the left leads to an overlook in 0.1 mile with limited views of the North Shore.

0.7   Trail intersection with the Tettegouche Trail; continue straight ahead.

0.9   "The Drainpipe." Here, a very rocky SHT ascends steeply. At the top of the Drainpipe, bear left on the SHT passing a trail to the right.

1.7   Trail intersection; continue straight ahead on the SHT passing trails to the left and right.

1.9   Spur trail on the left leads to panoramic views from Raven Rock in 0.2 mile.

2.3   Trail intersection; continue straight ahead leaving the SHT which turns left.

2.5   Spur trail to the right leads to the Conservancy Pines in 300 feet.

3.0   Trail intersection; turn right on the trail to Tettegouche Camp, passing the trail to Palisade Valley on the left.

3.3   Pass a trail on the left and in about 100 feet come to the camp's service road. Follow the road to the right through camp, and turn left just beyond Cabin C.

3.8   A bridge crossing Mosquito Creek.

4.2   A spur trail on the right leads to Nipisiquit Lake; continue straight ahead.

4.4   Trail intersection; continue straight ahead passing the trail to the left.

4.7   Trail intersection; continue straight ahead passing the Papasay Bypass to the left.

4.9   Spur trail on the left to Papasay Ridge in 80 feet with a view of the Sawtooth Mountains (47° 21' 26.8" N 91° 14' 32.9" W).

5.0   Five-way trail intersection; take the second trail to the left, a snowmobile, hiking, and skiing trail.

5.2   Cross a wooden bridge. In another 350 feet, cross a snowmobile trail and continue straight ahead on the hiking and skiing trail.

5.6   The spur trail on the left leads to the Lake Superior Overlook.

6.5   Trail intersection with the SHT completing the circuit portion of this hike; continue straight ahead.

6.8   Trailhead.

Mic Mac Lake— Mount Baldy

5.4 M
DIFFICULT

TETTEGOUCHE STATE PARK

LENGTH	5.4 miles
TIME	3:15
DIFFICULTY	Difficult
ROUTE-FINDING	Easy-Moderate
MAPS & PERMITS	DNR Tettegouche State Park map. USGS quad: Silver Bay. A Minnesota State Park permit is required.
GETTING THERE	The trailhead is located on County Road 4, 9.1 miles from U.S. Highway 61 in Beaver Bay.
TRAILHEAD GPS	47° 21' 36.0" N 91° 16' 55.5" W

The hub of Tettegouche State Park is the site of a former logging camp on Mic Mac Lake. Five trails lead to this popular destination. The Minnesota Department of Natural Resources has renovated the camp cabins and made them available for rent. They make a pleasant weekend get away any season of the year. Each cabin comes with a canoe to use for fishing or just paddling around on the lake. You might try going out to the middle of the lake on a clear night, lying back and drifting with the wind while the stars make their journey around the North Pole.

Tettegouche History

Information provided by the Department of Natural Resources indicates that loggers named Mic Mac Lake after an Algonquin Indian tribe in their homeland of New Brunswick, Canada. These men worked for the Alger-Smith Logging Company which began cutting timber in the area in 1898.

In 1910, after harvesting most of the red and white pine, Alger-Smith sold the camp and surrounding land to the "Tettegouche Club." This club, a group of Duluth sportsmen, managed the land as if it were already a park—they forbid hunting. When the club folded in 1921, one of its members, Clement K. Quinn, bought the land and continued to treat it as a park. In 1971, Mr. Quinn sold the property to banker John deLaittre who continued the tradition of preservation.

141

The initial attempt to formally create a park for the people of Minnesota failed when the residents of Lake County objected to the potential loss of local tax revenues. For too long they had witnessed the gradual erosion of the county's tax base as more and more land found its way into state or federal ownership. Resistance was finally overcome in 1979 when the state agreed to sell the county state lands equal in value to the lands they purchased to create the park.

Besides the sometimes rugged country around the interior lakes, the park also offers visitors the largest waterfall in Minnesota. It is one of the two waterfalls on the Baptism River. In addition, there is the fascinating geology of Shovel Point. You can learn more about these attractions while you explore the park after your hike or on future visits.

While there are a considerable number of red and white pines from presettlement years left in the park, most of the forest vegetation has been replaced with aspen and birch, with some sugar maple and red oak on the ridges, and cedar and black ash in wetland areas. Other trees found in the park include basswood, yellow birch, and white spruce.

Of the fifty hikes described in this book, this route must have the highest ratio of overlooks to mileage. There are four overlooks, and two short, optional side-trips to view a small waterfall on a tributary stream of Palisade Creek and Floating Bog Bay on Tettegouche Lake. When you take this hike, consider stopping for lunch at Tettegouche Camp where you can wonder among the cabins and other outbuildings. Plan on a long day so you have time to linger at the overlooks, particularly Mount Baldy, where you will enjoy the views of blue lakes and rolling green hills and valleys. Like well-known Carlton Peak in Temperance River State Park, Mount Baldy is made of resistant anorthosite.

Fall is a great time to hike in Tettegouche when the deciduous trees put on their annual show. If you go in midsummer, you may be able to snack on blueberries that seem to do rather well on the exposed, rocky soil at some of the overlooks.

The steepest part of the hike is at the very beginning as you walk up the dirt road leading to Tettegouche Camp. About half way to the camp, a hiking trail to the south begins the circuit that will take you by overlooks, across streams, past lakes, to the summit of a peak, and through several different forest communities. The bottom part of the circuit makes its way along ridges around Tettegouche Lake, while the top portion leads to Mount Baldy before circling back to the service road.

Frogs and Toads

On the day I hiked this route, the trails seemed almost alive with hopping toads and frogs. Their breeding season over, they had turned their backs on the ponds and lakes and were making tracks of their own. I had to watch carefully where I stepped. Their numbers made it difficult to understand how some populations could be engaged in a struggle for survival. Their moist, permeable skin, and reliance on bodies of water for reproduction and development, make them susceptible to the harmful effects of environmental changes brought on by humans.

One toad and at least seven frogs make their home in northeastern Minnesota. They fill the air with their raspy mating choruses long before the songbirds of summer arrive with their more pleasing notes. However, in some parts of the world, the calls of these creatures, and the creatures themselves, have disappeared. Species are declining or have gone extinct from Brazil, Puerto Rico, the Andes Mountains, Norway, Australia, and North America, especially California and the Pacific Northwest.

In his article for *Audubon*, Jon Luoma writes about some of these cases and some of the possible causes. For example: the Golden Toad, discovered in 1964 in a Costa Rican rain forest. In 1987, biologists, counting 1,500 breeding toads, considered the frog abundant. However, they have not been able to find any since 1990 and the toad is presumed extinct without any known cause. In Australia, the same is true for the Gastric Brooding Frog. Newly discovered in 1973, and described as abundant in 1976, none have been found since 1980.

These are just a couple of the cases that demonstrate what has been happening around the world. While the cases of disappearing frogs may be natural (frog populations are naturally erratic), because so little is known about their ecology, scientists can only speculate about the causes. Unfortunately, most of them originate with humans.

There are man-made chemicals in the environment that pass easily through the frogs' skin. Their moist skin may also make them sensitive to increases in ultraviolet radiation coming through the earth's thinning ozone layer. In the spring, melting snow packs may lead to sharp increases in the acidity of ponds where frogs lay their eggs. In industrial regions, acid rain may be leaching heavy metals into the water. In agricultural areas, pesticides and herbicides end up in ponds and small pools along streams and rivers. Other contributing causes include habitat destruction as forests and wetlands are cut, drained, or filled. Frogs are also lost as collectors look to provide food at fancy dinner tables or specimens for education and research.

While we might dismiss the loss of a few species of frogs as inconsequential, to ignore the causes allows them to persist and build. Like other indicator species, frogs are like the canary in a coal mine. They serve as a warning signal to the dangers of harmful changes in our environment. Who knows what the future holds for other animals and for our own species?

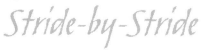

Stride-by-Stride

MILES	DESCRIPTION
0.0	Walk up the service road towards Tettegouche Camp. In 600 feet, pass the trail to Lax Lake on the right.
0.7	Trail intersection and the start of the circuit portion of this hike. Turn right onto the narrow hiking trail, leaving the road that continues ahead, and the trail to the left on which you will return to this point. The trail wanders through a predominately oak-maple forest.
0.9	A spur trail to the left leads to Tettegouche Lake Overlook in 145 feet. The main trail continues straight ahead.

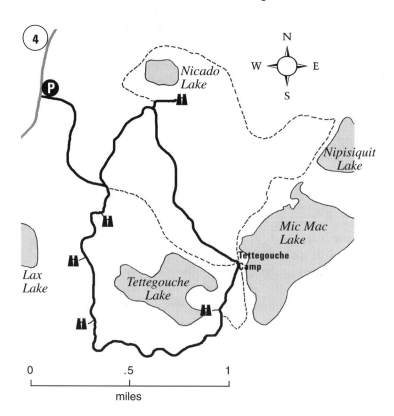

1.2   The trail to the right descends steeply to the shore of Lax Lake in 0.3 mile.

1.3   Spur trail to the right leads to Lax Lake Overlook in 200 feet.

1.6   Spur trail to the right leads to Cedar Lake Overlook in 200 feet.

2.7   Trail intersection; turn left passing the trail to Palisade Valley on the right.

2.8   Spur trail on the left leads to the shore of Floating Bog Bay in 200 feet.

3.0   The Palisade Valley Trail comes in sharply on the right as you reach the service road and Tettegouche Camp (47° 20' 47.7" N 91° 15' 40.6" W). The circuit hike continues on the Mount Baldy Trail on the other side of the road.

4.1   Trail intersection; the circuit continues on the trail to the left. The trail to the right leads to another trail intersection in 100 feet, where you bear right on a spur trail to reach the top of Mount Baldy in 0.3 mile. There are panoramic views of Mic Mac and Nicado lakes from the summit (47° 21' 33.1" N 91° 16' 1.5" W).

4.7   Trail intersection with the service road completing the circuit portion of this hike. Turn right and hike down the road to the trailhead.

5.4   Trailhead.

35

6.1 M
DIFFICULT-STRENUOUS

Matt Willis & Yellow Birch Trails

GEORGE H. CROSBY—MANITOU STATE PARK

LENGTH	6.1 miles
TIME	3:45
DIFFICULTY	Difficult-Strenuous
ROUTE-FINDING	Moderate
MAPS & PERMITS	DNR George H. Crosby—Manitou State Park map. USGS quad: Little Marais. A Minnesota State Park permit is required.
GETTING THERE	Take Minnesota State Highway 1 to Finland. Turn right on County Road 7 and drive about 7 miles to park entrance on the right. The trailhead is at the parking lot near Bensen Lake.
TRAILHEAD GPS	47° 28' 42.1" N 91° 6' 39.8" W

This hike travels through large sections of white birch and maple forest, and small forest swamps of yellow birch and white cedars. While the trail through the swamps is wet in places, it's possible to pick your way without getting too muddy. These tracts become the doorway to the lower reaches of the River Trail where large conifers shade the often turbulent Manitou River. One of the common trees you will find here is the northern white cedar, easily identified by its flattened, scale-like leaves and grayish bark that peels off in long, narrow, strips. Taxonomically the northern white cedar belongs to the cypress family of trees. Like the cypress, the cedar has an enduring, rot-resistant wood.

Northern White Cedar

The northern white cedar grows in coniferous and lowland hardwood swamps. While its presence usually indicates swampy, rich soils, it also grows along the rocky banks of streams and rivers. On this hike you will find this cedar growing in both habitats. Its range stretches from Nova Scotia, Quebec, Ontario, and southern Manitoba to New York, Ohio, Illinois, and west to Minnesota. It also grows at high elevations in the Appalachian Mountains south to North Carolina and Tennessee.

A very early name for the white cedar is *Arbor Vitae*. In *A Field Guide to Trees and Shrubs,* George A. Petrides notes the name is latinized French for "tree-of-life." It got this name after a brew of white cedar saved the lives of some men on Jacques Cartier's 1535–36 voyage from France to the St. Lawrence River. Wintering at the site of present-day Quebec, twenty-five of his men died of what was probably scurvy before someone concocted the life-saving drink. As a result, the northern white cedar became the first tree imported to Europe from the Americas.

The white cedar had many uses among Native Americans. James A. Duke, in *Medicinal Plants of the World,* writes that the Chippewa pricked cedar charcoal powder into their temples to reduce pain, used the leaves in cough compounds, and smoked the leaves in rituals of ceremonial cleansing. They also used the inner bark of young twigs to make soap and the wood to fashion ribs for birchbark canoes.

Trail Highlights

From the trailhead parking lot, the route leads south to the Matt Willis Trail which begins at the south end of Bensen Lake. Here the trail passes along the top of a large old beaver dam. Grass has overtaken the dam and it makes a lovely raised walkway now. Beyond the beaver dam, the trail continues south through white birch, box elder, balsam fir, and maples, occasionally crossing small bits of swamp where yellow birch and northern white cedars dominate.

As the trail approaches the south boundary of the park, it turns eastward and intersects the Beaver Bog Trail 2.1 miles from the trailhead. Beyond this point, the trail enters a second small swamp and intersects what must have been an old logging road. From this point on, the trail makes a gradual descent to the Manitou River for the next mile. As you approach the river giant pines become a more common sight. For some reason loggers didn't cut these trees down. Perhaps it was the steep slopes they grew on that saved them from the timberman's blade.

At the end of the Matt Willis Trail, the Manitou River Trail turns north to lead you against the current of the rapid waters of the Manitou River. Tall pines, spruces, and white cedars grow along the river bank. Where the river has carved high steep banks, the trail ascends a ridge past giant white pines whose soft foliage muffles the river's roar far below. As the Manitou River Trail nears the intersection with the Yellow Birch Trail, it returns to the river bank and crosses a small stream. The Yellow Birch Trail, aptly named for the many large yellow birches that line the path, leads west, away from the river, and returns the hiker to the trailhead from a satisfying hike over some challenging but spectacular terrain.

Stride-by-Stride

MILES	DESCRIPTION
0.0	Begin by hiking south on the road to Bensen Lake. In 675 feet, pass one end of the Bensen Lake Trail on the left leading to Campsites #20, #21, and #22. Continue along the road, walk through the picnic area, and pick up the trail near the shoreline amongst cedars and balsam firs.
0.5	Bear left passing a spur trail on the right to Campsite #19. The trail continues along an old beaver dam for about 300 feet before bearing left into the forest.
0.6	Trail intersection; leave the Bensen Lake Trail at this point, which continues to the left, by turning right onto the Matt Willis Trail. This new trail ascends through white birches, balsam firs, and maples.
0.7	Pass a spur trail on the right to Campsite #18.
0.8	Trail intersection; bear left passing the Superior Hiking Trail on the right. The trail descends through a small woodland swamp and ascends again into a birch-maple forest with little understory.
1.3	Intersection with a spur trail on the right in about 125 feet leading to an overlook with limited views. Beyond this point, the main trail enters a cedar-maple forest.
1.8	Cross a small stream. Notice the yellow birches mixed in with the maples.
1.9	The trail skirts an opening in the forest with a beaver pond for about 200 feet before bearing left back into the woods.
2.1	Trail intersection at a trail shelter; continue straight ahead on the Matt Willis Trail passing the Beaver Bog Trail on the left.
2.7	Trail intersection; turn left on an old, wide roadbed.
2.9	Cross a small stream after a short, steep descent. Beyond the stream, the trail continues to descend gradually.
3.2	Trail intersection; continue on the Matt Willis Trail by bearing right, passing the Cedar Ridge Trail on the left. The trail is rocky, crisscrossed with roots, and wet in places. Larger trees become more common.
3.5	Cross a small stream and turn right after climbing the bank on the other side. A spur trail to the left leads to Campsite #12.
3.6	Pass the River Trail going off sharply on the right. Continue ahead to the end of the sharp ridge where there are some very

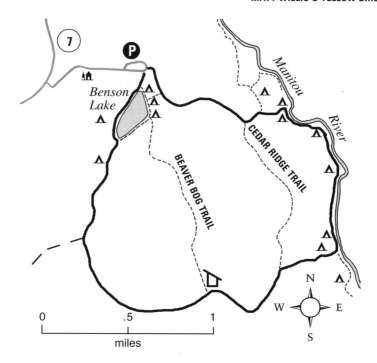

tall white pines. Turn left on the River Trail. The trail to the right at this point leads to Campsites #13–16. Pines, spruces, and cedars are dense along the river from this point on.

4.2 Pass Campsite #10 on the left.

4.6 Pass an unmarked trail on the left. In about 200 feet, bear right passing more unmarked trails on the left.

4.7 Bear right passing a trail on the left. The trail descends a set of wooden steps and rejoins the river.

4.8 Pass Campsite #8 on the left.

4.9 Trail intersection; turn left on the Yellow Birch Trail, leaving the River Trail as it continues upstream. The Yellow Birch Trail ascends steeply after crossing a small stream.

5.1 Continue ascent passing a trail on the right. In about 230 feet, continue straight on the Yellow Birch Trail, passing the Misquah Hill Trail on the right. Very large yellow birches and cedars grow along the trail.

5.5 Pass Cedar Ridge Trail on the left.

5.8 Pass Bensen Lake Trail on the left.

6.1 Trailhead.

36

4.1 M
DIFFICULT-STRENUOUS

Manitou River

GEORGE H. CROSBY-
MANITOU STATE PARK

LENGTH	4.1 miles
TIME	2:30
DIFFICULTY	Difficult-Strenuous
ROUTE-FINDING	Easy-Moderate
MAPS & PERMITS	DNR George H. Crosby—Manitou State Park map. USGS quad: Little Marais. A Minnesota State Park permit is required.
GETTING THERE	Take Minnesota State Highway 1 to Finland. Turn right on County Road 7 and drive about 7 miles to park entrance on the right. The trailhead is at the parking lot near Bensen Lake.
TRAILHEAD GPS	47° 28' 42.1" N 91° 6' 39.8" W

The George H. Crosby-Manitou State Park is the least developed in the state park system and that's the way its namesake wanted it. There are none of the conveniences normally found at other parks. There is no campground, no comfort stations with showers or even a flush toilet. Primitive campsites accessible only by backpackers help to ensure that the visitor's experience will be a true wilderness experience.

George H. Crosby, a mining magnate, donated the land for this park under the stipulation that it be managed so as to retain its wild nature. And wild it is. Hikers will find some of the most strenuous trails along the North Shore at Crosby-Manitou. There are many ascents and descents of hills and ridges, as well as the Manitou River gorge. Frequent open ridge tops provide panoramic views and an excuse to rest awhile; or you can rest in the cool spray of a Manitou River cascade, where the brown, tannin-stained water is churned to a froth. Along the way there are trees large enough to match the ruggedness of the land.

The Manitou River, the other namesake of the park, is Ojibwa for "Great Spirit." The spray spewed out by the many cascades and falls make this an appropriate name. In his book, *The Streams and Rivers of Minnesota*, Thomas Waters writes that the Manitou is unique among most of the rivers on the North Shore. The Manitou drains 103 square miles, including eleven small lakes and ten square miles of alder, tamarack, and cedar swamps. The water slowly released from the headwaters maintains a steadier flow of water then is typical of the other North Shore rivers. The last seven miles of this river flow through a deep gorge, the lower section of which lies within the park.

Yellow Birch

The last section of this hike is on the Yellow Birch Trail along which grow large, mature exemplars of this member of the birch family. The yellow to dark brown bark distinguishes it from the white birch. It can grow to be 80 feet tall, about 15–20 feet taller than the more common white birch, with a diameter of up to three feet. The yellow birch grows on the better soils of northern Minnesota where cool moist conditions exist. A variety of wildlife, including grouse, white-tailed deer, moose, rabbits, and red squirrels use the yellow birch as a food source.

Another distinguishing characteristic of the yellow birch is the odor and flavor of wintergreen in the crushed bark or broken twigs. No other birch tree has oil of wintergreen. The raw inner bark, either boiled or dried and pounded into a powder, makes a palatable energy food. Trees may be tapped like maples and its sap boiled down to a syrup. The sap, mixed with honey, can also be used to make birch beer. When you get to the Yellow Birch Trail, break off a piece of twig and chew on it for a bit of refreshing flavor at the end of a long hard hike.

Trail Highlights

This hike introduces you to the rugged nature of the park from the very beginning as the Humpback Trail ascends steeply over a series of ridges. From one ridge top, you get a good view of Blesner Creek. Along these ridges, the forest consists mainly of mature white birch and maple. As the trail approaches the river, it becomes more rocky and cedars begin to show up in the low moist areas. The Humpback Trail intersects the Manitou River Trail just above a high cascade. The roar of the water as it pours over the falls makes shouting necessary to communicate. After the falls, the River Trail climbs to the rim of the gorge and the roar of the river dims. The Superior Hiking Trail, coming in on the Middle Trail, joins the River Trail 0.1 mile past the cascade. As the trail follows the river downstream, you pass stands of large white cedars. Their dense shade and the coolness of the riverside, make this a good hike on hot summer days.

Two and a half miles into the hike, the Superior Hiking Trail descends steeply to the Manitou River, while the River Trail ascends another ridge with views of Lake Superior in the distance. On the other side of the ridge, the River Trail ends and the Misquah Hills Trail begins. A spur off this trail leads to the best overlook of the hike. The blue waters of Lake Superior lay spread out beyond the sea of green forest, from which you can hear the faint roar of the Manitou River. From the Misquah Hills Trail, the route follows the Yellow Birch Trail back to the trailhead.

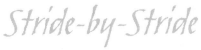

MILES	DESCRIPTION
0.0	The hike begins on the Humpback Trail at the west end of the parking lot. The trail ascends steeply to a rock outcropping.
0.2	Overlook with views of Blesner Creek and County Road 7 to the south.
0.6	Plank bridge.
1.2	Small boulder field. Walk across the boulders for about 100 feet and look for the trail as it ascends steeply on the right.
1.6	Trail intersection with the River Trail; bear right on the River Trail passing the trail to the left leading to Campsite #1.
1.7	Pass a spur trail on left to Campsite #2 by continuing straight ahead on the River Trail. In about 170 feet, there is a spur trail on left leading to the top of a cascade on the Manitou River. The main trail bears right at this point and descends to the base of the cascade.
1.8	Base of the cascade. In about 100 feet, the trail turns to the right and ascends a series of wooden steps and continues downriver along the top of the river gorge.
1.9	Trail intersection; continue straight ahead on the River Trail passing the Middle Trail on the right . At this intersection, the River Trail becomes a part of the Superior Hiking Trail.
2.0	Pass a spur trail on the left to Campsite #3.
2.2	Campsite #4. In about 400 feet the trail crosses a small bridge and turns away from the river passing through occasional stands of large cedars.
2.5	Trail intersection; from here the River Trail, and the hike, continues straight ahead while the Superior Hiking Trail bears left and descends very steeply for about 0.2 mile to the Manitou River and a bridge crossing. There is a good view of the river from the bridge.

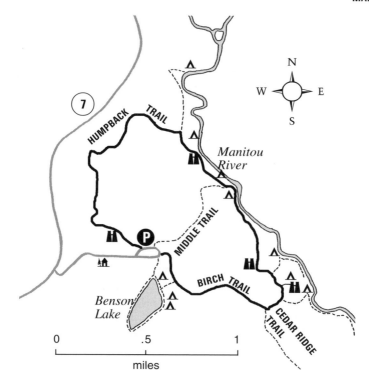

CONTINUING ON THE RIVER TRAIL

2.7 The first of a series of rocky ledges with limited views to the east. In about 400 feet, the trail begins to descend.

2.8 Trail intersection and the end of the River Trail. The trail to the left leads to Campsites #5 and #7. Bear right on the Misquah Hill Trail.

2.9 Spur trail to the left leads to an overlook in 540 feet and Campsite #6 beyond that. The views to the east and south, and of Lake Superior, from the overlook are well worth the detour. Look for large-toothed aspen at the overlook (47° 28' 34.1" N 91° 5' 46.0" W).

3.1 The end of the Misquah Hill Trail at an intersection with the Yellow Birch Trail going left and right; turn right. Very large yellow birches and cedars grow along the trail.

3.5 Pass Cedar Ridge Trail on the left.

3.8 Pass Bensen Lake Trail on the left.

4.1 Trailhead.

37 McDougal Lake Trail

0.9 M
EASY

SUPERIOR NATIONAL FOREST
TOFTE RANGER DISTRICT

LENGTH	0.9 mile
TIME	0:30
DIFFICULTY	Easy
ROUTE-FINDING	Easy
MAPS & PERMITS	A U.S. Forest Service sheet with map is available at the ranger district office in Tofte. USGS quad: Slate Lake East. No permit is required.
GETTING THERE	Drive west from Isabella for 10 miles on Minnesota State Highway 1 and turn left on U.S. Forest Road 106. The McDougal Lake Campground entrance is on the right in 0.5 mile. The trailhead is located at the parking lot, near the boat landing.
TRAILHEAD GPS	47° 38' 20.7" N 91° 32' 10.0" W

You might think that because this hike is so short it will have little to offer. This doesn't have to be the case. Being shorter, it invites you to linger and take a closer look at the plants and animals living along the trail. Life in the wild often proceeds at a much slower pace than what we are used to. Slowing down just a bit pushes open the door that has been standing just slightly ajar, giving us a broader look at the activities going on around us that we usually miss in our fast-paced lives.

The McDougal Lake Trail offers an easy walk along the shore of McDougal Lake, and through a mixed forest of white birch and balsam fir, with scattered pines and spruces. About halfway through the hike the trail passes briefly through a forest swamp. The charred remains of old growth pines along the trail are a testimony to past forest fires. Delicate wildflowers stand out boldly on the trailside or hide bashfully in the forest undergrowth. Small animals move about on the forest floor or through the canopy of trees. Walking quietly and slowly and stopping frequently to look and listen brings the world of the forest into sharper focus.

The trail starts out along the shore of McDougal Lake. Here you will find a conveniently placed bench looking out over the lake and up and down the shoreline. Viewers of wildlife know that animal activity is usually greater along the borders between two different types of habitats such as water and forest, or open field and forest. Before turning your back on the lake and going deeper into the forest, spend some time sitting quietly on the bench and see what presents itself.

An increased amount of plant and animal activity also exists in habitats that have a more natural diversity. A forest community with a wider age spread among its trees exhibits increased diversity: from young seedlings just poking their thin stems out of the leaf litter, to towering giants that have seen centuries pass, to dead snags that slowly drop decaying branches and will themselves one day fall crashing to the ground where they will rot and return nutrients to the soil. All of these add a richness to the forest. Like the way many different colored threads add to the richness of a tapestry, so to do the different ages of plants and animals add to the richness of the community. A study of the role of tree snags to breeding birds in northern Minnesota found that dead or partly dead trees over three feet tall did more to increase the variety of breeding bird populations in a forest than did the living trees and shrubs. Snags located in areas of shrubs and trees resulted in new bird species over areas of shrubs and trees that lacked snags.

Tree Snags

Snags are an important component of the forest community to many different types of breeding birds. Woodpeckers and nuthatches, which are primary excavators, carve nest sites in snags. Other birds, like swallows, chickadees, hawks, and owls use abandoned nest holes as their own. Song birds use snags as song perches from which they proclaim the surrounding territory theirs for breeding and foraging purposes.

Snags are also important to birds in procuring food. Besides the woodpeckers that drill into tree trunks looking for beetle larvae and other forms of insects, there are the bark gleaners, like chickadees and nuthatches, that probe under flaking bark and into crevices for food. Other birds may use the snags as perches from which they fly out to snatch insects out of the air and then return to the snags to resume scanning the air for more tiny morsels. Raptors, such as hawks and owls, also use snags as hunting perches. They search the ground for prey, pouncing quickly on unsuspecting quarry.

At the site of a second bench about two-thirds of the way through this hike, I watched adult yellow-shafted Northern Flickers bring food to nestlings in a cavity excavated in a dead aspen snag. The hungry cries of the youngsters drew my attention to the nest as they began screech-

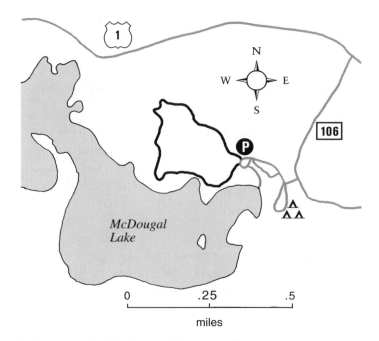

ing each time an adult arrived with a beak filled with caterpillars and other insects.

When you prepare for this hike, add a guidebook to flowers, birds, trees, or other wildlife to your pack, and spend an hour or two making your way slowly along this almost-one-mile trail. You may be astonished at what you discover.

Stride-by-Stride

MILES   **DESCRIPTION**

0.0   The beginning of the trail, marked with a sign, begins at the west end of the parking lot and sets out along the shore of the lake.

0.3   Bench with view of the lake. From here the trail turns away from the lake and passes through a forest swamp.

0.5   The trail bears to the right and onto a low ridge. In about 300 feet the trail descends from the ridge. Watch for charred stumps along the way.

0.6   Trailside bench.

0.9   Trailhead.

Flat Horn Lake Trail

SUPERIOR NATIONAL FOREST
TOFTE RANGER DISTRICT

2.0 M
EASY

LENGTH	2.0 miles
TIME	1:00
DIFFICULTY	Easy
ROUTE-FINDING	Easy
MAPS & PERMITS	The U.S. Forest Service provides a hiking sheet for this trail. Check with the district ranger's office in Tofte. USGS quad: Mitawan Lake. No permit is required.
GETTING THERE	Take Minnesota Highway 1 west from Isabella for about 6 miles and turn right on U.S. Forest Road 177. Go 0.8 mile and turn left into the Flat Horn Lake Recreation Area just after crossing the Little Isabella River. The trailhead is at the parking lot for the picnic area and swimming beach.
TRAILHEAD GPS	47° 39' 26.7" N 91° 27' 26.3" W

Flat Horn Lake is one of several lakes along the course of the Little Isabella River. The Flat Horn is a small lake, offering a short 2 mile hike over fairly level terrain. White birches, aspens, and balsam firs predominate in the surrounding forest, with scattered jack and white pines. There are many jack pines in the picnic and swimming area, and a stand of tall red and white pines at the east end of the lake. You'll see spruce in the soggy wetlands. White cedars help delineate other moist spots around the lake.

Eastern Garter Snake

Along with the many different trees around Flat Horn Lake, there are different animals to look for and watch. One that you may find on the trail is the Eastern Garter Snake. It is a wide-ranging reptile, from southern Canada to the Gulf of Mexico, and west to Minnesota and east Texas. It is the most common snake in Minnesota; you are likely to see more garter snakes than all the other snakes combined.

The garter snake takes its name from the striped garters that fashionable men once worn to hold up their socks. The Eastern Garter Snake has three stripes; a narrow stripe down the middle of the back, and one down each side. The stripes are usually yellow, but may be tinted brown, green, or blue.

The Eastern Garter Snake occupies a variety of habitats, including meadows, marshes, woodlands, stream banks, and even city lots. They feed on an equally wide variety of foods: frogs, toads, salamanders, fish, tadpoles, earthworms, leeches, small mammals, birds, and carrion. There seems to be a preference for prey found in or near water.

When picked up, garter snakes release musk from a gland near the base of the tail that has a strong odor meant to discourage predators from further aggression. They twist and turn trying to rub the musk onto the attacker. Afterwards, the odor lingers as a reminder of the encounter.

Garter snakes hibernate during the winter in large colonies in rotting tree stumps, chipmunk and woodchuck burrows, deserted ant mounds, and building foundations. They emerge from their dens in April and take advantage of their high density to mate before dispersing for the summer. Some mating may occur in the fall when the garter snakes regroup as females are able to store living sperm through the winter and use it to fertilize eggs in the spring.

Herpetologists (biologists specializing in the study of reptiles and amphibians) discovered that they can predict the color pattern of a snake if they have knowledge of how it escapes predators, how it feeds, where it breeds, and when it is active. They found that snakes that live in open areas like meadows, that are active during the day, forage widely for food, try to escape when threatened, and have little or no special means of defending themselves or threatening their attackers are likely to have a striped pattern.

The color pattern and behavior of snakes may be related because of the optical illusion of moving and fixed patterns. Stripes don't offer points on the snake's body for predators to fix their sight on, making it difficult for them to detect motion or gauge speed. Garter snakes, and other striped snakes, crawl away in a straight line when approached by predators who may not be aware the snakes are fleeing until they are gone.

Spots, on the other hand, are a disadvantage for moving snakes, but not for stationary ones. The broken pattern of spotted or blotchy snakes disrupts the outline of their bodies, making them more difficult to detect as long as they are lying still. However, when moving, their spots make them easier for predators to see and follow. To counter this disadvantage, spotted snakes are more likely to reverse direction during their escape and freeze. It's possible that the color pattern of snakes is genetically linked with their behavior.

Eastern Garter Snakes aren't a danger to hikers. They are not poisonous and do not show aggressive behavior when approached unless cornered and have little choice but to try and defend themselves. They will usually allow you to get close to them on the trail if you approach cautiously. I have walked past garter snakes without scaring them away. If you see a garter snake on the trail, look closely at its color pattern. Notice how it behaves if it crawls off the trail. See if you can follow it with your eyes.

Trail Highlights

The circuit hike around Flat Horn Lake follows the shoreline, or is only slightly away from the shore, except at the south end of the lake where it passes the old site of the Environmental Learning Center. The new Wolf Ridge Environmental Learning Center is near Finland where they offered their first class in the Fall of 1988. The Environmental Learning Center at Flat Horn Lake was a former Civilian Conservation Corps camp and was closed after the kitchen burned down. All that's left now are the concrete pads of razed buildings and parking lots.

On the west side of the lake, the circuit trail intersects several cross-country ski trails that are part of the extensive Flat Horn-Gegoka Trail System. These trails offer opportunities for exploring away from the lake, but may eventually run into wet areas unsuitable for hiking. Talk with a ranger at the Isabella Ranger Office and carry a map and compass if you go exploring on these trails.

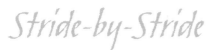

Stride-by-Stride

MILES	DESCRIPTION
0.0	This hike begins at the north end of the swimming beach near the lake shore. The trail enters a white birch forest with an open canopy and scattered conifers (jack and white pines, balsam firs, and white cedars). After 200 yards, the canopy closes and the trail begins to gradually ascend.
0.5	A stand of tall red and white pine trees at the eastern end of the lake. A faint trail on the right heads off in a southeasterly direction. Continue on the main trail along the lake shore and cross bridge over a small, rushing river flowing out of the lake.
0.9	Pass a trail, part of the Flat Horn-Gegoka cross-country ski trail system, on the right.

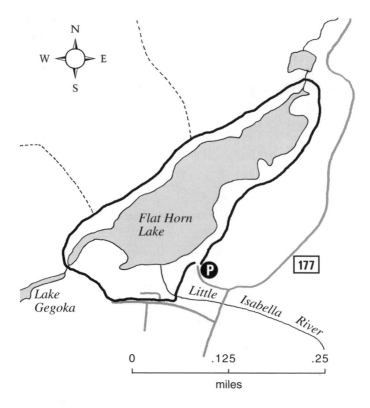

1.0 A short spur trail on left leads to the lake shore opposite the recreation area on the other side of the lake. The remains of a small wooden dock can be seen from this spot about 20–30 feet to the left.

1.2 Pass a cross-country ski trail on the right. The circuit trail emerges from a predominantly pine forest into one of mature aspen and birch as it makes its way around the west end of the lake.

1.4 Pass an unmarked trail on the right.

1.5 Cross a bridge over a small river flowing into the lake.

1.6 The trail emerges from the forest and bears left along the edge of a clearing, eventually reaching the former site of the Environmental Learning Center. Continue along the road.

1.8 Turn off the road onto a trail entering the forest on the left. A post with a hiker symbol on it marks the trail. In about 200 feet pass a trail on the right and come to a bridge over the Little Isabella River.

2.0 The trail emerges from the forest at the south end of the swimming beach.

Eighteen Lake

SUPERIOR NATIONAL FOREST
TOFTE RANGER DISTRICT

2.7 M
EASY

LENGTH	2.7 miles
TIME	1:30
DIFFICULTY	Easy
ROUTE-FINDING	Easy
MAPS & PERMITS	A U.S. Forest Service hiking sheet is available at the district ranger's office in Tofte. USGS quad: Sawbill Landing. No permit is required.
GETTING THERE	Turn right off Minnesota State Highway 1 onto U.S. Forest Road 172 at Isabella. In 0.8 mile, turn left onto U.S. Forest Road 369 and continue to Eighteen Lake Campground on the left in 1.6 miles. The trailhead is located at the parking lot near the boat ramp.
TRAILHEAD GPS	47° 38' 37.9" N 91° 20' 38.8" W

The Eighteen Lake Hiking Trail is an easy lake-side hike with several benches along the way for resting and viewing. Large pines tower over a variety of forest types, from mature mixed-conifer to dense stands of young softwoods. A diversity of wildlife takes advantage of these forest types. Woodpeckers excavate large holes in the trunks of dead tree snags and stumps looking for insects, and beaver gnaw on the softwood trees in the quest for construction materials and food. Belted Kingfishers flash along the shore making the lake echo with their distinctive rattlelike call. Openings in the canopy above the trail create sunny spots where a garter snake may lay soaking up a few rays to raise its temperature to an operating level. Pellets, with a diameter about the size of a quarter, litter the trail in scattered piles attesting to the presence of the elusive moose.

Moose Ecology

The moose is the largest member of the deer family in North America and the world. It is the tallest mammal in both North and South America and is second only to the bison in the Americas in terms of weight. Common characteristics of the deer family include their hoofed feet, antlers which they shed each year, and the fact that they are cud chewers.

Unlike deer and elk, moose have palm-shaped antlers with small prongs projecting from the edges. Deer and elk antlers consist of tines; they have a long main tine with smaller ones branching off it. Moose have large, pendulous snouts and a "bell" or "beard" hanging from their throats. In healthy bulls in their prime, the bells may reach three feet in length. While their distinctively long legs may give them a gangly look, moose are agile animals, both on land and in the water. Although moose are not aquatic animals, they are closely associated with water. They seldom venture far from it. Their long legs help them navigate shallow lakes and deep snow. In deep water they are powerful swimmers, able to cruise across a lake at speeds of up to six miles per hour with bursts of up to fifteen miles per hour.

Moose range across much of Canada and almost all of Alaska, and only dip down into the lower forty-eight in some of the northern-most states such as Maine, Michigan, and Minnesota, and down the Rocky Mountain chain to northern Utah and Colorado. They dwell in dense forests surrounding shallow lakes and swamps. They browse on woody plants, eating twigs, bark, and saplings in winter, and mostly softer aquatic vegetation and the tender tree shots and leaves of willows and aspens in summer.

Your chances of seeing a moose increase if you look for it near water early in the morning or at dusk. Otherwise, you might hear one banging through the brush if you happen to be hiking past a dense stand of young aspens. Studies have shown that over a long period of time moose can alter the structure of forests. Their browsing decreases the quantity of canopy trees in the area which allows more sunlight to reach the forest floor, fueling the growth of shrubs and herbaceous plants. Heavy browsing can also result in a shift in the relative abundance of some tree species. As moose tend to avoid spruces because of toxic chemicals in their leaves, they increase, while the abundance of balsam firs and dogwoods declines because moose prefer them.

Browsing also has an effect on the amount of nutrients in the soil. Browsed areas produce less litter in the form of fall leaves and other plant parts, reducing the amount of nutrients released into the soil through plant decay.

As you hike around Eighteen Lake, see how many different signs of moose you can find. Look for droppings and the browsed tips of young woody plants. Because of the dry nature of the moose's winter food, winter pellets look like small, compressed balls of sawdust. In the summer, moose droppings may resemble those of cows. The broken tops of willow and aspen trees that may have reached eight or ten feet is another sign of moose. Reaching up as high as possible, they will grab a branch in their mouth and pull down the top until it breaks in order to get at the upper leaves. Another sign of moose, and deer, is the rough ends to the twigs they have bitten off and eaten. Because moose lack sharp teeth they are not able to cleanly snip the twigs like chisel-toothed rodents do.

Trail Highlights

From the parking lot, the trail heads south along the lake shore through mixed conifers; red and white pines, balsam firs, and cedars, with white birch thrown in for contrast. There are large white cedars at the south end of the lake where the trail crosses a small stream. On the west side of the lake there are dense stands of young softwood trees, and many signs of moose. Occasionally the trail will ascend steeply, but shortly, onto a ridge from which there are broad views of the lake. These ridge trails help to skirt wet places along the lake shore and provide some hiking variety. Fortunately there are a number of benches along the way, and rock outcroppings, where you can sit awhile, catch your breath, and enjoy the lake and the breeze in the trees.

MILES	DESCRIPTION
0.0	The hike begins at the trail sign and heads south (to the left) along the lake shore among red and white pines, balsams, cedars, and white birches.
0.2	A bench on the lake shore under an awning of pines and cedars.
0.5	Cross a small wooden bridge at the southern end of the lake. Here the trail turns upstream where a plank bridge crosses it.
1.3	The trail descends to the lake shore and a bench.
1.4	The trail begins to make its way around a small cove. Look for giant white pines.
1.5	The trail makes a short, steep ascent of a ridge and then descends just as steeply.
1.6	The trail ascends a short steep slope to a bench.
1.9	The trail ascends steeply with a view of the lake to the south.

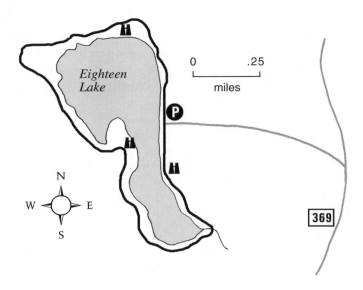

2.3 A small rock outcropping near the water's edge among red and white pines provides a good vantage point from which view the lake. Otherwise you can use the bench in about 200 feet.

2.4 The trail bears right and descends steeply to the lake shore.

2.7 Trailhead.

 *Divide Lake*

SUPERIOR NATIONAL FOREST
TOFTE RANGER DISTRICT

2.1 M
EASY

LENGTH	2.1 miles
TIME	1:15
DIFFICULTY	Easy
ROUTE FINDING	Easy
MAPS & PERMITS	A U.S. Forest Service map of this trail is available at the ranger office in Tofte. USGS quads: Isabella and Cabin Lake. No permit is required.
GETTING THERE	Turn east off Minnesota State Highway 1 in Isabella onto U.S. Forest Road 172. Drive 4.7 miles to Divide Lake Campground on the right.
TRAILHEAD GPS	47° 36' 36.5" N 91° 15' 21.9" W

The short distance and mostly gentle terrain make the hike around Divide Lake an easy one. There are several short ascents of ridges in order to skirt bogs at a few places around the lake. The bogs support large numbers of Blue Flag Irises, while fewer Pink Lady's Slippers grow along the trail. The woods along the lake's edge are thick with white birch and balsam firs which often grow in rich soils along streams, rivers, and lakes.

At the end of the hike, as you walk back to the trailhead along Forest Road 172, you will be walking along the crest of the Laurentian Divide. On the south side of the road and the divide, the waters from Divide Lake flow to Cross Cut Lake and on to Lake Superior by way of the Manitou River. On the north side of the road, the waters of Tanner Lake flow through many different streams, rivers, and lakes until they eventually reach Canada's Hudson Bay.

Blue Flag Irises

Blue Flag Irises grow in wet meadows, swamps, marshes, and along lakes and streams from Manitoba to Nova Scotia at the northern limit of its range and from Minnesota to Virginia at its southern limit. This perennial flower tends to grow in clumps that form from thick underground networks of rhizomes. The flower, which blooms in June, rises on a stalk from among narrow swordlike leaves. While the leaves and rhizomes are toxic to humans and most grazing animals, Native Americans and early colonists used very small amounts of dried rhizome as a cathartic and diuretic.

Pink Lady's Slippers

Pink Lady's Slippers, members of the orchid family, grow in a variety of habitats: moist woods and bogs, like those around Divide Lake, as well as dry woods, cliffs, and inland sandy soils. Orchids form the largest family of flowering plants in terms of the number of species. While there are many different kinds of orchids, they seldom, if ever, dominate a habitat. A leafless stalk bears the inflated, slipper-like flower of the Pink Lady's Slipper to a height of about 12 inches around late June. The genus name of the lady slippers group of flowers (*Cypripdeium*) is Latin for Venus' slipper.

At the northern limit of their range, Pink Lady's Slippers stretch across Canada from Saskatchewan to Newfoundland and Nova Scotia, and from Alabama to South Carolina in the south. Enjoy all wildflowers in their natural environment. Some, like the lady slipper, have a difficult time reproducing, even in the wild, and usually don't do well when transplanted to wildflower gardens. The requirements for healthy wildflowers can be very specific and they suffer and die when gardeners can't match these conditions.

The route around Divide Lake closely approaches the lake in places, but also moves away from it and onto ridges to get around lakeside bogs and wetlands. There are several overlooks, some with benches that provide convenient spots to stop and rest. The benches are also good places to sit and see what wildlife presents itself. Besides the benches, the campsite on Blueberry Point, which juts out into the lake, is an excellent vantage point from which to view the lake and all its goings on. The morning and evening hours are the best times to catch glimpses of wildlife. Scat along the trail indicates that moose frequent the area in winter. Because of its short length, wide trail, and gentle terrain, this trail would be a good one to use in winter for your early adventures on snowshoes.

Stride-by-Stride

MILES **DESCRIPTION**

0.0 The hike begins on the boat access path to the lake and turns right just before descending the wooden steps. Soon

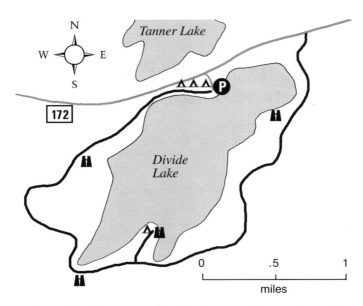

the trail crosses two plank bridges and ascends a ridge along the west side of the lake.

0.2   A bench with a view of the lake.

0.5   Cross a small bridge over a stream flowing out of the lake.

0.6   A rock gibbon constructed to keep fish from migrating out of the lake. The gibbon also serves as a bridge across the shallow stream.

0.7   Another bench with a view of Crosscut Lake to the south. Beyond this point the trail passes along a narrow ridge separating Divide and Crosscut lakes.

0.8   Trail intersection; the spur trail on the left leads to Blueberry Point in about 400 feet. The circuit trail bears right and away from the lake at this point.

0.9   The trail crosses an old beaver dam and returns to the lake shore briefly before turning away from the lake once again.

1.5   Pass a swinging bench with a view of Divide Lake.

1.6   The trail reaches the eastern most end of the lake before turning away from the lake and ascending to Forest Service Road 172.

1.7   Reach Forest Road 172; turn left and walk along the road to return to the campground and the trailhead.

2.0   At the crest of the hill on your way back to the campground you cross the Laurentian Divide. Tanner Lake is on the right side of the road.

2.1   The trailhead.

Hogback Lake

SUPERIOR NATIONAL FOREST
TOFTE RANGER DISTRICT

LENGTH	3.2 miles
TIME	2:00
DIFFICULTY	Easy-Moderate
ROUTE-FINDING	Easy
MAPS & PERMITS	A hiking sheet is available from the district ranger's office in Tofte. USGS quads: Silver Island Lake and Wilson Lake. No permit is required.
GETTING THERE	Turn right off Minnesota State Highway 1 onto U.S. Forest Road 172 in Isabella. Drive 12.3 miles to the Hogback Recreation Area on the right.
TRAILHEAD GPS	47° 38' 40.4" N 91° 8' 39.0" W

Hogback Lake takes its name from the sharp ridges that run generally east-west in the area. The major one you will meet on this hike runs between Hogback and Canal Lake, extending to between Mound Lake and Scarp Lake. The ridges provide good vantage points from which to view sparkling lakes snug in a thick setting of thick green forest. But the ridges are an interesting geological feature in their own right.

Hogbacks

The earth's crust consists of many layers of rock laid down in horizontal beds. Easily eroded strata alternate with resistant ones like the tiers of a layer cake. When massive forces within the earth's crust cause these layers to tilt, their edges, become exposed to the surface. Hogbacks result when extreme tilting turns the layers almost perpendicular to the horizontal. The ridges slowly take shape as the soft layers are eroded from either side of the resistant layers. Erosion is more pronounced during periods of glaciation. With the retreat of the great ice sheets, lakes may form in the depressions gouged out of the softer rock layers with narrow bands of resistant rock forming barriers between them.

This explains how hogbacks form, but how did these sharp ridges come to be called hogbacks? Anyone familiar with the feral hogs of southern states should make the connection right away. When agitated, a narrow band of bristles running along the spine of wild boars stands on end, looking like the edge of a razor. Razorback is a name applied to wild boars in some regions of the country, most notably Arkansas.

Like Hogback Lake, Scarp Lake takes its name from the sharp ridges in the area. A scarp, an abbreviation of escarpment, refers to a vertical or steep cliff which has resulted from erosion or faulting.

Trail Highlights

White birch and balsam fir make up the bulk of the forest you will be hiking. There are white pines near the northeast corner of Hogback Lake, white cedars around the southeast end of Scarp Lake, and scattered maples on the ridges. From the trailhead, the trail heads east along the shore of Hogback Lake. At the east end of Hogback, the trail turns away from the lake and climbs a hogback ridge north of Scarp Lake. The route continues east along this ridge passing between Mound and Scarp lakes. The trail eventually descends the ridge, rounds the east end of Scarp Lake, and climbs another hogback and heads west.

At the west end of Scarp Lake, the trail follows the portage trail to Canal Lake. This trail parallels a small canal that loggers used in the 1930s to move timber from Scarp Lake to Canal Lake and over to Hogback Lake. The trail continues along the shore of Canal Lake to a point of land between it and Hogback Lake. Here the trail once again turns east and ascends the first ridge of this route and intersects the trail running back to Hogback Lake and the trailhead.

Stride-by-Stride

MILES	DESCRIPTION
0.0	A sign marks the start of the trail at the east end of the picnic area parking lot. From there it heads east along the lake shore, shortly crossing a gibbon and entering a conifer forest.
0.3	The trail bears left away from Hogback Lake at its eastern end.
0.4	Trail intersection and the start of the circuit portion of this hike. The trail to the right leads to Canal Lake from which you will return to this point near the end of the hike. To begin the circuit, bear left on the trail to Scarp Lake. The trail travels along a sharp ridge, or hogback.
0.7	Spur trail on the right leads to a campsite in 250 feet on a peninsula in Scarp Lake. The main trail continues along the narrow ridge with views of Scarp Lake on the right and Mound Lake on the left.

169

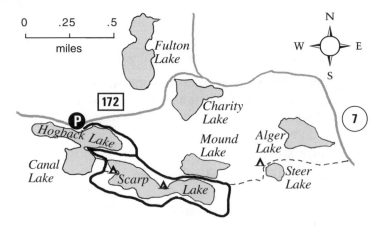

0.9 Cross a small stream flowing into Mound Lake.

1.1 Trail intersection; trail on the left provides another access route to this circuit hike from County Road 7. A campsite on Steer Lake can be reached in 0.4 mile from this intersection. Bear right to continue the circuit hike. The trail descends from the hogback and makes its way around the eastern end of Scarp Lake. On the southside of the lake the trail once again ascends another hogback ridge.

2.2 Trail intersection; the Lupus Lake Trail bears off to the left. This trail is no longer maintained by the Forest Service and is heavily overgrown and difficult to travel. The Scarp Lake Trail continues to the right.

2.3 Spur trail on the right leads to a campsite in about 0.2 mile.

2.4 Come to a small stream flowing out of Scarp Lake. Cross the stream, turn left and follow it to Canal Lake in about 400 feet. At Canal Lake, turn right and follow the trail along the lake shore. The trail eventually comes to a very narrow strip of land between Canal Lake and Hogback Lake (47° 38' 33.5" N 91° 8' 6.8" W).

2.5 The trail makes a very hard right turn and ascends the sharp ridge between Canal and Hogback lakes. Before ascending the ridge you may want to walk out to the end of the point where a narrow channel about 5–6 feet wide allows boats access from one lake to the other.

2.8 Trail intersection and the completion of the circuit portion of this hike. To return to the trailhead continue straight ahead passing the Scarp Lake Trail on the right.

2.9 Return to Hogback Lake.

3.2 Trailhead.

Ninemile Hiking Trail 42

SUPERIOR NATIONAL FOREST
TOFTE RANGER DISTRICT

4.3 M
MODERATE

LENGTH	4.3 miles
TIME	2:30
DIFFICULTY	Moderate
ROUTE-FINDING	Moderate
MAPS & PERMITS	A hiking sheet is available from the district office in Tofte. USGS quad: Cramer. No permit is required.
GETTING THERE	At Schroeder, drive 10 miles on County Road 1 to the intersection with County Road 7. Turn right and drive four miles to the Ninemile Lake Campground entrance on the left.
TRAILHEAD GPS	47° 34' 41.1" N 91° 4' 23.4" W

This is a pleasant hike with the route confined mostly to high ground. Where the trail dips to the lowlands, it crosses streams and wetlands on bridges. The forest consists mainly of maples on the ridges, and white birch and balsam fir at the lower, wetter elevations. From the start, the route gradually ascends onto a ridge where an overlook provides views of a valley that makes up part of the headwaters of the Caribou River. The name of this river will always be a testimony to the woodland caribou which once roamed this region until overhunting and destruction of their habitat led to their extirpation.

Beyond the overlook, the trail descends to the intersection that begins the circuit portion of the hike. From there the trail continues to descend into the narrow valley seen from the overlook. As you walk down the slope of the ridge, notice the change in the forest makeup from predominately maple to mostly white birch and balsam. On the valley floor, a small stream flows into a beaver pond on the right side of the trail. On the other side of the bridge, the trail once again climbs a ridge covered with large white birches and maples.

The white birches on this second ridge provide evidence that a catastrophic disturbance occurred long ago. The presence of large, multiple trunks growing from a single stump is an indication that fire or logging almost destroyed the tree. However, from the stump and root system, slender saplings sprouted and the tree began to grow again. In a way, the white birch is the forest's equivalent of the Hydra, a creature of mythology that was nearly impossible to kill; when one of its heads was cut off, two more would grow back in its place.

In the case of this forest, it is most likely that logging was the big event. Additional evidence that the cause might have been fire, would be the presence of a heavy fire scar on the uphill side of the remaining stump. As twigs and branches fall and wind and water slowly move them downhill, they tend to accumulate against the uphill sides of trees. When fire sweeps across the forest floor, the small piles of tinder burn hotter and longer than the litter on the other sides of the trees, leaving heavier, blacker scars on the uphill sides.

The stroll along this second ridge is much like a walk through a park. The understory is open and it is possible to see long distances through the trees. Contrast this with the forest you pass through later after the trail has descended from the ridge and the undergrowth is dense. The difference is in the canopy. On the ridge, the canopy is well developed and it blocks much of the sunlight from reaching the forest floor. In the later case, however, there are few large trees, and the canopy is almost nonexistent. More light reaches the ground and a dense understory is the result.

Striped Coralroot

If you keep a sharp eye out as you stroll this ridge, you might see a slender, dull purplish plant growing out of the dry leaf litter on this and other trails in northeastern Minnesota. It is the striped coralroot, a saprophytic orchid that shows no trace of green. Lacking chlorophyll and the ability to produce its own energy, the striped coralroot gets its nourishment from organic material in the soil's humus layer. The slender, leafless stalk, growing 8–20 inches tall, bears 10–20 very small purplish-red flowers that bloom in July and August. The name comes from the resemblance of the much branched rootstock to coral.

The striped coralroot doesn't fit the image most people have of orchids being lovers of a hot climate. In central North America, its range is restricted to the rich soils found in the forests of Ontario, Quebec, Michigan, Wisconsin, and Minnesota.

Other saprophytes found in our region include the pinesap and Indian pipe; however, these are not orchids. They belong to the Indian pipe family. These two plants get their energy from fungi that grow in association with the roots of trees such as oaks and pines. The pinesap is a red, pink, or yellow plant with nodding flowers that make it look like a miniature candlesnuffer. The Indian pipe is white with a translucent stem and a single nodding flower. When the Indian pipe's fruit ripens, or when it is picked, the plant turns black. For this reason it is also known as the corpse-plant according to Mrs. William Starr Dana, who also notes that Indians used it as an eye-lotion.

At the northern section of the trail, it passes a small pond from which frogs may sing like sirens trying to lure you into the woods, away from the security of the trail. Here the trail is at its wettest, but it is not too bad and your boots will dry quickly as you climb the last ridge that will take you south and back to the trailhead.

Stride-by-Stride

MILES	DESCRIPTION
0.0	The hike begins across County Road 7 from the campground entrance. If you are not staying at the campground, you will find parking near the boat ramp. The trail ascends gradually from the start through a forest of white birch, maple, and balsam fir. In about 455 feet continue straight ahead across a snowmobile trail going right and left.
0.2	Pass an overgrown trail on the left.
0.3	Bear right, passing an unmarked trail on the left.
0.4	Intersection with the snowmobile trail again; turn right and follow it for about 20 feet and then bear left as the snowmobile trail continues to the right. The trail ascends a ridge, makes a sharp turn to the right, and continues to ascend gradually along the ridge with a valley on the right.
0.6	An overlook on the right provides limited views of the valley. The trail begins to descend gradually beyond this point.
0.7	Trail intersection beginning the circuit portion of this hike; turn right and descend into the valley. White birches and balsam firs become more common and the maples less frequent.
0.9	Cross a bridge over a small stream flowing into a beaver pond on the right. Afterwards, the trail ascends gradually onto a broad, maple-forested ridge. Notice the birches growing in clumps around the remains of old stumps. The hiking through this open maple forest is pleasant, like a walk through a city park.
1.9	The trail turns north.

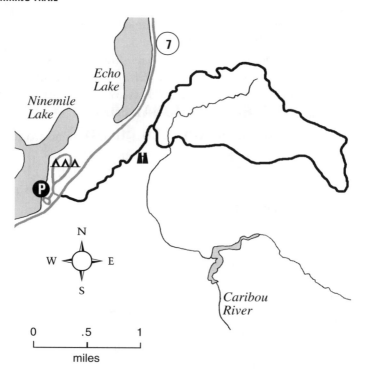

2.3   The trail begins to bear in a westerly direction and shortly begins a gradual descent.

2.5   A small pond comes into view through the trees on the left.

2.9   Cross a small stream on a three-board bridge. The trail is rocky at this point. Eventually it bears right, ascends a ridge, and travels back into maples once again.

3.5   Trail intersection completing the circuit portion of this hike. Continue straight ahead passing the trail on the left that began the circuit.

3.7   Pass the overlook on the left.

3.9   Intersection with the snowmobile trail. Follow it for about 20 feet and then bear left onto the hiking trail.

4.2   Cross the snowmobile trail for last time.

4.3   Reach County Road 7 and the trailhead.

Ennis, Blackstone, & Secret Lakes

3.7 M
MODERATE

SUPERIOR NATIONAL FOREST
KAWISHIWI RANGER DISTRICT

LENGTH	3.7 miles
TIME	2:30
DIFFICULTY	Moderate
ROUTE-FINDING	Moderate
MAPS & PERMITS	Fisher Map F-10. USGS quad: Snowbank Lake. No permit is required.
GETTING THERE	From Ely drive east on Minnesota State Highway 169 and County Road 18 for about 18 miles to U.S. Forest Road 438. Turn left on U.S. Forest Road 438 and go 2 miles to trailhead parking lot on the right.
TRAILHEAD GPS	47° 59' 9.4" N 91° 29' 52.2" W

Late September and early October is an excellent time of the year to hike the Blackstone Lake and Ennis Lake trails. The pleasantly cool sunny days go well with the warm glow from autumn's changing leaves. Aspens and maples provide much of the brilliance, while graceful red and white pines, and gnarly jack pines, contribute their evergreen to the palette of rapidly changing colors. The white blooms of pearly everlasting, and the blue of asters show that some small flowers don't easily give up their hold on summer. There is still plenty of wildlife to see; birds such as energetic Black-capped Chickadees, Rose-breasted Grosbeaks, Red-breasted Nuthatches, Gray Jays, and White-throated Sparrows. Garter snakes still take advantage of the sun's fading warmth to bask along the trail, well camouflaged among newly fallen leaves.

Wolves

Another animal that frequents these trails, but which you are not likely to see, is the wolf. Their droppings and tracks appear occasionally, the tracks showing up best in muddy places. You can usually determine wolf tracks by their size. If you open your hand with the fingers spread out wide, and then curl the fingers in at the second and third joints, what you have left should just about fill a wolf print. The scat is usually long and cylindrical, up to 6 inches in length.

Sections of northeastern Minnesota are a mosaic of wolf pack territories that may range in size from 48–120 square miles. Wolves are strongly territorial. Being at the top of the food chain requires that they roam and maintain large areas in order to ensure an adequate food supply and protection for their pups. A pack delineates its territory with the use of urine and feces scent-markers and howling.

A study of wolf howling and its role in maintaining a pack's territory, conducted by Fred Harrington and David Mech in the Superior National Forest, showed that whether to howl or not is a complicated matter for wolves. The overall response rate Harrington and Mech got to their howls was an unexpectedly low 29 percent. They learned that howling has both a benefit and a cost. The benefit of howling is that it advertises the pack's position and allows nearby wolves to change their course of travel so as to avoid an encounter. Wolves generally prefer to avoid encounters between packs due to the high risk of injury and death. The cost to a pack for howling is that it gives away the pack's position to other wolves that may be intent on an encounter. Harrington and Mech decided that to avoid accidental encounters between packs, wolves should respond to howling, but to avoid deliberate encounters they should remain silent and retreat, which is what the wolves tended to do most often with some exceptions. From the exceptions, the biologists learned that howling responses were not associated with the pack's entire territory, but to specific resources and sites within it, namely food and newborn pups.

Harrington and Mech got higher responses from wolf packs and lone wolves that were attending to recent kills. The more recent the kill, and consequently the more food the wolves were still likely to get from the carcass, the more likely they were to respond to howls. The men also found that packs were more likely to respond if pups were present. In both of these instances, wolf packs behaved as though the cost of responding, while it might lead to deliberate encounters, is worth the effort because of the essential resources that had to be protected. In both cases again, neither resource is one wolves can easily move, and so moving is not an option.

You may want to try howling on some of your hikes to see if you get a response. What a thrill that would be. Harrington and Mech found little difference in response rates between night and daytime howling. They usually howled at night though because the wind tends to be calmer making it easier to be heard and to hear.

Trail Highlights

This hike consists of a 1.3 mile circuit around Blackstone Lake with a 1.8 mile round-trip hike ending at a cliff that provides a panoramic view of Ennis Lake. From the trailhead and intersection with the Flash Lake portage trail, the route turns south past Blackstone Lake with two short spurs leading to the lake shore. Once off the Blackstone circuit and on the trail to Ennis Lake, the route ascends a rocky trail to a ridge overlooking a pond in a narrow valley. The trail descends from the ridge past the pond, crosses a stream, and ascends a red pine-covered ridge at the north end of a small unnamed lake. From here the route continues along the ridge, the trail marked with large cairns through the red pines. Eventually the route descends through aspens, white birch, and mixed conifers to cross a steep walled, narrow valley where maples grow thick in the moist soil of the valley floor. After making the steep climb out of the valley the route comes to the high cliffs at the north-west corner of Ennis Lake. This is an excellent lunching spot where you can refuel the body while drinking in the view.

To resume the Blackstone circuit hike, retrace your steps to the south end of the loop. Here the route turns east along a very narrow ridge that separates Blackstone Lake to the north and Secret Lake to the south. At times it is possible to see both lakes through the jack pines growing on the ridge. At the east end of Blackstone Lake, the route crosses a portage trail between Blackstone and Flash lakes. This portage trail is not on the Fisher F-10 map. Along the north side of Blackstone Lake the trail passes through a stand of white, jack, and red pines. At the north-west corner of Blackstone Lake, the trail skirts a beaver dam and the circuit is soon completed. From here it's 0.4 miles back to the trailhead.

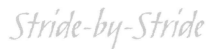

Stride-by-Stride

MILES	DESCRIPTION
0.0	The trail heads south from the parking area, passes under a powerline, crosses a small bridge, and skirts a wet meadow.
0.1	Intersection with the portage trail to Flash Lake to the left. Turn right on the trail to Secret and Ennis lakes. The trail is rocky and crisscrossed with roots.
0.3	Trail intersection with the north end of the Blackstone Lake Loop to the left; bear right. In about 200 feet pass a short spur trail on the left to Blackstone Lake.
0.4	Spur trail on the left leads to a campsite on Blackstone Lake in about 365 feet.

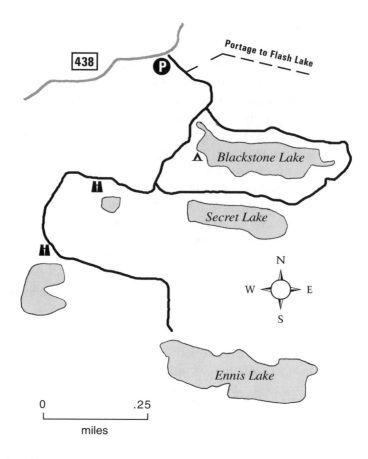

0.5 Trail intersection with the south end of the Blackstone Lake Loop. Bear right on the trail to Ennis Lake.

0.9 Overlook from a short cliff of a lake south of the trail. Look for a beaver lodge in the northeast corner of the lake.

1.3 The trail descends steeply into a narrow valley with maples growing on its floor, and then steeply ascends the other side.

1.4 Cliffs at the northwest end of Ennis Lake; an excellent place for lunch (47° 58' 35.0" N 91° 29' 51.2" W). From here retrace your steps to the south end of the Blackstone Lake Loop.

2.3 Intersection at the south end of the Blackstone Lake Loop; turn right.

2.4 The trail passes along a narrow jack pine-covered ridge separating Secret Lake on the right and Blackstone Lake.

2.7 Trail turns north around the east end of Blackstone Lake.

2.9 Intersection with an unmapped portage trail between Blackstone and Flash lakes. To the left the portage trail leads to Blackstone Lake in 85 feet. Continue straight ahead. In 100 feet, the main trail turns left off the portage just before reaching Flash Lake. Pass through a stand of mixed pines at the north end of Blackstone Lake.

3.4 The trail reaches a small beaver dam at the northwest end of Blackstone Lake. Make your way around the dam until you pick up the main trail once again. In about 200 feet, come to the trail intersection completing the loop around Blackstone Lake and the circuit portion of this hike. Turn right.

3.6 Trail intersection with the Flash Lake portage; turn left.

3.7 Trailhead.

44

6.3 M
MODERATE-DIFFICULT

Cross River Wayside

TEMPERANCE RIVER STATE PARK

LENGTH	6.3 miles
TIME	3:45
DIFFICULTY	Moderate-Difficult
ROUTE-FINDING	Moderate
MAPS & PERMITS	DNR Temperance River State Park map. McKenzie Map 102 (Lutsen and Tofte). USGS quads: Tofte and Schroder. A permit is not required if hikers use the parking lots along U.S. Highway 61.
GETTING THERE	The trailhead is located on U.S. Highway 61 in southern Cook County at the parking lot just west of the Temperance River.
TRAILHEAD GPS	47° 33' 16.1" N 90° 52' 28.9" W

Cross River got its name from a cross erected at the mouth of the river by Father Frederick Baraga, a missionary priest, to mark his safe passage across Lake Superior after being caught in a storm during the crossing. Father Baraga, called "the snowshoe priest" by the Ojibwa, immigrated to the U.S. from Yugoslavia in 1830 to work as a missionary among the Native Americans. He was responsible for translating the Bible into Ojibwa, and writing the first Ojibwa grammar book and dictionary.

Father Baraga shuddered at the thought of the long paddle along the lake shoreline when he and an Indian guide set out in a canoe from Wisconsin's South Shore for Grand Portage. Since the weather was favorable and the lake calm, the two set out across the lake hoping to eliminate almost 150 miles of paddling. However, once in the middle of the great lake, a storm arose and the two feared for their lives. They had to work hard to keep the canoe from being swamped by the large waves. Eventually they drew near to the North Shore, but then had to find a way to land the canoe without getting it smashed by the waves against the rocks. A wave, perhaps sent from heaven, carried the canoe safely over the bar at the mouth of the Cross River, delivering them into the calmer waters of this small lagoon. In honor of their deliverance, Father Baraga erected a wooden cross at the site and the river got its name. Today a cement cross commemorates this historic event.

The Cross River drains 91 square miles of the North Shore along the border of Cook and Lake counties. There are five major falls in the last six miles of its dash to Lake Superior. Along a section of the river followed by the Cross River Trail that is a part of this circuit hike, the river has cut a deep, narrow gorge through the layers of lava flows underlying the region. The Ojibwa called the river *"Tchibaiatigo zibi"* or "wood of the soul river." Trying to look at the river from the rim of the gorge can be as difficult as trying to look into a person's soul. Although in places you can hear its roar, it's not possible to see the river far below because the gorge is deep and narrow and the walls steep.

For a time, loggers used the Cross River to transport timber to Lake Superior where they then made large rafts of the logs and towed them to a sawmill. In the winter, lumberjacks stored the logs in a reservoir. In the spring, with the reservoir swollen with meltwater, they opened the dam. The result was a flood of water and logs rampaging down the river. However, the use of Cross River for this purpose was short lived after too many logs reached Lake Superior with their ends splintered like well-used toothpicks from repeatedly ramming the gorge walls and rocks along the way.

Trail Highlights

From the trailhead at the parking lot on U.S. Highway 61, the trail heads north on the Superior Hiking Trail along the western side of the Temperance River. Look for large kettles along the river near the beginning of the hike. After about a mile, the trail reaches the upper cascade and turns west heading across country to the Cross River. Where the trail climbs a ridge, the going is rather strenuous. The trail is steep and there are no switchbacks that would help lessen the grade.

Fortunately, once on the ridge the going is fairly level as the trail tries to faithfully follow the contour. There are occasional views of the North Shore where the forest opens up along the way.

You will reach Cross River after slightly more than three miles from the trailhead. Here the Superior Hiking Trail descends steeply to cross the river and continue its way down the North Shore. The circuit hike leaves the Superior Hiking Trail and follows the Cross River Trail as it descends gradually along the rim of the Cross River gorge for about three-quarters of a mile. There are many impressive views of the gorge, and occasionally of the river far below. At a shelter the circuit turns back to the east to return over level terrain to the Temperance River.

181

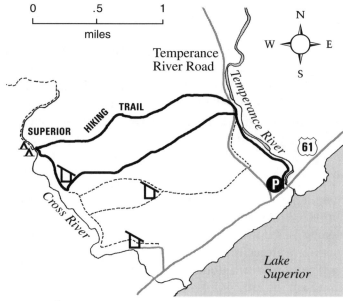

Stride-by-Stride

MILES   **DESCRIPTION**

0.0   This hike begins on the Superior Hiking Trail (SHT) as it ascends the west side of the Temperance River. Look for old kettles abandoned by the river along the lower portion of the trail.

0.2   Trail intersection with the footbridge over the Temperance River on the right; continue straight ahead hiking up river on the SHT.

0.4   Trail intersection; pass a trail coming in sharply on the left.

0.7   Trail intersection; continue ahead on the SHT passing a cross-country ski trail on the left.

0.8   Trail intersection beginning the circuit portion of this hike. Bear right to the river's edge, passing a trail to the left. Continue up river and reenter the forest in about 100 feet. In another 300 feet, with the upper falls of the Temperance River on the right, continue straight ahead past an unmarked trail on the left.

1.1   Cross the Temperance River Road (Forest Road 343) and continue hiking on the SHT. The trail soon begins to ascend a ridge, first moderately and then more steeply.

2.0   A small overlook on the left provides views of the North Shore, including Taconite Harbor to the southeast.

2.7   The trail enters a clearing providing views of the North Shore.

3.1   Trail intersection; leave the SHT, which continues to the right, by turning left on the trail which descends to U.S. Highway 61 along the east side of Cross River. Before continuing the circuit hike, you may want to make the short walk down the SHT to get a close look at Cross River.

3.6   An overlook on the rim of the gorge provides a view of the river far below.

3.7   The river rushes through a narrow gorge.

3.8   Trail intersection at an Adirondack shelter; turn left, leaving the Cross River Trail, and hike east on a cross-country ski trail passing through a forest of white birch, aspen, and balsam fir.

4.6   Trail intersection; bear left passing the trail on the right.

5.3   The trail enters a clearing; bear right across the clearing.

5.5   Temperance River Road; turn right and walk along the road for about 130 feet before turning left onto a hiking trail. Do not take the gated hiking and skiing trail about 50 feet further on. In about 120 feet, reach the trail intersection along the Temperance River completing the circuit portion of this hike. Turn right on the SHT to return to the trailhead.

5.9   Trail intersection; bear left, staying close to the river, passing the trail on the right.

6.1   Trail intersection at the footbridge over the Temperance River; continue straight ahead.

6.3   Trailhead on U.S. Highway 61.

3.2 M
EASY-MODERATE

SUPERIOR NATIONAL FOREST
TOFTE RANGER DISTRICT

LENGTH	3.2 miles
TIME	2:15
DIFFICULTY	Easy-Moderate with a steep ascent to the peak.
ROUTE-FINDING	Easy-Moderate
MAPS & PERMITS	McKenzie Map 102 (Lutsen and Tofte). USGS quads: Honeymoon Mountain and Tofte. No permit is required.
GETTING THERE	Drive 5 miles east of Tofte on U.S. Highway 61 to U.S. Forest Road 336. Turn left and drive about 2 miles to the parking lot on the left side of the road.
TRAILHEAD GPS	47° 37' 42.9" N 90° 47' 6.5" W

It never fails that every time I see the footprints of a black bear on the trail, the hair stands up on the back of my neck and a chill races along my spine. Goose bumps prickle my skin and I look cautiously over my shoulder every so often until I have left the tracks far behind. Logic and facts about black bears tell me that I have very little to worry about, but it's hard to shake off the fear held over somewhere deep within my psyche from boyhood stories heard at midnight around campfires. Despite this uneasiness I always look forward to finding bear tracks, as I did on the way to Leveaux Peak. They give a hike a whole different feeling.

The most fascinating thing about black bears is the physiology they have evolved so they can hibernate for long periods; up to five and six months. During this time, they do not eat, drink, or eliminate any body wastes. How bears can do this is of interest to scientists specializing in the treatment of kidney and bone diseases in humans.

Writing for the *Canadian Geographic*, Wayne Lynch notes that bears are successful at starving. When we humans do it, either willingly or not, our bodies burn precious muscle protein, as well as fat, and we become weak in addition to lighter. Bears, on the other hand, burn very little if any muscle protein; they burn only fat during hibernation. As a consequence, when bears leave their dens in spring, they may look like ninety pound weaklings but all they've lost is a lot of fat. They are still very strong animals.

Bears get the little water they need to survive hibernation from the fat-burning process. And since they metabolize so little protein during their big sleep, bears don't need to eliminate urea, a toxic by-product of protein metabolism. Even the small amount of urea they do produce is not a problem. It is simply broken down into harmless components and reabsorbed by the body.

When illness confines us to our beds for a couple of weeks, our bones begin to lose calcium and osteoporosis sets in. Bears, asleep in their dens for up to six months, don't have to worry about getting brittle bones, or curvature of the spine. It's as if they were getting intravenous feedings of Wonder bread all that time. But seriously, the only Wonder bread a bear is likely to get is on a raid of some luckless campers' food cache.

The Leveaux Peak Hiking Trail shares a common trailhead with the Oberg Mountain Trail. Together they form a hike of about 5.5 miles which is easily doable in half a morning and an afternoon. Plan on spending the morning hiking the Leveaux Peak circuit first, and the afternoon lunching on Oberg and enjoying the many overlooks it has to offer. Not that Leveaux is a slacker when it comes to overlooks.

From the trailhead, the route to Leveaux Peak passes through a forest of balsam firs, spruce, and white birch. A small clearing a quarter mile from the start provides a glimpse of the rocky-sided peak. Shortly afterwards, the trail crosses the Onion River and enters a predominately maple forest with an open understory.

The trail leads right up to the base of an escarpment and boulder field at the bottom of the steep rock face. The trail skirts this cliff a short way and then climbs steeply to the summit by way of switchbacks that lessen the grade. A bench situated nicely under a cedar tree offers itself as a resting place for those in need. There is a small looping trail off the main circuit around Leveaux Peak. The smaller circuit has views of nearby Carlton Peak, the North Shore, and Lake Superior. Back on the main circuit around the peak is an overlook of the headwaters of the west branch of the Onion River and low ridges fading into the distance. Immediately after this last overlook, the trail descends via switchbacks and heads back to the trailhead.

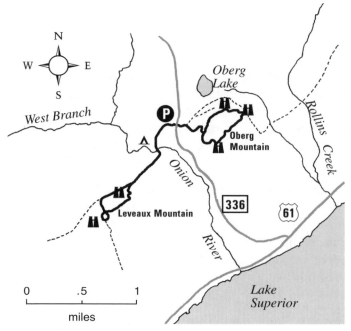

Stride-by-Stride

MILES   DESCRIPTION

0.0   The hike begins on the Superior Hiking Trail (SHT) as it heads west from the parking lot through white birches, balsam firs, and spruces.

0.3   The trail enters a small clearing from which you can see Leveaux Peak off to the left.

0.5   Spur trail on the right leads to a campsite. In about 300 feet, the SHT turns left and descends to a bridge crossing the Onion River.

0.6   Bridge over the Onion River. The trail ascends and enters a forest dominated by maples.

1.0   Trail intersection and the beginning of the circuit portion of this hike. Continue straight ahead on SHT passing the trail on the left.

1.1   Trail reaches the base of Leveaux Peak just below a towering rock face and boulder field. In about 300 feet, the SHT bears right; continue straight ahead on the trail to Leveaux Peak. The trail makes a steep ascent via switchbacks. A bench in the shade of a large cedar tree provides an excellent rest opportunity part way through the climb.

1.3   Trail intersection; pass the trail on the left and continue straight ahead to reach a small loop trail on the west side of the summit. You will shortly return to this intersection and continue the hike on the trail to the left.

1.4   Trail intersection and the beginning of the smaller loop on Leveaux Peak. Continue straight ahead passing the trail on the left. Reach an overlook in about 500 feet on the right side of the trail with views of the North Shore and Carlton Peak. Better views can be seen at a second overlook in 175 feet.

1.5   Trail intersection; bear left passing a trail on the right to Chateau Leveaux and Cobblestone Cabins. Just past this point is the foundation of an old fire tower (47° 36' 56.9" N 90° 47' 49.6" W).

1.7   Trail intersection completing the small loop. Turn right to return to the main circuit in about 200 feet. Turn right again at the next intersection to continue the main circuit.

1.9   An overlook on the left side of the trail provides panoramic views to the north of the headwater region of the Onion River and low ridges beyond. From this point the trail descends gradually and then steeply.

2.1   Pass a log bench at a switchback on the steep descent from the summit.

2.2   Trail intersection completing the main circuit of Leveaux Peak. Turn right to return to the trailhead. The trail gradually descends to the Onion River.

2.6   Cross the Onion River.

3.2   Trailhead.

46

2.3 M
EASY-MODERATE

Oberg Mountain

SUPERIOR NATIONAL FOREST
TOFTE RANGER DISTRICT

LENGTH	2.3 miles
TIME	1:45
DIFFICULTY	Easy with a short, moderately steep climb of Oberg Mountain.
ROUTE-FINDING	Easy
MAPS & PERMITS	McKenzie Map 102 (Lutsen and Tofte). USGS quads: Honeymoon Mountain and Tofte. No permit is required.
GETTING THERE	Five miles east of Tofte, turn north on Forest Road 336 (also known as Onion River Road). Drive about 2 miles to the parking lot on the left side of the road. The trailhead to Oberg Mountain is on the right side of the road just before turning into the parking lot.
TRAILHEAD GPS	47° 37' 42.9" N 90° 47' 6.5" W

Oberg Mountain and its neighbors on either side, Leveaux Peak to the southwest and Moose Mountain to the northeast, are part of a series of mountain peaks and ridges known as the Sawtooth Mountains. Their origin dates back as much as 1.1 million years when the earth's crust from Lake Superior to as far south as Kansas began to rift or pull apart. Great flows of basaltic lava flowed out of the rift. Layer on top of layer of lava flowed across the land. Eventually the rifting stopped and the subsiding of underground lava caused the Lake Superior Basin to form. As the basin slowly grew deeper, the surrounding layers of lava flows tilted anywhere from 10 to 20 degrees toward the lake pushing up their edges to form the ridges. Imagine a giant teeter-totter; as one end, say the end out in the basin, sinks, the other end, the one away from the basin, rises. You can see the tilting of the great lava flows in dramatic fashion at Palisade Head and Shovel Point north of the Baptism River.

While Oberg Mountain provides some of the most dramatic and panoramic views along the North Shore, it is also a place where your attention is drawn to the close-at-hand.

Rivaling the views of Leveaux Peak, the North Shore and Lake Superior, Moose Mountain, Rolling Creek watershed, Oberg Lake, and the receding ridges of the Sawtooths, are the flowers that grace the trail. The West End Garden Club has printed a brochure especially for this trail. Called *A Guide to the Wildflowers of Oberg Mountain*, they are available from a small box near the trailhead. The Club asks that if you take one of the guides to help identify the many flowers on the mountain, that you return it to the box at the end of your hike for others to use.

Wildflowers

There are a lot of wildflowers for you to see on Oberg Mountain. Since the Oberg Mountain Trail is such a short one, you should have plenty of time to stop in between the overlooks, as well as at the overlooks, to study the flowers. Take your time to learn about some of the beautiful plants that call Oberg home.

Two cinquefoils, members of the rose family, grow on Oberg. The Three-toothed Cinquefoil is said to have strawberrylike blossoms that brighten the mountaintops of the Alleghenies, the coast of New England, and the shores of the Great Lakes. The Rough Cinquefoil, according to Mrs. William Dana Starr, is a "rather weedy-looking plant" common in dry soils. Its flowers last through the summer. The genus name for the cinquefoils, *Pontentilla*, refers to the powerful medicinal properties these plants were once thought to possess.

The Bluebead Lily is easily identified after the shiny blue fruits have ripened. But beware, the fruits are poisonous. There are 3 to 6 berries perched at the top of a stalk. Another name for this wildflower is Yellow Clintonia in honor of a former governor of New York, DeWitt Clinton, and yellow being the color of the flowers.

Yarrow, a member of the sunflower family, is another easily identifiable wildflower on Oberg, as well as the rest of the eastern two-thirds of North America. Tiny white flowers form dense, flat-topped clusters at the top of a stem that grows from 1–3 feet high. The blossoms appear throughout the summer and into the fall. According to Mrs. Starr, whose book, *How to Know the Wild Flowers*, is a source of interesting information about wildflowers, writes that the genus name, *Achillea*, derives from the belief that Achilles used it to cure the wounds of his soldiers. People must do strange things with plants, because she goes on to say that English botanists referred to yarrow as "nosebleed," "because the leaves being put into the nose caused it to bleed." Swedes call it field hop in recognition of its use in brewing beer.

Finally, although not even close to being the end of the Oberg flowers, is the bunchberry. This low-to-the-ground plant has the look of Christmas about it with its tight cluster of small, shiny red berries above a whorl of green leaves. It is one of the most common flowers growing along the trails of northeastern Minnesota. This flower is a member of the dogwood family which consists mainly of small trees and shrubs. The bunchberry is one of only two herbs in the family. While the berries are edible, they do not have much of a taste, and the fruit is difficult to separate from the seed. However, cooks and bakers may use bunchberries in combination with other, more flavorful berries, to make the tastier berries go further.

Trail Highlights

The route of the Oberg Mountain Trail shares a common trailhead with the Leveaux Peak Trail. Hike northeast on the Superior Hiking Trail for about 0.2 miles to reach the spur trail leading to the circuit around the summit. The ascent is rather moderate and lasts for about 0.3 miles. A bench part way up provides a resting place if necessary.

On the summit of Oberg, a 1.4 mile circuit trail connects eight overlooks that provide views of the surrounding countryside that almost completes a full turn of the compass. The overlooks start with a view of the rocky face of Leveaux Peak, and the narrow valley the Onion River has carved between the two peaks. The overlooks end with a view of Oberg Lake from high atop a rocky perch. In between are views of the North Shore, Lake Superior, Moose Mountain, and the headwaters of Rolling Creek. Stretching up and down the shore and inland are the Sawtooth Mountains. Bring a flower guide on this hike, and a lunch or some snacks and plan on staying for a while.

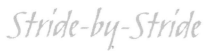

Stride-by-Stride

MILES	DESCRIPTION
0.0	The hike begins on the Superior Hiking Trail (SHT) leading northeast to Moose Mountain and Lake Agnes.
0.2	Trail intersection; turn right on the trail to Oberg Mountain, leaving the SHT as it continues to the left towards Moose Mountain. The trail to Oberg Mountain ascends steeply via switchbacks.
0.4	Bench at a switchback part way up the ascent.
0.5	Trail intersection beginning the circuit portion of this hike. Continue straight ahead passing the trail on the left. Come to the first overlook, with views of Leveaux Peak, in about 250 feet. The Onion River drains the narrow valley between the

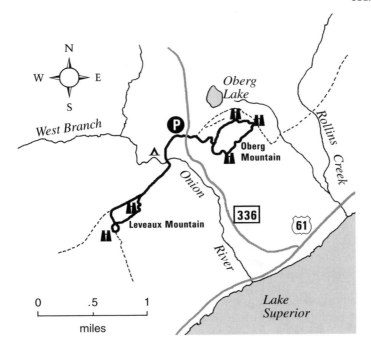

two peaks. Mature maples predominate on the summit of
Oberg Peak, along with large aspens.

0.6 Second overlook providing more dramatic views of Leveaux
Peak and the North Shore to the southwest.

1.0 Third overlook with a picnic table and views to the northeast.

1.1 Fourth overlook; a fifth one, providing views of Lutsen and
Moose Mountain, is reached in another 300 feet.

1.3 The sixth overlook at the rim of a very steep, high rock face
on the north side of Oberg Mountain. From here you get the
first glimpse of Oberg Lake to the left. Moose Mountain rises
on the other side of the Rolling Creek drainage. A seventh
overlook in about 500 feet provides an even better view of
Oberg Lake and the headwaters of Rolling Creek. The stream
flowing from Oberg Lake is a part of this drainage.

1.5 A spur trail to the right leads to an overlook with excellent
views of Oberg Lake and a beaver pond at the outlet.

1.9 Trail intersection completing the circuit portion of this hike.
Turn right to return to the SHT.

2.2 Trail intersection on the SHT; turn left to return to the
trailhead.

2.3 Forest Road 336 and the trailhead.

Lookout Mountain

CASCADE RIVER STATE PARK

LENGTH	3.0 miles
TIME	2:00
DIFFICULTY	Moderate with one very steep climb.
ROUTE-FINDING	Moderate
MAPS & PERMITS	DNR Cascade River State Park map. USGS quad: Deer Yard Lake. A Minnesota State Park permit is required.
GETTING THERE	The park is located in Cook County 9 miles southwest of Grand Marais and 21 miles northeast of Tofte on U.S. Highway 61. Enter the park and follow the signs to "trail parking."
TRAILHEAD GPS	47° 42' 32.9" N 90° 31' 16.9" W

Lookout Mountain lies just outside the Cascade River State Park boundary along the Superior Hiking Trail. While the circuit hike to Lookout Mountain is a relatively short three miles, a portion of it involves a steep climb to the summit that gives it a moderate to strenuous degree of difficulty. However, once at the summit, there is a great overlook of the forested interior of the rugged North Shore. Here you can catch your breath and enjoy lunch or a snack. You can also rest easy knowing that the rest of your journey is all downhill from there.

As it heads west from the trailhead, the route crosses the Cascade River and then Cascade Creek, which is not a tributary of the larger river but flows directly into Lake Superior. The steepest part of the hike comes after the creek as the trail climbs to the summit of Lookout Mountain. Lookout Mountain, and its attending ridge, is supported by diabase, a type of igneous rock injected into the cracks of older rocks below the Earth's surface where the molten material hardens. There are a couple of benches at the overlook, but if you walk beyond them out onto some rock ledges you will get better views. From the overlook, you can see east and north across the forested drainage of Cascade Creek to other ridges rising above forested valleys.

During my rest at the overlook, a flock of cedar wax-wings came over the mountain from behind me and drifted down into the valley below.

With the bright sunlight shimmering off the silky texture of their feathers, they seemed a harbinger of fall. The swooping turns they made through the air made them seem like the yellow leaves of autumn that would soon be flying on the wind. On the ground nearby, a Black-throated Green Warbler hunted insects. This bird with a green back, yellow cheeks, and black throat was bulking up for a long migration flight to Central America.

Black-capped Chickadee

Another bird that you are very likely to see at the overlook, and just about anywhere else in northeastern Minnesota, is the Black-capped Chickadee. This small, gray-and-white bird, with a formal looking black cap and bib, and a distinctive *chick-a-dee-dee-dee* call, is a well-known, cheerful visitor to birdfeeders in town and country. By late summer, early fall, the year's young have fledged and gathered into flocks. These groups stay together through the cold months of a northland winter foraging and roosting.

The fledging process of Black-capped Chickadees is a gradual one. Mary Holleback describes the process in an article she wrote for *The Wilson Bulletin*, an ornithological journal. At first, even after the young have gained independence from the nest, they rely on the parents for food. To reduce aggression by the parents and to increase their chances of receiving food, the young persist in the submissive behavior they displayed while in the nest. During the first 8–10 days out of the nest, the fledglings beg quite often and the adults show little offense towards them. After this short period, however, the young are feeding more independently. They also beg less and the adults show more aggression towards them. Holleback attributes this change in adult behavior to the gradual cessation in the youngs' submissive behavior. The benevolence that once existed within the family is gradually replaced with intolerance.

About 20 days after fledging, the families have broken apart, the young joining into flocks associated with at least one adult that is not a parent, whose territory they will inhabit. Along with the adult, each group consists of the young from several different families, with the young of a single family mostly joining different groups. By the time winter comes around, the flock is prepared to spend the long winter months foraging and roosting. Their lighthearted chattering and uplifting disposition form an attitude perfect for surviving the long, harsh season of cold temperatures and scarce food supplies. Whatever the season, these bundles of energy are always a pleasing sight to see along the trail.

From the overlook, and just beyond the shelter, the route leaves the Superior Hiking Trail and descends from the mountain through white birches and balsam firs. In late summer, thimbleberry plants crowd the trail. The large red berries make pleasant snacking; their tart flavor lingers on the tongue, and the juices seem to provide a little burst of energy.

Stride-by-Stride

MILES   DESCRIPTION

0.0   The hike begins on the Cascade River Trail by climbing a short flight of steps, passing under powerlines, and crossing an unmarked trail before reaching the bridge over the Cascade River.

0.1   Trail intersection at the bridge; cross the bridge, turn right on the Superior Hiking Trail (SHT).

0.3   Bear left at a fork in the trail.

0.5   Trail intersection; continue straight ahead on the SHT passing the ski trail on the left and the trail to the right.

0.6   Trail intersection; turn left passing a ski trail to the right.

0.8   Trail intersection; turn right on the SHT passing a ski trail to the left. The trail crosses Cascade Creek in about 200 feet.

0.9   Trail intersection; continue straight ahead on the SHT crossing a ski trail going right and left. The trail ascends steeply at times.

1.2   A spur trail on the right leads to an overlook in 165 feet with views to the north across the watershed of Cascade Creek.

1.4   Trail intersection; continue straight ahead on the SHT passing the spur trail on the left which leads to a backpack camping site. Reach Lookout Mountain overlook in 60 feet which has views to the east and north. The trail continues past the overlook to an Adirondack shelter in about 160 feet.

1.5   Trail intersection just beyond the shelter; turn left on a hiking trail leaving the SHT which continues straight ahead. This new trail descends from Lookout Mountain.

2.2   Trail intersection with a ski trail; turn left. In about 150 feet come to another intersection; turn right passing the trail to the left.

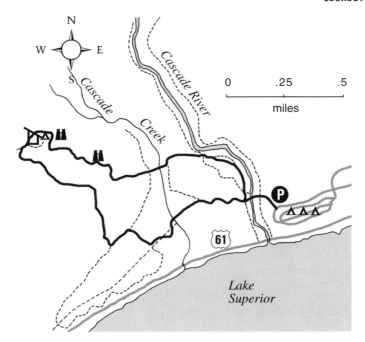

2.3   Trail intersection; turn left following the trail along the powerline corridor.

2.4   Trail intersection; turn left on the Wild Flower Trail leaving the trail which continues straight ahead.

2.5   Trail intersection; continue straight ahead, cross a bridge over Cascade Creek, turn left, and ascend a short distance along the east side of the creek. In about 100 feet, the trail comes to another intersection; turn right passing trails going straight ahead and to the left. About 130 feet further on, the trail, which is again traveling along the powerline corridor, comes to yet another intersection. Continue straight ahead passing the trail on the right.

2.6   Trail intersection just inside the forest; turn right passing the trail to the left.

2.8   Trail intersection; turn right passing the trail to the left. In about 80 feet, come to the intersection at the bridge over the Cascade River completing the circuit portion of this hike. Cross the bridge and continue straight ahead to return to the trailhead.

3.0   Trailhead.

48

7.9 M
STRENUOUS

Cascade River

CASCADE RIVER STATE PARK

LENGTH	7.9 miles
TIME	5:00
DIFFICULTY	Strenuous
ROUTE-FINDING	Moderate
MAPS & PERMITS	DNR Cascade River State Park map. USGS quad: Deer Yard Lake. A Minnesota State Park permit is required.
GETTING THERE	The park is located in Cook County 9 miles southwest of Grand Marais and 21 miles northeast of Tofte on Highway 61. Enter the park and follow the signs to "trail parking."
TRAILHEAD GPS	47° 42' 32.9" N 90° 31' 16.9" W

The route of this hike takes you up the west side of Cascade River, staying mostly on the rim of the river gorge, and returns down the east side spending more time along the riverbank. For practically the entire way the river is either within sight or hearing range. Near the start, the trail crosses the Cascade River below one of its many cascades. According to Thomas Waters, in *The Streams and Rivers of Minnesota,* this river drains an area of 120 square miles. There are many lakes in its headwaters, which ensure a steady flow of water through out the summer and fall months. The cascades occur along a series of erosion-resistant bedrock ledges. The river drops 900 feet in its last three miles before pouring itself into Lake Superior, with a final 120 foot drop through a twisting gorge in the last quarter mile.

The tree vegetation in the park is a boreal hardwood-conifer forest. Areas of aspen, white birch, balsam fir, and spruce alternate with stands of maple growing on higher ground on the west side of the river. Northern white cedars grow in the moister soils. Tall white pines, scattered along the entire route, rise above the usual forest canopy.

A mile and a half into the hike, a 0.3 mile spur trail ushers you to a 20 foot waterfall along a narrow side canyon of the main river gorge. The trees and close walls of the ravine keep it well shaded; and the moisture from the falls keeps the air cool and moist. A lush growth of ferns and mosses covers the rock walls. Shade-tolerant flowers and cedar trees add to the soft texture making this a peaceful place. Its distance from the road and distance off the main trail almost ensures that you will have this place to yourself for as long as you might want to stay.

Henry Mayhew, a pioneering founder of the town of Grand Marais, is believed to have prospected for copper along this tributary somewhere above the falls. In *Geology on Display,* a fine book on the geology of North Shore state parks, author John Green notes that Mayhew made a small excavation in his search for mineable deposits of copper ore. While stories in the Grand Marais newspaper in 1891 seemed to indicate that Mayhew's efforts would prove fruitful, nothing ever came of the excavation. However, this doesn't mean that mineable quantities of copper and other minerals don't exist, just not on the North Shore. Green indicates that geologists have located sizable deposits of copper, nickel, iron, and cobalt many miles inland from the lake.

Native American Copper Mining

The idea that Europeans settlers could find copper deposits around Lake Superior came from the earliest contacts explorers had with the native peoples. They found tribes from the St. Lawrence River to the Gulf of Mexico using copper implements and ornaments. They also learned that much of this copper had come from the Lake Superior region.

George A. West, in *Copper: Its Mining and Use by the Aborigines of the Lake Superior Region,* describes how the Indians mined the green metal. First they searched rock outcroppings for green streaks that indicated the presence of malachite which is often found in association with other copper-bearing minerals. They then built a large fire over the rock, and, after getting it very hot, threw water on the rock causing it to fracture. Next, the Indians used stone mauls to break away the cracked pieces of rock. The stone these mauls were made of was very brittle, and so they didn't last long before the workers had to find another one. As a consequence, Indians littered the areas around their copper pits with the splintered remains of hundreds of thousands of mauls. In the process of mining copper, these early miners excavated trenches 5–15 feet wide, 6–10 feet deep, and up to 20 feet long. In some cases, the Indians used their canoe paddles as shovels.

After separating the copper from the fractured bits of rock, a toolmaker in the tribe worked the metal into one of many items. To strengthen the copper so it could be given a thin edge, the Indians annealed the metal, repeatedly heating the piece being worked on and then dipping it in water. In this way, Indians were able to fashion spear and arrow-points, knives, axes, wedges, piercing implements, fishing implements, and ornaments such as beads, bracelets, rings, and pendants.

Stride-by-Stride

MILES	DESCRIPTION
0.0	The hike begins on the Cascade River Trail by climbing a flight of steps, passing under a powerline, and, in 440 feet, crossing an unmarked trail going right and left.
0.1	Trail intersection at the bridge crossing the Cascade River, and the beginning of the circuit portion of this hike. Cross the bridge and turn right on the Superior Hiking Trail (SHT), passing two trails to the left.
0.3	The trail forks; take either one as they rejoin in about 330 feet.
0.5	Trail intersection; turn right, passing two trails on the left, and descend the "96 Steps." At the bottom, bear left on the SHT passing a spur trail to the right.
1.5	Trail intersection; the spur trail on the right leads to a small waterfall in 0.3 mile. The main trail bears left and ascends very steeply. The 15–20 foot waterfall at the end of the spur trail is located in a small box canyon on a tributary stream of the Cascade River. The main trail, after ascending steeply, levels out and moves away from the river so that it's just within hearing range. This section of the trail passes the site of an old mine.
1.8	Cross a bridge over a small wet-weather stream.
2.4	Cross a bridge over a tributary stream. After a steep ascent, the trail passes over level terrain through a maple forest.
2.9	Cross a bridge over a small stream.
3.3	Cross a bridge.
3.6	The trail crosses a bridge, turns right, and reaches a point high above the river that provides an excellent view of Hidden Falls upriver. Beyond this point, the trail passes above a recent landslide where a section of the steep river canyon wall has collapsed onto the riverbank. Soon the trail reaches County Road 45. Turn right and walk along the road crossing the bridge over Cascade River.
3.9	Turn left off County Road 45 onto the road providing access to a small parking lot for the SHT. Pass the SHT on the right and head downriver by walking past the parking lot and under the bridge.
4.4	Hidden Falls.
4.9	The trail enters private property. Please stay on the trail.

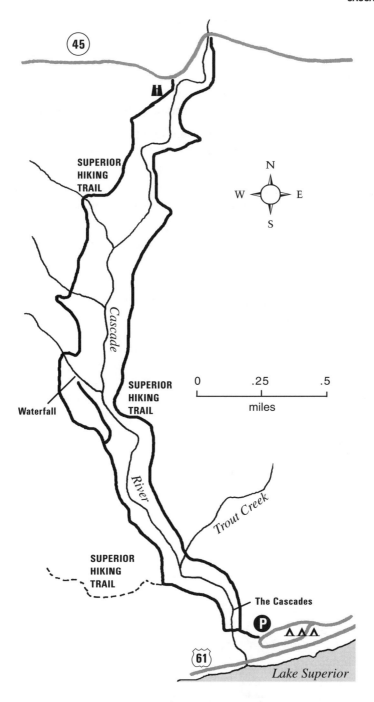

5.1 The trail ascends a steep flight of log steps to a ridge crest. Once on the ridge the trail descends very gradually as it passes along the edge of the river gorge.

6.7 The trail leaves private property still making its gradual descent through tall white pines.

7.0 Pass a spur trail on the right leading to a campsite.

7.1 Cross a bridge over Trout Creek.

7.3 The trail bears left and ascends a steep, sharp ridge.

7.4 Trail intersection; continue straight ahead, passing a very short spur trail on the left leading to a cross-country skiing trail in about 20 feet.

7.5 Trail intersection; turn left on the SHT passing a spur trail to the right. Before going on, stop here to look back upriver at the cascades.

7.6 Trail intersection; bear right on the SHT passing a trail to the left. In the next 800 feet, pass three more trails to the left.

7.8 Trail intersection at the east end of the bridge over Cascade River completing the circuit portion of this hike. Turn left to return to the trailhead.

7.9 Trailhead.

Pincushion Mountain **49**

GRAND MARAIS OVERLOOK

4.4 M
MODERATE

LENGTH	4.4 miles
TIME	2:30
DIFFICULTY	Moderate
ROUTE-FINDING	Easy
MAPS & PERMITS	A map of the Pincushion Mountain trails is available at the Tourist Information Center in Grand Marais. Or call the Grand Marais Chamber of Commerce at 1-888-922-5000. USGS quad: Grand Marais. No permit is required.
GETTING THERE	Take the Gunflint Trail (County Road 12) at the west end of town. Drive 2 miles and turn right on Pincushion Drive (County Road 53) and drive 0.2 mile to the parking lot.
TRAILHEAD GPS	47° 46' 14.7" N 90° 19' 1.4" W

The first time I heard the name Pincushion Mountain I thought of the small red, tomatolike cushion my Mom kept her pins in when she wasn't using them. As it turns out, this image isn't far from what the namers of this peak had in mind. A 1930s forest fire left only stark, burnt trees protruding at different angles from the otherwise denuded knob, making it look like a pincushion. Today the forest has grown back and only the name persists offering but a hint of Grand Marais' history.

The area to the west of Pincushion Mountain is interlaced with 15 miles of cross-country skiing trails. During the "off season," hikers and mountain bikers use the trails, ignoring the "Do Not Enter" signs that direct one-way traffic during the skiing season.

The route of this hike incorporates the large Pincushion Mountain Loop with a short side trip to the summit of the peak. From the trailhead, which also serves as the Grand Marais Overlook, the route heads north, first through an open forest of widely spaced aspens and spruces. After crossing a short rise and turning east, the forest thickens. From here on the trails pass through a mixed deciduous-conifer forest of aspen, white birch, balsam fir, and spruce. The only exception is Pincushion Mountain where you will find stunted jack pines and ash trees growing in the thin rocky soil.

Pincushion Mountain offers panoramic views in all directions. To the southwest are the Sawtooth Mountains, looking like the worn teeth on an old rust-stained saw. The gentle sloping of resistant lava flows formed these ridges. While one end of the flows tilts down and under the lake, the opposite end rises, creating the ridges. Breaks along the ridgeline form the notches that separate the "teeth" of the giant saw blade.

To the north, the summit looks out over Devil Track River Canyon. While you can't see the river, you can make out the break in the forest canopy that marks its course. The Chippewa called this river *Manido bimadagakowini zibi,* "spirits (God) walking-place-on-the-ice river." In *Minnesota Geographic Names,* Warren Upham writes: "The Ojibway applied this name primarily to Devil Track lake, and thence, according to their custom, to the outflowing river. The name implies mystery or something supernatural about the lake and its winter covering of ice, but without the supremely evil idea that is given in the white men's translation."

In *Pioneers in the Wilderness,* a history of the settling of Grand Marais and Cook County, author Willis H. Raff relates another story about the name origin of Devil Track River. Sam Zimmerman, who arrived at Grand Marais as a 22 year old in 1874, had a limp caused by severe burns to his right leg that he suffered as a youngster. At the end of the trapping season of 1881–82, Sam froze both legs. He was rushed on board a mail-carrying tug and taken to St. Luke's Hospital in Duluth where doctors amputated his right leg. But that didn't slow Sam down. After recuperating from the ordeal, Sam continued to trap, getting around, at times, with a ski on one foot and a snowshoe on his peg-leg. Folklore suggests that Indian trappers, upon seeing the strange tracks Zimmerman left in the snow, began calling the stream along which he trapped "Devil's Track." Soon the settlers gave the name also to the lake just over the hill from which the stream flowed. While it makes a good story, Willis is clear to point out that the Chippewa name for the lake and river had been in use long before Zimmerman started walking its snow-covered banks with his peg-leg.

Once the side trip to Pincushion Mountain is over and you're back on the main circuit, the route turns west along the edge of Devil Track River valley. You can see plenty of sky through the trees on the right because the land slopes steeply to the river canyon 900 feet below. One half mile past the Pincushion Mountain spur, the Superior Hiking Trail bears off to the right and begins its descent to the river. From this inter-section, it's 0.4 mile down to the river. The guide to the Superior Hiking Trail describes the canyon as "deep and remote." If you're ready for a slightly longer hike, you might consider hiking down to the river.

Stride-by-Stride

MILES	DESCRIPTION

0.0 The hike heads north from the parking lot passing a signboard with information about the Superior Hiking Trail (SHT). Almost immediately pass trails going right and left by continuing straight ahead. Ignore the "Do Not Enter" signs. They apply only during the skiing season.

0.1 Trail intersection; continue straight ahead passing a trail to the right. The forest up to this point is open with widely set spruces and aspens. After crossing a short rise the woods becomes thick with white birch, aspen, and balsam fir.

0.4 Trail intersection (#4 on the signpost) beginning the circuit portion of this hike; pass a trail coming in sharply from the left and turn right leaving the trail that continues straight ahead.

0.8 Trail intersection (#19); continue straight ahead, passing the trail to the left.

1.7 Trail intersection (#8); the main trail continues to the left. The short 0.2 mile spur to Pincushion Mountain leads straight ahead. About 145 feet from the main trail, the spur turns to the right passing a trail to the left. In another 145 feet, climb a large rock outcropping, turn left, and continue along the ridge for 650 feet to the summit (47° 46' 27.9" N 90° 17' 3.5" W). Retrace your steps to return to the circuit trail.

2.0 Back on the circuit trail after a round trip to the summit.

2.5 Trail intersection with the SHT which descends steeply on the right; continue straight ahead. Pass a shelter in 0.2 mile.

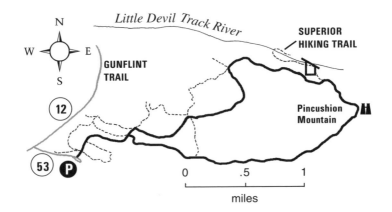

203

3.1   Trail intersection (#7); turn left, passing the trail to the right (the "North Advanced Loop"). In 85 feet, take the left fork, passing the one to the right.

3.6   Trail intersection (#13); continue straight ahead, passing the trail to the left. In 85 feet, at trail intersection #6, take the left most of the three trails.

3.9   Trail intersection (#5); bear left passing the trail to the right. In 75 feet, take the left fork.

4.0   Trail intersection (#4) ending the circuit portion of the hike; continue straight ahead, passing the trail to the right. In 75 feet, take the left fork.

4.3   Trail intersection; continue straight ahead, passing the trail to the left.

4.4   Trailhead.

Mucker Lake– Border Route

5.4 M
DIFFICULT-STRENUOUS

SUPERIOR NATIONAL FOREST
GUNFLINT RANGER DISTRICT

LENGTH	5.4 miles
TIME	3:45
DIFFICULTY	Difficult-Strenuous. While only 5.4 miles long, wet conditions along the trail from beaver dams and streams can make the going strenuous for short distances.
ROUTE-FINDING	Difficult. Finding your way past beaver dams can make route-finding difficult.
MAPS & PERMITS	Fisher Map F-13. USGS quad: South Lake. Part of this hike is in the Boundary Waters Canoe Area Wilderness. A self-registration permit box is located near the start of the hike.
GETTING THERE	Drive north on the Gunflint Trail (County Road 12) for about 34 miles to Forest Route 317 and turn right. Go one-half mile to a small parking area on the side of the road.
TRAILHEAD GPS	48° 4' 42.4" N 90° 34' 2.1" W

A map of the bedrock geology of Minnesota reveals a narrow band of rock type along the border between Minnesota and Canada north of the Gunflint Trail that stands out from the rest of the bedrock in northeastern Minnesota. Looking at a map of the Boundary Waters Canoe Area Wilderness you discover that in this area are many long and narrow, east-west tending lakes. The lakes lie in a bedrock composed of relatively soft sedimentary rocks between ridges of harder, erosion-resistant diabase dikes. Differential erosion by streams, and later glaciers, resulted in the long, deep lakes and steep separating ridges.

The sedimentary bedrock, known as the Rove Formation, is about 1.9-2.0 million years old. It consists of shales, siltstones, and sandstones formed from deposits on the floor of a large inland sea that once covered central and northeastern Minnesota, northern Wisconsin, and Michigan's Upper Peninsula. In the area of Jay Cooke State Park, similar deposits, known as the Thompson Formation, were deformed by great pressures within the earth's crust. The Rove Formation, however, did not experience these pressures and it remains undeformed to this day. About 1.1 billion years ago, during the period of great rifting in the Lake Superior Basin, a series of diabase sills and dikes were intruded into the sedimentary rocks.

Although the east-west lakes are the result of glaciers, their development began long before the glaciers arrived. The rock structure determined that streams would run mostly east-west. But stream erosion alone doesn't account for the deep lakes. To produce them glaciers were needed. When they came hundreds of millions of years later, they flowed from north to south, perpendicular to the east-west running streams. As great ice sheets came and went, they plucked softer sedimentary rock from the valleys, and overrode the ridges of the resistant diabase dikes.

Trail Highlights

The Mucker Lake-Border Route circuit heads east from the trailhead at Mayhew Lake to Hoat Lake. This trail stretches along a valley floor following an abandoned logging road that parallels a small stream flowing east to Hoat Lake. Just northwest of Hoat Lake, the Mucker Lake Trail heads northeast past two beaver dams where the going can be wet crossing the outlet streams. Keep in mind, however, that this is a wilderness trail. It's going to be more challenging than the nicely maintained trails found in the state parks. Judging by the prints and scat along the trail, more moose than people frequent this area.

As the trail approaches Mucker Lake from the south, it turns east and then north, skirting the lake, and ascends a ridge to an intersection with the Border Route Trail. The white birches and balsam firs that were prevalent at lower elevations, give way to jack pines on the ridge.

The route now follows the Border Route Trail west and descends to the north shore of Mucker Lake. Huge red and white pines, and large northern white cedars grow along the trail, hints of what used to grow here in greater abundance before the logging years. At the northwest end of the lake, the trail crosses an outlet stream flowing north to South Lake, turns left upstream, and climbs a ridge with an overlook of Mucker Lake. From here the route ascends via switchbacks to another overlook that provides panoramic views of Sock and Dunn lakes.

Turning from the overlook, the route crosses a knob and comes to an intersection, where a trail leads to a campsite on Sock Lake. About 0.7 mile past this spur, the Border Route Trail intersects another spur trail

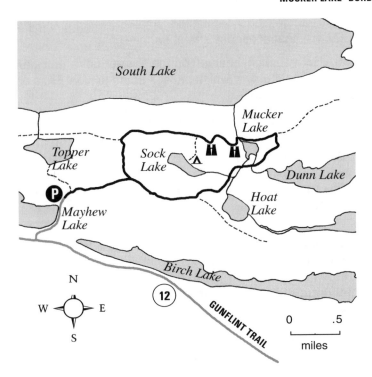

that descends into the valley on the left and reconnects with the Mucker Lake Trail to return to the trailhead. Fall would be an excellent time to make this hike. Lower water levels will help to keep your feet drier, and the changing of the autumn leaves make the views from the overlooks more spectacular.

Stride-by-Stride

MILES   DESCRIPTION

0.0   Walk ahead on Forest Road 317.

0.1   Boundary Waters Canoe Area Wilderness (BWCAW) permit box at a fork in the trail. Fill out a permit at this point before continuing on the right fork, the Mucker Lake Trail. The left fork provides access to Topper Lake in about 0.4 mile.

0.4   BWCAW boundary. The road narrows to a foot path.

0.7   Trail intersection and the start of the circuit portion of this hike. You will return to this point from the Border Route Trail via the trail on the left. Proceed by continuing straight ahead on the Mucker Lake Trail.

207

0.8   Trail intersection; bear left in a small grassy clearing, passing the trail that continues straight ahead.

1.4   Trail intersection; bear left on the Mucker Lake Trail, passing the trail to the right which passes south of Hoat Lake and on to East Otter Lake.

1.5   Cross a small stream flowing east to Hoat Lake which is visible to the right.

1.8   Beaver dam at the north side of Hoat Lake. Follow the trail which is just to the left of the stream flowing north to Mucker Lake. In about 250 feet the trail comes to a small wetland in a narrow valley. Make your way along the base of the slope on your left. In another 400 feet, the trail reenters the forest.

2.0   The trail comes to yet another beaver dam and for the next hundred feet or so is likely to be under water. To continue cross the stream and push on straight ahead until you reach drier ground bearing in mind that this is a wilderness trail.

2.2   The trail crosses a stream and begins to ascend to the Border Route Trail.

2.5   Trail intersection with the Border Route Trail. This intersection is marked with blue ribbons and a small rock cairn. Also, a small sign indicating the Border Route Trail is nailed to a jack pine at this intersection. To continue the circuit, turn left on the Border Route Trail. The trail soon comes to and passes along the north shore of Mucker Lake.

2.9   Stream crossing at the northwest corner of Mucker Lake. After crossing the stream, turn left and continue up stream. In about 150 feet, the trail turns right, climbs the steep bank, and enters a small grove of old pines overlooking Mucker Lake. In the grove, the trail turns sharply to the right.

3.4   Overlook providing glimpses of Dunn and Sock lakes.

3.7   Spur trail on the left leads to a campsite on the north shore of Sock Lake.

4.0   Border Route Trail turns sharply to the left.

4.4   Trail intersection; turn left and descend to the Mucker Lake Trail, leaving the Border Route Trail which continues straight ahead. The trail descends quickly to the valley floor and crosses a small stream before reaching the Mucker Lake Trail.

4.7   Trail intersection; turn right on the Mucker Lake Trail and retrace your steps to the trailhead.

5.4   Trailhead.

MINNESOTA STATE PARKS

Banning State Park
PO Box 643
Sandstone MN 55072
320-245-2668

Bear Head Lake State Park
9301 Bear Head Lake State Park
Road
Ely MN 55731
218-365-7229

Cascade River State Park
HC 3, Box 450
Lutsen MN 55612-9705
218-387-1543

George H. Crosby-Manitou State Park
c/o Tettegouche State Park
474 Highway 61 East
Silver Bay MN 55614
218-226-3539

Gooseberry State Park
1300 Highway 61 East
Two Harbors MN 55616
218-834-3855

Jay Cooke State Park
500 East Highway 210
Carlton MN 55718
218-384-4610

McCarthy Beach State Park
7622 McCarthy Beach Road
Side Lake MN 55781
218-254-2411

Moose Lake State park
4252 County Road 137
Moose Lake MN 55767-9237
218-485-5420

Savanna Portage State Park
HCR 3, Box 591
McGregor MN 55760
218-426-3271

Split Rock Lighthouse State Park
2010-A Highway 61 East
Two Harbors MN 55616
218-226-6377

Temperance River State Park
Box 33
Schroeder MN 55613
218-663-7476

Tettegouche State Park
474 Highway 61 East
Silver Bay MN 55614
218-226-6365

MINNESOTA STATE FORESTS

Fond du Lac State Forest
Area Forest Supervisor
Box 220
Highway 33 South
Cloquet MN 55720
218-879-4544

Kabetogama State Forest
Area Forest Supervisor
PO Box 432
Tower MN 55771
218-753-4500

Nemadji State Forest
Moose Lake Area Forest
Supervisor
Route 2, 701 South Kenwood
Moose Lake MN 55767
218-485-5400

Savanna State Forest
Area Forest Supervisor
Box 9
Hill City MN 55748
218-697-2476

SUPERIOR NATIONAL FOREST

Gunflint Ranger District
PO Box 790
Grand Marais MN 55604
218-387-1750

Isabella Work Station
759 Highway 1
Isabella MN 55607
218-323-7722

Kawishiwi Ranger District
118 South 4th Avenue East
Ely MN 55731
218-365-7600

LaCroix Ranger District
320 North Highway 53
Cook MN 55723
218-666-0020

Laurentian Ranger District
318 Forestry Road
Aurora MN 55705
218-229-8800

Superior National Forest
Forest Supervisor's Office
8901 Grand Avenue Place
Duluth MN 55808
218-626-4300

Tofte Ranger District
PO Box 2159
Tofte MN 55615
218-663-8060

VOYAGEURS NATIONAL PARK

Voyageurs National Park
3131 Highway 53
International Falls MN 56649-8904
218-283-9831

CITY OF DULUTH

Public Works
Forestry Division
110 North 42nd Avenue West
Duluth MN 55807

BIBLIOGRAPHY

Aguar, C. E. *Exploring St. Louis County Historical Sites*. Duluth MN: St. Louis County Historical Society, 1971.

Ballum, J. M. "The use of soaring by the Red-tailed Hawk (*Buteo jamaicensis*)." *Auk*. 101:519–524, 1984.

Bent, Arthur Cleveland. *Life Histories of North American Birds of Prey*. New York: Dover Publications, Inc., 1961.

Breckenridge, W. J. *Reptiles and Amphibians of Minnesota*. Minneapolis MN: University of Minnesota Press,1944.

Brodie, E. D., III. "Genetics of the garter's getaway." *Natural History* 99(7): 45–51, 1990.

Burt, W. H., and R. P. Grossenheider. *A Field Guide to the Mammals*. Boston MA: Houghton Mifflin Company, 1964.

Caras, R. A. *North American Mammals*. New York: Galahad Books, 1967.

Choate, E. A. *The Dictionary of American Bird Names*. Boston MA: Gambit, 1973.

Clark, W. S., and B. K. Wheeler. *A Field Guide to Hawks of North America*. New York: Houghton Mifflin Company, 1987.

Collins, H. H., Jr. *Complete Guide to American Wildlife*. New York: Harper and Row, 1959.

Conant, R. *A Field Guide to Reptiles and Amphibians of the United States and Canada East of the 100th Meridian*. Boston MA: Houghton Mifflin Company, 1958.

Dana, W. S. *How to Know the Wild Flowers*. New York: Dover Publications, 1963.

Davis, W. J. "King of the stream." *Natural History*. 97(5):38–45, 1988.

Duke, J. A. and Wain, K. K. Medicinal plants of the world. Computer index with more than 85,000 entries. 3 vols. 1981.

Dunn, J. L., and E. A. T. Bloom, Chief Consultants. *Field Guide to the Birds of North America, Second Edition*. Washington, DC: National Geographic Society, 1987.

Erichsen-Brown, C. *Use of Plants for the Past 500 Years*. Aurora, Canada: Breezy Creeks Press, 1979.

Ewins, P. J., J. R. Miller, M. E. Barker, and S. Postupalsky. "Birds breeding in or beneath osprey nests in the Great Lakes basin." *Wilson Bulletin* 106:743–749, 1994.

Fritzen, J. *Historic Sites and Place Names of Minnesota's North Shore.* Duluth MN: St. Louis County Historical Society, 1974.

Goodrich, L. J., S. C. Crocoll, and S. E. Senner. "The Broadwinged Hawk." *The Birds of North America.* Philadelphia PA: American Ornithologists' Union and The Academy of Natural Sciences of Philadelphia, 1993.

Gruson, E. S. *Words for Birds: A Lexicon of North American Birds with Biographical Notes.* New York: Quadrangle Books, Inc., 1972.

Harrington, F. H. and D. L. Mech. "Wolf howling and its role in territory maintenance." *Behavior* Vol. LXVIII, Parts 3–4: 205–249, 1979.

Heinselman, M. L. *The Boundary Waters Wilderness Ecosystem.* Minneapolis MN: University of Minnesota Press, 1996.

Hereid, N., and E. D. Gennaro. *A Family Guide to Minnesota's North Shore.* Minneapolis MN: Minnesota Sea Grant, University of Minnesota, 1993.

Jacobson, G. L. "A 7,000 year history of White Pine." *White Pine Symposium Proceedings.* Stine, R. A., Editor. St. Paul MN: Minnesota Extension Service, University of Minnesota, 1992.

Johnston, C. A. and R. J. Naiman. "Aquatic patch creation by beavers." *Ecology* 71(4): 1615–1621, 1990.

King, F.A. *Minnesota Logging Railroads.* San Marino CA: Golden West Books, 1981.

LaBerge, G. L. *Geology of the Lake Superior Region.* Phoenix AZ: Geoscience Press Inc., 1994.

McInnes, P. F., R. J. Naiman, J. Pastor, and Y. Cohen. "Effects of browsing on vegetation and litter of the boreal forest" *Ecology* 73(6): 2059–2075, 1992.

Meyer, R. W. *Everyone's Country Estate.* St. Paul MN: Minnesota Historical Society Press, 1911.

Murie, O. J. *A Field Guide to Animal Tracks.* Boston MA: Houghton Mifflin Company, 1954.

Naiman, R. J., G. Pinay, C. A. Johnston, and J. Pastor. "Beaver influences on the long-term biochemical characteristics of boreal forest drainage networks." *Ecology* 75(1): 905–921, 1994.

Niemi, G.J., and J. M. Hanowski. Role of snags to breeding birds in northern Minnesota. St. Paul MN: Technical Report, Department of Biology and Lake Superior Basins Study Center, University of Minnesota.

Ohmann, L. F. and R. R. Ream. *Wilderness Ecology: Virgin Plant Communities of the BWCA.* North Central Forest Experiment Station, St. Paul, MN (USDA Forest Service Research Paper NC-63), 1971.

Ojakangas, R., and C. Matsch. *Minnesota's Geology*. Minneapolis MN: University of Minnesota Press, 1982.

Olfield, B., and J. J. Moriarty. *Amphibians & Reptiles Native to Minnesota*. MinneapolisMN: University of Minnesota Press, 1994.

Palmer, R. S., Editor. *Handbook of North America, Vol. 5*. New Haven CT: Yale University Press, 1988.

Preston, C. R., and R. D. Beane. *The Birds of North America*. Philadelphia PA: American Ornithologists' Union and The Academy of Natural Sciences of Philadelphia, 1993.

Rogers, L. L., and E. L. Lindquist. "Supercanopy white pine and wildlife." *White Pine Symposium Proceedings*. St. Paul MN: Minnesota Extension Service, University of Minnesota, 1992.

Sansome, C. J. *Minnesota Underfoot*. Bloomington MN: Voyageur Press, 1983.

Searle, R. N. *State Parks of the North Shore*. Minnesota Parks Foundation, 1979.

Schwartz, G. M., and G. A. Thiel. *Minnesota's Rocks and Rivers: A Geological Story*. Minneapolis MN: University of Minnesota Press, 1954.

Swhwartz, G.M., and G. A. Thiel. *Minnesota's Rocks and Rivers*. Minneapolis MN: University of Minnesota Press, 1963.

Summer, J. P. "Flight display in two American species of Buteo." *Condor* 76:214–215, 1974.

Two Harbors Centennial Commission, in cooperation with the Lake County Historical Society. *Two Harbors 100 Years: A Pictorial History of Two Harbors, Minnesota and Surrounding Communities*. Dallas TX: Taylor Publishing Company, 1983.

Vanderboom, R. *Minnesota State Parks Guide*. Milwaukee WI: 1989.

Waters, T. F. *The Streams and Rivers of Minnesota*. Minneapolis MN: University of Minnesota Press, 1977.

West, G. A. *Copper: Its Mining and Use by the Aborigines of the Lake Superior Region—Report of the McDonald Massee Isle Royale Expedition*. Bulletin of the Public Museum of the City of Milwaukee. Vol. 10, No. 1, 1928.

Zumberge, J. H. *The Lakes of Minnesota: Their Origin and Classification*. Minneapolis MN: University of Minnesota Press, 1952.

INDEX

Italic numbers indicate map references.

yellow birch 151
Twin Lakes Trail 134–135

V

Voyageurs National Park 112–116, 210

W

Whisky Jack Lake 87–89, *88*
white birch 171–172
white pine 46, 72–73, 83–84
white-tailed deer 28, 103–104
Willard Munger State Trail 37, *39*
wolves 175–176

Y

yarrow 189
yellow birch 151
Yellow Birch Trail 146–147, 149, *149*